Tracey Thorn was singer and songwriter with Everything
 Girl from 1982–2000. At that point she semi-retired from
 c business to bring up her family. She has since recorded
 e solo albums, *Out of the Woods, Love and Its Opposite* and
 el and Lights. She lives in London with her husband Ben
 t and their three children.

tor *Bedsit Disco Queen*

'V warm and utterly without prima donna pretensions, how
 anyone not love Tracey Thorn? For anyone who sat on
 as a teenager, listening to records and fantasising about
 a band – most of us, then – *Bedsit Disco Queen* is the
 their dreams' *Mail on Sunday*

intensely readable account of thirty years of being in love
 sic . . . Most would recognise Thorn's distinctive,
 ep voice, with its rich blend of melancholy and
 ning. Her written voice is similarly distinctive: warm,
 as ve, sweetly funny, but most of all honest' *Daily Telegraph*

y and wise chronicle of the post-punk era and a life
 pping in and out of the limelight, this is second to none'
 nt on Sunday

cey Thorn grew up to be a genuine pop star her
 roll anecdotes are stellar. Part memoir, part social
 ntary and part reflection on the past few decades of
the music industry, Thorn's account is both heart-breaking
and hilarious' *Elle*

'Thorn takes a refined route down the music memoir path, much as she has been carving her niche in the music industry since 1979 … A nuanced and unusually reflective autobiography' *Sunday Express*

'In prose as in song, Thorn has a lovely, lulling, disarming tone, with steel beneath the self-effacement' *Evening Standard*

'Always a reluctant, almost accidental pop star, Thorn has written one of the best books about ambivalence I've ever read' *Guardian*

'As idiosyncratic, clever and entertaining as you'd hope. Like Thorn's lyrics, *Bedsit Disco Queen* is pared down and stripped of artifice, yet still manages to be both funny and revealing, full of insight and remarkably modest' *Scotsman*

'It's no surprise that *Bedsit Disco Queen* is an immensely likable book … Thorn is observant, funny, modest and dry' *New Statesman*

BEDSIT DISCO QUEEN

HOW I GREW UP AND TRIED
TO BE A POP STAR

TRACEY THORN

virago

... Press
... Press

A CIP catalogue record for this book
is available from the British Library.

ISBN 978-1-84408-868-3

Typeset in Bembo by M Rules
Printed and bound in Great Britain by
Clays Ltd, St Ives plc

Papers used by Virago are from well-managed forests
and other responsible sources.

MIX
Paper from
responsible sources
FSC FSC® C104740
www.fsc.org

Virago Press
An imprint of
Little, Brown Book Group
Carmelite House
50 Victoria Embankment
London EC4Y 0DZ

An Hachette UK Company
www.hachette.co.uk

www.virago.co.uk

For Ben

And all the effort that it took to get here in the first
place
And all the effort not to let the effort show

'Downhill Racer', from *Temperamental*, 1999

And all the ... ... to perform his ... a ...
peace
And all the life ... ... in the space ...

— William Shakespeare, *Hamlet* ( )

AUTHOR'S NOTE

My story spans a full thirty years. I was only sixteen when I bought an electric guitar and joined a band. A year or so later, I formed an all-girl band called the Marine Girls and began playing gigs, and signed to an indie label and started releasing records.

Then for eighteen years, between 1982 and 2000, I was one half of a group called Everything But The Girl. In that time we released nine albums and sold around nine million records. We went on countless tours and promo trips, had hit singles and flop singles, were reviewed and interviewed to within an inch of our lives.

I've been in the charts, out of them, then back in again. Been signed, dropped, re-signed, mixed and remixed. I've seen myself described as an indie darling, a middle-of-the-road nobody and a disco diva. As Bono once sang: 'There's nothing you can throw at me, that I haven't already heard.' The career I've had has been one that's existed mostly on the margins, outside of the genre-specific accounts of the period. I haven't always fitted in, you see, and that's made for some uncomfortable moments over the years. But it's also forced me to face up to the realities of what a pop career is, and to realise that there are undoubtedly thrills and wonders to be experienced, but just as often there are doubts and mistakes. Moments of boredom and shame. Trivial irritations and petty humiliations. Violent lifestyle swings from luxury to squalor and back again – sometimes within minutes.

If you like those kinds of stories, stories where the lead characters seem to blunder through life, much as you do through your own, then you might like this one. The experience of writing it has sometimes been very like drowning, except that I've spent months, instead of seconds, with my past life flashing before my eyes. It's been strange, and disconcerting; it has made me confront what I've done with my life, take a close look at who I once was and how that has a bearing on who I am now. And so often I've heard David Byrne singing just over my shoulder, 'How did I get here?'

Or even, on occasion, 'My God, what have I done?'

March 1997

I'm in a hotel in Perth, Australia. To be more specific, I'm in the air-conditioned penthouse suite of a hotel in Perth, gazing through the huge wrap-around windows at the limitless expanse of blue sky and ocean beyond. In the centre of the living room, next to the mushroom-coloured leather sofa and the shagpile rug, stands a white baby grand piano. It's a pure 1970s luxury rock 'n' roll hotel-room setting, beyond parody.

Ben and I have come out here a few days before the start of our latest sold-out Australian tour, to 'acclimatise' and get over jet lag. In other words, lie on the beach, get a tan and lounge around in penthouse suites with baby grands. And now we're sitting here, languidly waiting for room service or something, when the phone rings. It's our manager in London.

'You won't believe the conversation I've just had,' she says. 'I've had a call from U2's management office. You've been offered the support slot on their American stadium tour!'

This too is beyond parody. It's the kind of moment when you expect to be shaken awake any minute by your mum and told to get up for school.

Ben covers the receiver with his hand while he tells me the news. We're both laughing and shaking our heads in disbelief. Have they muddled us up with someone else?

'What d'you reckon?' he says to me. 'Should we do it, or what?'

I can't really think what to say. I wish it wasn't up to me, but I know why Ben's asking. It's not a foregone conclusion at all, you see, and Ben knows me well enough to have guessed this immediately.

I look around the room at the view, the grand piano, everything.

It's a top moment, obviously. And I'll be able to dine out on it for ages. But here's what I say—

PART ONE

PART-TIME PUNKS

I'd always kidded myself that it was punk that got me started. It was certainly the answer I gave in interviews when I was asked about the beginnings of my musical career. I even had a box of punk singles upstairs that seemed to support my claim, and if, when I did the sums and realised I was only thirteen when many of them were released, it ever gave me pause for thought and made me wonder whether I'd actually bought some of them after the event, well, that wasn't anything I was going to own up to.

It's not that the punk version of my story is a complete lie; more that it's a compression of a story that begins just after punk. It's a simplification of a truth that's a little more complicated than journalists tend to like answers to their questions to be; an acknowledgement of the fact that, if they were confused by my liking for punk, it would hardly have made matters easier to start trying to draw fine distinctions between punk and its immediate aftermath, or to define the precise delineations of post-punk.

In terms of chronology, a year or two either way might have made all the difference. If I'd been born a couple of years earlier or later, I wouldn't have been thirteen when punk happened, and everything that followed it might have just passed me by. Maybe being thirteen when it all began was the reason for everything. If I'd been born a couple of years later, I might simply have been too young to have been attracted to something so ostensibly dangerous and threatening. A couple of years earlier, and I might have been a year too old to have been so completely taken in by what could have seemed a mere fad, a musical novelty aimed at impressionable, easily scared children and their easily scared parents.

As it was, in 1976 I was almost too young. But not quite.

I grew up in the suburbs, in Brookmans Park, a little satellite town about twenty miles north of London. It was once a proper village, and during the war had been considered just far enough from London to be safe for evacuees. And so for my parents it represented an idyllic escape from the blitzed London they had both grown up in. In the early 1950s they had left Kentish Town and headed out to safety, away from the bomb sites and the terraced streets now riven with sudden gaps, to a classic little semi on an unmade road, with potholes that my mum filled every morning with the sweepings from the coal fire.

By the 1960s when I was born, Brookmans Park was still clinging to its green-belt status, while gradually and unavoidably merging into the rest of the homogeneous sprawl that surrounded London. By the 1970s, once I had outgrown the innocent attractions of fields to play in, shops near enough to walk to and quiet roads to ride your bike on, it represented for me everything that was suffocating and inhibiting about small-town life. Near enough to London that you could almost see

it if you peered hard enough down the railway line, it was just far enough away to bear no resemblance, and like other modern suburbs it turned its back resolutely on all that the city seemed to offer or threaten, depending on your point of view.

But growing up in a place like Brookmans Park meant that I was hardly at the epicentre of punk when it began. I wasn't really there when it was all happening, so why is it that my memory has fixed that moment in my mind as being the starting point and the reason for everything that followed?

To show you just what I mean about having kidded myself that I was a true child of punk, I will share with you some of the home truths from my diary for 1976. Granted I was only thirteen, and the diary itself is clearly a work-in-progress – the handwriting, for instance, going through dramatic changes as I try out different styles, slanting to the left for a bit, or suddenly getting very, very tiny. There are scribbled love hearts, stickers, extra bits of paper taped in with now dried-out, yellowed Sellotape and so many asterisks and exclamation marks it's like trying to read Braille.

But even making allowances for my tender age, as a story of someone discovering, and falling for, pop music it doesn't get off to a very promising start. In 1976, the number of records I bought was – seven.

'Rock On' by David Essex
The Love Hangover LP by Diana Ross
'This Time I'll Be Sweeter' by Linda Lewis
The Beach Boys Greatest Hits
The Eagles Greatest Hits Vol. 1
'With Your Love' by Jefferson Starship
'I Want More' by Can

Now, I'd be happy to hear *any* of these records if you put one on right now, and I'm not ashamed of them at all. But they are none of them quintessential punk classics.

I can find only four other mentions of music all year:

16 Jan – I hear a record on the radio by Nilsson and I like it.
3 April – Brotherhood of Man win the Eurovision Song Contest.
22 June – I am happy that The Real Thing are number one.
29 Oct – I describe *Songs in the Key of Life* as 'brilliant'.

Here we are then: 1976, pop's Year Zero, the year punk gets started, and I think it's fair to say that I am completely untouched by it. In fact, pop music doesn't seem to impinge on my life much at all. What this diary mostly reveals is that I'm more interested in boys and what's on the telly. School features heavily, of course. And the weather. The twenty-second of June for instance, is notable for the fact that I get 85 per cent in my music exam and the summer is turning very hot. This is marked by a little shining sun around the date, which appears every day for three solid weeks. 'Weather STILL boiling,' I keep recording, with ever-increasing numbers of exclamation marks. This is the famous heatwave summer of 1976. But of the other famous events of punk's inaugural year, well, there is simply no mention. In February the Sex Pistols played at St Albans art college, just down the road. But I was apparently too pre-occupied with the weather forecast to notice.

In November they released 'Anarchy In The UK', and then on 1 December appeared on the *Today* programme with Bill Grundy and made pop history by saying 'sod' and 'fucking rotter'.

But did I even see it? My diary makes no mention of it, concentrating instead on the fact that I 'watched *Superstars*. Washed hair and had a bath.'

In 1976, the truth is I was not even a part-time punk.

But opening up my diary for 1977 is something of a shock. Sellotaped to the inside front cover is a photo of Johnny Rotten, and on the facing page I have written 'Never mind the bollocks . . . here's my diary'. I must have cheated and stuck the photo in and written that slogan towards the end of the year, because the first half of 1977 reveals no evidence of any such sea change having taken place. In fact, I seem to be losing interest in music.

Records bought pre-June 1977: zero.

Then, suddenly, it happens. Something happens. Number of records bought from June 1977 to end of year – eight.

'In The City' by The Jam
'Lights Out' by Dr Feelgood
'All Around The World' by The Jam
'Something Better Change' by The Stranglers

My Aim Is True by Elvis Costello
'Gary Gilmore's Eyes' by The Adverts
'Grip' by The Stranglers
'London Girls' by The Vibrators

Other mentions of music between June and December that year include:

14 July – on *TOTP* are The Commodores, Supertramp and the SEX PISTOLS, whose name I have surrounded with a sort of starry biro halo. I describe their appearance as being a 'film of them doing "Pretty Vacant". Phew!' (I have finally had my socks blown off.)

7 Aug – see Sex Pistols on *London Weekend Show* – they are 'absolutely brilliant'.

31 Aug – 'Charts are really chronic now apart from Jam, Stranglers, Adverts, Boomtown Rats and Mink DeVille' (Right, so really chronic, apart from being mostly fantastic.)

29 Sept – I'm listening to new wave on *Your Mother Wouldn't Like It*.

20 Nov – listening to punk records on Radio Luxembourg.

10 Dec – see The Clash on *So It Goes* ('fantastic, I luv 'em').

So at some point in June 1977, later than I had liked to remember, but not so late as to be totally embarrassing, I discovered punk, and it triggered in me a passion for pop music and a record-buying spree which was new and obsessive, and which carried on for years. Up until that point I had only half cared about music, but this moment marked the point when

I changed – not as many of my immediate elders changed, from people who liked Genesis into people who liked The Clash – from someone who had barely noticed pop music and didn't seem to care much either way, into someone who cared about very little else.

Mind you, I should also be honest and admit that at this stage my interest was still largely that of your average hormonally afflicted Bay City Rollers fan – i.e., I fancied them.

7 Aug – 'Steve Jones – CCORR!!!'

6 Oct – 'J. J. Burnel is so hunky!! Luv his jeans!!*???!!**

3 Nov – 'David Bowie was on *TOTP*. Boy, he's so hunky'

1 Dec – 'Bob Geldof is so gorgeous'

And so on, and so on . . .

At this point I was simply having fun with it all in a quite uncomplicated way, still just a fourteen-year-old pop fan. Sadly this phase didn't last long, and as it began to occur to me that liking punk was, or was supposed to be, somehow different to liking David Essex, things got more awkward, especially at home.

It goes without saying that the teenage years can be 'difficult', and that problems at school and with your parents are perhaps more the rule than the exception – but even given all this, the period of punk, and of punk's influence, was a particularly problematic time to be a teenager. Punk demanded a stance of such antagonism and rejection (a 1976 press handout from the Sex Pistols has them saying 'We hate everything') that it seemed impossible to carry on being civil to your parents while claiming to like The Stranglers. The two appeared to be utterly incompatible, to a degree that I'm not sure has ever been the case since, and certainly wasn't before. Bear in mind, too, that thirty-odd years ago the generation gap between teenagers and parents was a lot wider than it is today. It has been steadily closing since, so that now it is almost a cliché to observe that many parents like the same records as their kids and happily go with them to Glastonbury.

Well, may I just say that it wasn't like that for me and my parents, whose musical tastes were rooted in the pre-rock cool of Sinatra and Glenn Miller, and extended into the present only as far as the unarguable musicality of someone like Stevie Wonder. They had used to enjoy listening to me play the piano, and had no objections to my David Cassidy collection, but by late 1977 they were reeling in shock at what had happened to me.

I wasn't supposed to have gone to the bad like this; it wasn't in the script at all. I was the youngest child in the family, and like all youngest children, exploited my position mercilessly. My brother Keith had been born in 1953. Then in 1960 came my sister Debbie, after which my mum was abruptly informed by the doctor at the end of her hospital bed that medical complications meant she would not be able to have any more children. Two years later, in defiance of this inept prediction, I was born, though I did my best to prove the doctor right by attempting to die as soon as I appeared. I had apparently mistimed my first breath and inhaled a lungful of amniotic fluid instead of air, and so had drowned before I was even born. The midwife who delivered me, in the front bedroom at home, had been on a training course only the week before, where she had learned for the first time how to perform neonatal resuscitation. Presented with her first opportunity to practise her new skills, she gave me the kiss of life and saved me, though I would spend some time in an incubator at the hospital with pneumonia. It would be eighteen months or so before the doctors were able to reassure my parents that my brain hadn't been damaged by that initial lack of oxygen.

All in all, it was the kind of arrival likely to confer upon any child a special status within the family. Throughout my childhood this had worked in my favour, but now, as I entered my teens, the level of attention and expectation that was focused on me was all of a sudden proving to be troublesome.

I had always been bright and done well at school, along with being something of a goody-goody. I was chatty, too, and indulged, so when I rebelled against school dinners as a picky primary-school child, I was allowed to walk home every day for lunch with my mum – a special private time of our own, where we'd sit in the kitchen and I'd regale her with tales of the morning's events and entertain her with impressions of all the teachers. If I wanted the same food every lunchtime – a crusty cheese roll – and if I wanted to eat Jacob's Cream Crackers for breakfast, well, that was all right. It was allowed. Mealtimes might be punctuated with cries from my mum of 'Tracey! Eat your peas!' but it wasn't really serious. It was just who I was. The fussy one, the youngest. I wasn't really a problem. I was an avid reader, which also marked me out as clever, and that was to be respected. I had my weekly piano lessons, and impressed everyone with my endless practising and my jolly Scott Joplin tunes. Within the cosy structure of the family I felt central, liked for who I was. Special.

But as I attempted to forge a new and adult persona for myself, using punk-rock singles as a kind of catalyst to bring into being, with a lot of unexpected heat and light, a person who was ME, really, truly ME, and not just a mini-version of my parents, the bond between us was stretched to breaking point. Having been chatty, I became sullen. Dinner-table conversation had always been light-hearted, never analytical, in our house and there was no tradition of friendly debate, so now if I disagreed with things my parents said there would be

a brief, terse exchange, the stakes would be raised within minutes, a sharp insult might be flung – 'Fascist!' 'Ignorant!' – and
I would leave the room. Not a row as such, but an absence of
friendly communication, which left me feeling unlistened to,
my opinions worthless.

Instead of confrontation, I opted for secrecy. In a timid way
I would make minor adjustments to my fashion style. On 10
September 1977 my diary records that I 'changed my sloopy
jeans into drainpipes. They're really tight and straight!!! Look
dead punky!!! Saw *Starsky and Hutch*.' Then on 18 October I
had my hair cut 'all spiky at the front – looks punky', though
I have to admit I can't find any photographic evidence to back
this up, and I wouldn't be at all surprised if it only looked spiky
up in my bedroom and was flattened down each time I went
downstairs. Later, a proper confrontation would be triggered
by a sweary badge from Stiff Records, carefully hidden by me
in my bedroom, and yet somehow 'found' by my mum. Her
shock at my apparently casual reaction to something which
was, to her, profoundly offensive left me wondering whether
I truly had betrayed some kind of unspoken and universal value
system, or whether she was overreacting.

As for the music emanating from my bedroom, it was
beyond the pale. Nothing in life so far had prepared my parents for a daughter who suddenly loved ugly, swearing rock
groups instead of Diana Ross. You can see their point, really.

When I was ten I thought my brother was God
He'd lie in bed, and turn out the light with a fishing
    rod
I learned the names of all his football team
And I still remembered them when I was nineteen

Strange the things that I remember still –
Shouts from the playground, when I was home and ill
My sister taught me all that she learned there
When we grew up, we said, we'd share a flat
    somewhere

When I was seventeen
London meant Oxford Street

Where I grew up there were no factories
There was a school, and shops, and some fields and
    trees
And rows of houses one by one appeared
I was born in one, and lived there for eighteen years

Then when I was nineteen
I thought the Humber would be
The gateway from my little world
Into the real world

But there is no real world
We live side by side
And sometimes collide

When I was seventeen
London meant Oxford Street
It was a little world
I grew up in a little world

'Oxford Street', from *Idlewild*, 1988

GIG BUDDY

20 January 1978

'TERRIBLE NEWS – the Sex Pistols have split up, torn up their contract, Malcolm's quit and Sid's in hospital with an OD ... This is the end of punk, really.'

Whaaat? Hang on a minute there, I mean, it's only just started for me! This is the problem with 'movements' in pop music – you're forever trying to keep up. No sooner do you become a fully paid-up devotee of the latest craze than someone, a journalist usually, comes along and declares it's dead. All over. I think my diary entry is probably just something I copied out of the *NME* and I'm sure it felt suitably apocalyptic to declare punk well and truly finished. Especially since hardly anyone I knew had even had time to get into it. And yet, did punk being dead make any major difference to my life? Not a bit of it. It had, as I say, only just started for me, and whatever you want to call it – post-punk if you like, new wave, whatever – it was taking me over.

*

The local record shops were still largely the bastion of greasy-haired, leather-jacketed Status Quo fans ('greebos', we called them), and even if they did stock the records I wanted – and usually they didn't – they were not appealing locations for a girl to hang out in. But in those days before internet shopping there was another way of accessing things that were unavailable locally, and so I started relying on the mail-order lists in the back of the *NME*, filling in tiny little order forms and mailing them with a postal order. Illicit-looking seven-inch brown cardboard envelopes would arrive at the door for me from Small Wonder Records. The Clash, X-Ray Spex and Patrik Fitzgerald singles arrived in this way, and seemed all the more precious for being so hard to come by.

If I was going to get out there and engage with this stuff, though, I needed allies. At school I made an effort to befriend the smattering of cool girls who wanted to go to gigs, and while I had reservations about how much I actually LIKED my new girl-gang, it was a typically pragmatic kind of teenage friendship: they were my friends because I needed them. There was Joanne, who I noticed had stuck some torn-out pictures of The Jam on the inside of her desk lid. There was Amanda, whose dad was a policeman and Denise, who dated Paul Young before he was pop star Paul Young. And Dee, who had unspecified problems at home, which led to our French teacher beginning every lesson by fixing her with a concerned gaze and gently asking, 'Are you *coping*, Dee?' We'd get dolled up in our skinniest trousers, outsized pale blue policeman shirts borrowed from Amanda, cheap stilettos and school blazers smothered with button badges, and someone's dad would drop us off outside Hemel Hempstead Pavilion, where, over the next few months, I saw Ian Dury, Siouxsie and the Banshees, the Buzzcocks, Subway Sect and the Boomtown Rats. On one occasion we even managed to get tickets to see The Jam recording an *In Concert* programme at the BBC studios in Regent Street. Afterwards I breathlessly noted in my diary that 'Outside, Paul Weller and Rick Buckler walked right by me!!'

The school we attended was something of an anomaly, an ex-girls' grammar which had recently gone comprehensive, which meant that although it was a single-sex school it was by no means posh. But, like most girls' schools, it could be a scary place, with that intense, emotionally manipulative atmosphere that swirls around teenage girls. In the spirit of the times the gang I'd hooked up with could be bitchy in the extreme, and my allegiance to them demanded a shift in my behaviour at school. Up till now I'd always been well behaved, a bit of a swot in fact, but now I began to get into trouble more. My diary describes incidents of being sent out of lessons, or told off for 'being insolent'. It was a continuation of the conflict at home – liking this new music seemed to demand that you behave badly.

I may have had qualms about whether or not these girls were true friends, but the alternative to hanging out with them was too awful to contemplate as I discovered when, in a momentary lapse of judgement, I agreed to go to the Knebworth Festival with a couple of boys from down the road. They had a car, and they were going anyway, and had some spare tickets, and . . . Oh, you know. It was a day out, after all. In the car the whole way there they insisted on singing along to a tape of *The Lamb Lies Down on Broadway* by Genesis, while I scowled and made sarky comments. When we got there it turned out Peter Gabriel was on the bill, and they were beside themselves with excitement. Later on Frank Zappa played too, by which time I was more or less comatose with boredom. (Ironically, the day was billed as Not Another Boring Old Knebworth.) I only woke up at the end of the night when

The Tubes DROVE ONSTAGE IN A CAR! Now that's more like it, I thought.

In my heart I knew I needed to find a proper gig buddy – someone who wanted to go to the same gigs as me, but was outside the somewhat charmless circle of the girls at school. I wanted to be able to go out without having always to engage with the inevitable dramas and constantly shifting loyalties of the gang. As if by magic, the person I needed without even consciously realising it turned up in the unlikely form of the brother of a schoolfriend of my sister's. Huw was five years older than me. He wasn't at school like everyone else I knew, but was at art college studying to be a photographer. Old enough to have been following music since before punk, he had some perspective on it all, and was also literate and political. The girls at school didn't like him, were suspicious of him even, but that made it all the better. I found him interesting and good company, and for some reason he decided to take me under his wing. He'd been out to New York for a while in 1976 and had hung out with the band Suicide, and when they came over to support The Clash on tour, Huw went along with them and photographed the whole tour. In 1978, he started a local fanzine called *The Weekly Bugle* and, discovering my passion for bands, asked me to write something for it, and on this basis we went to gigs together, looking for things to review. We started out locally and spent a few evenings trawling round the pubs that had bands on – the Duke of Lancaster and the Horn of Plenty, but it was all hippy hangovers and pub-rock losers. We saw Paul Young with his group Streetband, and I succinctly described them in my diary as 'really boring', apparently not spotting any likelihood that he was destined for pop stardom.

Because Huw had a car, we started driving up to London to see bands, and in their wisdom my parents had decided that

Huw was safe to be with, their logic being that the five-year age gap (he was twenty-one and I was sixteen) meant that he would look after me. (Huh?) There was some truth in this assumption, in that our relationship was never anything more than platonic and he never tried to get off with me.

Much more importantly, he offered me an entry into the world I was longing to be part of, or at least get close enough to look at – the world of London and bands and gigs. At the Music Machine in Camden, we saw Patrik Fitzgerald, who had come up with a kind of romantic/acoustic version of punk. It was unheard of at this time for anyone to pick up an acoustic guitar without expecting, and possibly deserving, to get beaten up, but somehow the very riskiness of what Patrik did made him seem truly punky. When Huw managed to get us backstage passes to interview him for the fanzine, I felt I was at the heart of urban hipsterdom – I might as well have been Julie Burchill interviewing the Pistols.

Over the next few months we went to an amazing series of gigs. When Siouxsie and the Banshees played at the Roundhouse, they were supported by Spizz Oil, who gave the loudest live performance I have ever witnessed, and which Huw, being something of an extremist when it came to things like volume, insisted we experience from near the stage, in front of the PA, where it was so hair-flatteningly loud that I was nearly sick. We saw The Human League at the Nashville, in the 'Being Boiled' days, when they were a very serious and theoretical concoction of post-punk electronica – the pop songs and the shop girls a long way off in an unimaginable future – and I swear that I stood next to David Bowie at the bar.

We went to the Lyceum a lot, usually to the Sunday gigs, where we'd lounge around on the greasy carpet upstairs, watching boys with mohicans slouching in and out of the

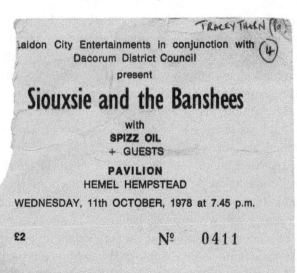

Girls' Boudoir (the ladies' loo). It's quite hard now to convey just how scuzzy and down-at-heel everywhere was during the 1970s. When you went to gigs at places like the Hope and Anchor or the Nashville, it really did feel like stepping into an alternative and entirely punk-designed universe. Maybe my impressions of this time were informed by being a nice suburban girl from a relatively middle-class home, but even so, in the decades before 'design' was a widely used word, or concept, it's salutary to remember the grubby grottiness of it all. Sticky, floral carpets, damp dripping walls lined with stickers and posters, and behind the bar, beer on tap or spirits. I don't remember anyone ever having a glass of wine or a bottle of lager, and there was no such thing as an alcopop. Cocktails hadn't been invented. Everyone smoked, everywhere, all the time, and ate crisps and pies. Personal grooming came nowhere near the standards which are now considered the bare

LYCEUM BALLROOM
Box office open 12 - 6 Mon. - Sat.
8.00 p.m. (Normal Sessions)
Telephone: 836 3715

SUNDAY
JUNE **17**

at 7.30 p.m.

Straight Music presents
THE CURE

ST JULY   7-30
N̲o̲   238

This portion to be retained
[P.T.O.

LYCEUM BALLROOM
Box office open 12 - 6 Mon. - Sat.
8.00 p.m (Normal Sessions)
Telephone: 836 3715

SUNDAY
JULY **29**

at 7.30 p.m.

Straight Music presents
**The
Pretenders**

N̲o̲   569

retained
[P.T.O.

LYCEUM BALLROOM
Box office open 12-6 Mon-Sat
8 pm (Normal Sessions)
Telephone : 836 3715

SUNDAY
SEPTEMBER **7**

at 6.30pm

Straight Music presents
**Echo and the
Bunnymen**

N̲o̲   1073

retained
(P.T.O.)

LYCEUM BALLROOM
Box Office open Evenings only
8.00 p.m. (Normal Sessions)
Telephone: 836 3715

SUNDAY
MAY **27**

at 7.30 p.m.

Straight Music presents
GANG OF FOUR

N̲o̲   308

This portion to be retained
[P.T.O.

LYCEUM BALLROOM
Box office open 12-6 Mon-Sat
8pm (Normal Sessions)
Telephone: 836 3715

SUNDAY
NOVEMBER **2**

at 6.30p.m.

STRAIGHT MUSIC presents
BUZZCOCKS

N̲o̲   1312

This portion to be retained
(P.T.O.)

minimum of what's acceptable. In other words, we were all a bit dirtier and smellier, as were the places we frequented.

The Lyceum was no exception, and despite having a sort of faded grandeur, it often felt like a decidedly dodgy place to be spending an evening. It also offered the most extraordinarily mixed line-ups: the UK Subs playing with The Fall, who got glasses chucked at them – presumably by UK Subs fans, who might have found The Fall a bit difficult and upsetting – or The Members playing with the Mekons. There was one night we went to where the billing was Delta 5, the Mekons, Gang of Four – plus The Specials. The Leeds University punk-funk politicos versus the heroes of 2 Tone in a meeting that makes no sense at all in the category-specific descriptions of the period, but which I promise you I saw. It was a memorable night.

I'd never taken much in the way of drugs before, my attempts to experiment having been limited to cough tablets called Do-Dos, which in sufficient quantity made you feel speedy; and also a small plastic bag of unidentified multi-coloured pills which my friend Katrina came to school wielding as a trophy following a backstage encounter with Velvet Underground survivor Nico. Not knowing what they were, she was reluctant to take them – my friend, that is, not Nico, who I don't think was renowned for her drugs squea-mishness – so she sold them to me, and I thought the sensible thing to do would be to take them one at a time, so that any unexpected effect would not be too greatly magnified. For the next few nights I secretly took one each night at home, and I think they were probably barbiturates, as all that happened was I got a really good night's sleep.

But this evening, on the train up to town, I had taken some blues – speed in tablet form. At first I felt great, but as the evening wore on I began to wonder if I really liked this some-what jaw-clenching experience. Was it my imagination, or did

Gang of Four sound even edgier and choppier than usual? They seemed to be gripping their guitars as tightly as I was my drink. Were those Delta 5 girls shouting just a bit louder than was strictly necessary? And were The Specials' songs usually this bloody fast? Back at home, I sat up in bed most of the night staring straight ahead of me, counting every lost minute of sleep as the morning, when I would have to get up and dressed and off to school, loomed ever nearer, and my belief that strong stimulants were not for me became a firm and lasting conviction.

It's Sunday 30 April 1978. The Anti-Nazi League have organised a huge rally, kicking off with speakers in Trafalgar Square and marching from there to Victoria Park in Hackney, where several bands are due to perform. I have somehow persuaded my parents to allow me to go, so a group of us from school – Dee, Amanda, Kym and Shelley – are going up on the train. I'm wearing a dark blue men's suit jacket with badges up and down the lapels: TRB (Tom Robinson Band), Rock Against Racism and The Clash. Amanda is wearing her pink leopard-skin trousers, which I covet desperately. This is *sooo* exciting. We are going to see loads of bands we like AND stop the Nazis, all in one day. We go to Trafalgar Square first with everyone else and listen to some speeches, one of them by Tom Robinson. A steel band plays. Then we all start marching the five miles towards Hackney, a huge crowd, eighty thousand or so, though the figure will always be disputed by the organisers and police.

We get to the park. It's a very urban park, more tower blocks than trees. I've never seen a park like it before; it's a kind of punk park. We're just in time to hear the end of X-Ray Spex, and then see Patrik Fitzgerald. Before The Clash come on we try to get down nearer the front, but it's difficult pushing through, and in the huge crowd I manage to lose the other girls. At first I think I'll spot them any minute, but as I try and shove my way forward we become irrevocably separated, and I begin to realise that I'm not going to find them. Suddenly I feel even younger than my fifteen years. I may have been going to gigs in London and experimenting with drugs, but this is only half of who I am. I'm not the cool girl at school, not at this moment, anyway. I'm like a very small child, peering through the grown-ups' legs, trying to find my mum and dad. All at once everyone else around me looks a lot older, and tougher, like proper Londoners. I'm only up from the suburbs for the day, and now I'm lost.

I decide to stick it out now I'm here, and stay at the front to watch The Clash. They're fantastic – I'm nearer than I've ever been before (or since) to Joe Strummer! – and I'm thrilled to be seeing them, but I'd enjoy it more if I wasn't basically feeling completely shit-scared. After The Clash finish, I make my way to the back of the crowd again. It's less oppressive here where it thins out, and I have another look around, but it's hopeless – there are so many people. I'm not sure what to do. Should I stay or should I go? I can't just give up, it seems so wimpy. So I stick it out for a bit longer, still half wondering if I might see someone I know, and only when I look at my watch and realise it's getting late and I need to get home by the promised time do I accept the fact that I'm going to have to find my way from Victoria Park back to Brookmans Park by myself.

Leaving the park, I tag along with the few stragglers who are heading off already – the show isn't over yet – and find myself walking towards Mile End tube station through an unfamiliar and scarily urban landscape. There's been a lot of talk before the rally today of possible violence from racist skinheads and the like, so I'm walking with my head down, eyes darting from side to side, wishing I wasn't wearing a big pink Rock Against Racism badge. Can't stop and take it off, though – that would be pathetic. Others who've left the park at the same time as me seem to have peeled off in different directions, and I am now completely alone walking along Mile End Road, and while I'm loath to admit it, one of the reasons I feel so unsettled is that I am the only white person on the street. The shops are all Asian, as are the few people I pass, and I'm not sure how I look to them. Should they like me because I've just been to an anti-Nazi rally? Or do I look like a horrible little punk, of uncertain political views?

I get to the tube station, my tail between my legs. No one bothers me in any way, of course, and with the help of the Underground map that even a little suburbanite like me can follow, I make my way back to Highbury and Islington station, where I bump into Dee and Kym.

'Where were you? What happened?' they ask.

'Dunno, must have got lost. No, no, I'm fine. Yeah, it was great, wasn't it? Clash, yeah, brilliant!'

Can we just go home now, please?

You never knew the teenage me
And you wouldn't believe
The things you didn't see
Some pretty, some ugly
And the lovely mirrorball
Reflected back them all
Every triumph, every fight
Under disco light

C'mon, girl, it's all right
C'mon, girl, it's gonna be all right now

Well, I guess some boys adored me
But the one I loved ignored me
And caused me in the end
To murder my best friend
And though I got her letter
It never did get better
So I got out of my head
Then I joined a band instead

C'mon, girl
It's too late
C'mon, girl
It's too late now

Some good times I remember
My birthday that September
We lay down on the lawn
And counted until dawn
The stars that we lay under
And is he still I wonder
The fairest of them all
Mirror, mirrorball

C'mon, girl
It's too late
C'mon, girl
It's too late now
C'mon girl
Let it all go
C'mon, girl
It's too late now

It's gonna be all right
No, it's never gonna be all right
But it's too late now
Let it all go

'Mirrorball', from *Walking Wounded*, 1996

It's been good times enough
To but my mind to rather
Way up down on that bed
And round it still lasts
For sure what we up holla
And is me still I reckon
The fairest for me of all
Mirror, mirror but...

C'mon girl
It's too late
C'mon girl
It's too late now
C'mon girl
Let it all go
C'mon girl
It's too late now

It's gonna be all right
No, it's never gonna be all right
But it's too late now
Let it all go

Michael, from Wedding Wanted, 1996

TOKEN GIRL

It's August 1979, and I have just bought my first electric
guitar. It's a black Les Paul copy which I bought for sixty
quid from a bloke in London Fields, via a small ad in the back
of *Melody Maker*. I'm amazed at myself – where have I found
the audacity to buy this, well, very masculine icon? And it does
feel masculine – that's one of the things I like about it. It's
heavy, for a start. I hadn't realised it would be. I get a strap with
it in the case, and I hang it round my neck and almost immediately it makes my shoulder ache. I love the feel, the weight
of it. I get it home, take it out and fondle it. Then try to play
it a little. And here's the thing: I don't have an amp, or even a
lead, and if I'm going to be really honest, I'm not certain I
even realised you needed one. I had never paid any attention
to what happened behind and around guitar players in bands,
and so I think I imagined that the point of an electric guitar
was that you plugged it into the electricity socket in the wall
and somehow a loud noise came out. I still have a lot to learn.

I sit in my bedroom and quietly play my unplugged electric

guitar, and it is, of course, even quieter than an acoustic guitar would be. I practise like this for a while, and get into the habit of making very little noise. This is good too, because I am self-conscious in our small house, and I feel very watched by my parents. I don't want the confrontational aspect of making a loud noise and having rows about it. I just want to be allowed to be on my own and get on with playing, without anyone noticing. I become quite secretive about my music, and I go to great lengths not to be overheard. When, shortly afterwards, I borrow an amp from someone, I can't bring myself to turn it up very loud, and so the quietness thing begins, born of necessity and ignorance and embarrassment. Only later will it become a kind of manifesto.

What had prompted this decisive step was my growing conviction that I wanted to be in a band myself. Like many other fundamentally shy and awkward teenagers both before and since, I'd realised that joining a band could be a shortcut to the kind of local status and prestige I dreamed of. I was uncertain about my looks, being a skinny, flat-chested, slightly androgynous girl, and thought I had a better chance of making an impact if I became *someone*. And being in a band surely made you a *someone*.

I had met up with a couple of boys from nearby St Albans Boys School – Dave Foster and Ade Clarke – and in the summer of 1979 they told me they had formed a band. Just a few days later I announce in my diary that: 'Jane Fox and I have decided to try and form a band sometime' – this despite the fact that neither of us had any instruments (it was just before I bought my guitar), or any songs, or even knew each other very well. It just seemed like an entirely reasonable proposition – we liked lots of bands and we had lots of records and went to gigs, so what was to stop us?

Meanwhile all around me, in the quiet of their own bedrooms, countless other teenagers (mostly still boys, if the truth be told) were having the same idea. It has been repeated so often that it is now a cliché, but it is a fact that punk groups, like no other groups before them, inspired in those of a certain age the conviction and desire to take part in what was happening rather than simply to watch and listen. Perhaps previous bands had inspired those with genuine musical talent to buy instruments, start practising and dream of one day being good enough to perform. But after 1977 it seemed there was no need to fanny around wasting time on things like practising, or honing your craft – you could just buy an instrument, get together with anyone else who had one and go out and do a gig. Right now. For teenagers with the patience and attention spans of goldfish, this was enormously appealing. There was the added bonus that the grown-ups hated it all, and so wouldn't try to spoil it by being supportive (i.e. interfering). You didn't want or need anyone's help, the whole point was to Do It Yourself. And so that's just what we did.

The first local band I had any real contact with was The Toys. Top dogs at the time on the St Albans school band scene, they were what would probably now be described as a jangly pop band, more Postcard than Rough Trade. Their main strength lay in Gez Sagar's vocals, which were unusually strong and tuneful by local standards – by any standards, in fact – and I would later practise at home, singing into a borrowed mic, trying to sound like him. In contrast to the majority of other bands at the time, they wrote mostly love songs, slightly world-weary and bitchy, and because of this were very popular with the girls.

In June 1979 I was impressed beyond reason to discover that they had actually managed to put a record out – it was a seven-inch, four-track EP called 'My Mind Wanders' – and my diary for 21 June says: 'Got *NME*. Gez Sagar's band The Toys have got an EP out and Danny Baker gave it a pretty good review.' Then, fantastically, Huw came up with the suggestion that we interview them for his fanzine. His idea was that we would both interview them but I would write the piece. This sounded great to me, and I didn't like to disillusion him by admitting that I had not the faintest clue what you were supposed to do once you had an interview on tape, or how you turned it into an article.

So we spent the evening in the pub, me with a tape recorder, while they mucked about throughout the 'interview', taking the piss out of Huw and flirting with me in a very old-fashioned, sexist way. Didn't they realise I was a serious journalist, and a bit of a feminist too? They left messages and phone numbers for me on the tape while I was in the loo, and of course this section of the tape was the bit that most excited my interest when I got it home later. Huw was very cross with them and wanted me to write a dismissive piece, saying how silly they were. But they were a band, for God's sake – I fancied them! And what's more, they made me want to be in a band too. I loved the camaraderie they displayed, the being-in-a-gang aspect of it all, and I knew I wanted some of that for myself.

The phone rang at home one evening. It was Dave Foster.

'I hear you've got yourself a guitar,' he said casually.

'Yeah, that's right. I'm thinking of forming a band with Jane Fox.'

'Well, we could do with a second guitarist, why don't you come over and rehearse with us? You know, we could see how it sounds.'

Hey, this was cool. I was being asked to join a band. As the token girl! I liked the idea, so I kept quiet about the fact that I couldn't play yet, and got my dad to give me a lift over to Dave's house.

I learned a few of their songs, and they were, if not madly enthusiastic about my guitar-playing, at least tolerant of my ineptitude, and three days later Dave rang to tell me I was officially in the band, which was called Stern Bops.

And did I mind being let into the band as the token girl? No, I don't think I did. In fact, I thought there was a certain sex appeal to being the only girl. Clearly being onstage with a guitar was sexy anyway. But standing next to a load of blokes just enhanced the sexiness if you were the only girl. I was also quite clear that this was a good way to get a boyfriend who was in a band, one of my current ambitions, and indeed that did happen, as pretty soon I started going out with Ade, the bass player. But even that wasn't the whole story. When it came to boys in bands, I didn't want just to go out with them, I wanted to BE them.

The very next Saturday after being invited to join, I went over to rehearse at Dave's house and then we all went out together in the evening to see The Specials and Madness at Hatfield Poly. This was the 'being part of a gang' that I'd been hoping for. Lucy O'Brien wrote in her book *She Bop*: 'Being in a band gives you instant power. No wonder boys love it.' She was talking about her own experience of being in a teenage all-girl band, but I found that being the only girl in a band had the same effect. Almost overnight it seemed my status had improved, and I was Someone.

Over the half-term holiday I spent every day rehearsing with them, and after a few days plucked up the courage to show them some lyrics I had written. These included 'Trendy Last Wednesday', in which I drew a cunning link between the fickleness of pop fashion and the inconstancy of boyfriends: 'I was trendy last Wednesday / Like wearing leather trousers and expressions of hate / Yeah, I was trendy last Wednesday / But now I'm out of date'. And 'Julie', my ode to Julie Burchill, whom I worshipped and adored. At home I had pinned to my bedroom wall that iconic black-and-white *NME* shot of her and Tony Parsons leaning against a brick wall, though I had ruthlessly cut Tony out of the photo, knowing exactly who the talent was, and my song was written in her defence – as if she needed my help. 'Everybody hates you, Julie / Everybody hates you, but they can't see / What you're really like, Julie / Everybody hates you – except for me'.

I went on to make a career out of being a songwriter, you know. As Morrissey would say, these things take time.

Despite their obvious flaws, the boys loved these songs of mine. Theirs weren't much better – one of our more popular numbers was called 'Down The Horn' and was about, well, going down the Horn of Plenty for a drink. We were off and running now. The only real problem in the band was Paul, the singer, who was neither very keen nor very good, and so when he failed to turn up for a rehearsal one day, the boys turned to me.

'What about you, Trace? Can you sing?' they asked.

Could I sing? I had no idea – it had never occurred to me.

I had sung a bit at school, in the choir, but it was hardly an Aretha-style gospel training – it was more that we got together at lunchtime in the music room and sang *Joseph and His Technicolor Dreamcoat*. Since I'd got into punk, I'd spent a lot of time singing along with records at home, but that didn't mean I knew what I sounded like. The singer I most wanted to sound like was Patti Smith, whose *Horses* album I had played endlessly, but it was already clear to me that her style of singing required a level of confidence and assertiveness that I was pretty sure was beyond me. In fact, I was worried that any kind of singing ultimately demanded self-confidence more than anything else. Playing rhythm guitar in a band was one thing: it was quite easy to hide behind your guitar, and behind what the other guitarist was playing, but being the singer put you fair and square in the middle of the stage (not that there were any stages yet) and at the front of the whole band. I wasn't a natural show-off, so was that really where I wanted to be?

At the same time I was intrigued by the idea, and flattered to be asked. Too embarrassed even to try as long as everyone was looking at me, I made what was probably a fairly unique request.

'Um, I'll have a go. But I can't do it if you're all looking at me. Can I go inside the wardrobe and sing from there?'

The others looked at me strangely, possibly beginning to worry about the apparent absence of any stage personality in this girl they had just recruited, but to their credit they agreed, without killing themselves laughing, and so in I went. From inside my hidey-hole I sang David Bowie's 'Rebel Rebel'. I emerged to a very positive response, the others all declaring that I sounded like Siouxsie Sioux – I was trying very hard to – and while I was quite pleased with myself, I wasn't sure that I would be able to do it in front of an audience. We could hardly take the wardrobe around with us. Anyway, the strain of trying to sing like Siouxsie had already given me a sore throat, so the very moment that opened my eyes to the possibility of being a singer was tinged with the disappointment of acknowledging that I would never be a Siouxsie or a Patti Smith. And at that time, I wasn't really sure what other type of girl singers there were.

It was decided. I would stay on rhythm guitar, and Paul would remain the singer. Though not for long – he soon left, and Ade took over on vocals.

The boys were disappointed, and I came away from the

rehearsal wondering if I'd let them down. The thought worried away at me during the bus ride home. Why didn't I want it more? Or, not that exactly, for in many ways I really did want it, desperately. But why was I so ambivalent about the very concept of attention, both wanting and not wanting it? Making music is never just about making music. It's about being heard, fighting for your personal vision – your own version of events – to be listened to, given weight. It's about making people sit up and notice you, and acknowledge your worth. But while I wanted all this, I seemed to want it in an invisible kind of way. I wanted to be heard without having to be heard, or perhaps more specifically, without having to be looked at.

I only have one old rehearsal-room tape of the Stern Bops to remind me of what we sounded like, plus a couple of tracks we recorded for other people's compilations. The cassette – which has 'Some good stuff' scrawled on one side, and 'DO NOT PLAY EVER' written menacingly on the other – captures a fairly classic rackety, punky, poppy garage band. Very tuneful and punchy, jangly like our local heroes The Toys, but a little bit heavier and chunkier due to the two guitars. Our drummer, who was a ginger-haired skinhead, dressed permanently in a pale blue Fred Perry and Doc Martens, attacks every corner of the kit. Possibly with his Doc Martens. We're obviously influenced by the Buzzcocks, The Undertones and The Specials, and as my one little press cutting about us, from the *St Albans Review* of April 1980, says: 'They do a nice line in pop originals, that combine echoes of the 60s beat-group sound with a modern up-tempo zest'! We were never likely to set the world on fire, but we were good enough.

On 2 November 1979 we did our – and my – first ever 'gig', playing at a party at Dave's house. We had rehearsed hard for it, and it went off OK until some gatecrashers barged in,

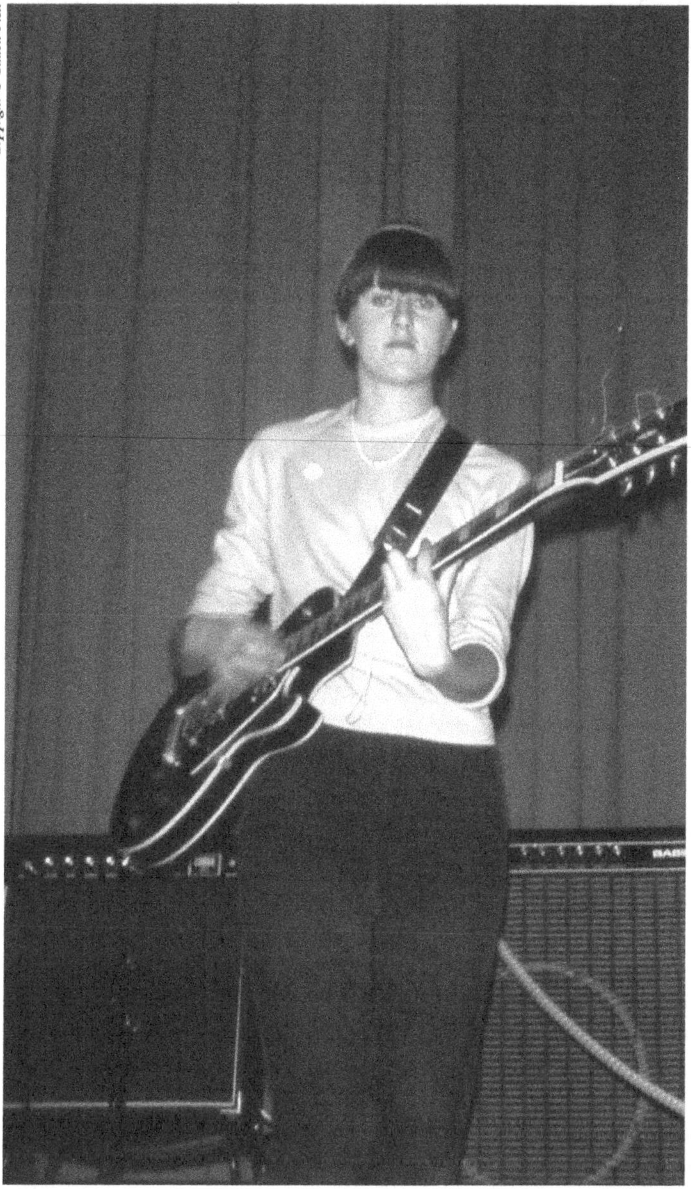

a fight broke out and Dave's dad got beaten up and the police were called. Apart from that, it was a lovely evening.

Two days later we did our second gig, at the Randall Hut, which was the location for the boys' school youth club. We played seven songs including 'Julie', 'Stern Bops' (our theme tune, which I had quickly written), 'Down The Horn' and 'Barbed Wire Love' – possibly our political song, though the lyrics now escape me. 'Not many people there, but the few seemed to like us', says my diary.

It's Christmas 1979, and you can tell Ade and I are the perfect post-punk romantic couple – he gives me The Cure single, and I give him 'Time Goes By So Slow' by The Distractions. I also get *London Calling* by The Clash, the Mekons LP and a book by Leonard Cohen. Style-wise, we are now fully into our 2 Tone-inspired look – Ade wears very short, almost skin-head hair, fatigues or narrow suit trousers, DMs and a

Harrington jacket. I have a bob held back with a hairband, and wear pedal pushers with flats or stilettos and an old anorak of my mum's. Sixties-style round-neck jumpers from The Spastics Society shop. An old khaki mac, tightly belted and worn with stilettos to emulate a photo I have on my wall of Jean Shrimpton. A straight-cut floral dress, also from The Spastics shop, worn to look like the lead singer of The Mo-dettes.

Because of his look, Mum is not very happy about me seeing Ade, and given the regularity with which violence breaks out at the gigs and parties we go to, she fears, quite reasonably, that we will be targeted. In these excessively tribal post-punk days there seem to be fights all the time, and my parents are shocked at this development – they had, after all, based a whole lifestyle choice on the deeply held belief that suburbia was a safe place. Suddenly this doesn't seem to be the case any more.

In August that year, when Gez from The Toys threw a party, some skinheads started a fight and one of our friends needed four stitches in his face. At The Specials' gig at Hatfield Poly with the rest of the Stern Bops, another friend of ours was mistaken for the wrong kind of skinhead (i.e. a nasty racist one) and clobbered over the head with a metal bar by some vigilantes from the Socialist Workers Party. In November, at our school disco, Dave and Ade got beaten up and the police were called, and a year later, when my school held another disco, my diary records casually: 'Not too much trouble – police were there loads of the time'. What does this say about the times, that a police presence at a suburban girls' school disco was taken for granted?

The culmination of my own personal experience of this atmosphere of violence will come later still, when on the way out of a party at Hatfield Poly there is an outbreak of fighting and a boy I am with gets stabbed in the head. I don't even remember seeing it happen. One minute we are standing aimlessly around, waiting for a lift, then there is a sudden scuffle, he is on the ground and there is blood. I have had a certain amount to drink and become almost hysterical at the sight of the blood, and convinced it is a lot more serious than it turns out to be. An ambulance is called and I go with him to the hospital, where he is stitched up, and then on to the police station where, still drunk and blood-spattered, we attempt to help them with their enquiries.

I don't go home that night as I am staying at Jane Fox's house, and the next day we go straight out, so that by the time I finally get back home the police have already called round to my house to get my statement, to the complete horror of my parents, who I haven't yet thought to tell of the previous night's events. So I arrive home with quite a lot of explaining to do.

The next day the police come back again to talk to me, but as I say in my diary: 'I found it hard to remember exactly what happened, and cocked it all up something terrible'. I am put in an awful quandary when the police ask me to describe what I had been wearing – this is apparently so that they can identify people described in other statements and get a full picture of what happened. But the previous night, I had changed outfits after I left home and before going to the party. For some reason I had decided to wear a very tight pair of black plastic trousers and some ridiculous stilettos and looked, well, a bit extreme, in a classic 'you're not going out dressed like that' kind of way. Ever one to avoid confrontation if at all possible, I had preferred to change at a friend's house rather than have a row at home.

But now my plan has backfired, and here I am in our lounge at home with a policeman, both my parents lurking just outside in the hall, and if I tell him what I'd been wearing my

mum will be furious. On top of being in trouble for nearly getting stabbed, I'll be in trouble for wearing tarty trousers. Faced
with the choice of perverting the course of justice or being told
off by my mum, I do the obvious thing and lie to the police.

Suburbia, I a.m., you're walking home again,
Shopping bags and broken glass
I hate going thru the underpass
I wish there was some other way round
But you got beaten up by the playground
And it's no use, we'll have to go thru
The deserted shopping centre, pedestrian walkways
I thought they were meant to
Make things better, but it's just emptier
And scary at night time
Hatfield at this time
This is the place I live
Where is everyone? Are we the only ones?

Hatfield 1980, I'm seeing my first knife
My first ambulance ride
I hold your hand the whole way, crying
Get home the next day
Police have already been, well, you can imagine the
        scene
And if I'm going home
I better change my clothes
This is the place I live
Where is everyone? Are we the only ones?

'Hatfield 1980', from *Temperamental*, 1999

DIY

All of a sudden, it seemed as though everyone I knew was forming a band. Like the biggest playground craze of all time, it swept through the schools of suburbia offering an escape route to every nerdy, bullied kid who'd never cut it on the sports field. Turn your back for five minutes and yet another alliance had been formed at the school bus stop, or in the art room, and the fun of thinking up another name for a band would begin. And once we'd worked out how to start a band, we all turned our attention to the job of running the whole show ourselves, taking self-taught crash courses in the recording, processing and selling of our own music. The punk and post-punk period had seen an explosion of indie labels being set up from Rough Trade through to Small Wonder, Mute, Fast, Zoo and Factory, but even these labels seemed a few rungs above us on the music-biz ladder. For a start, they were all city-based labels – Rough Trade in west London, Factory in Manchester – and living out in the suburbs it was still easy to feel cut off from what was happening in town, and a bit country-cousin next to their urban hipness.

In St Albans we had our very own Waldo's Records run by Phil Smee, who released the wonderful 'Happy Birthday Sweet Sixteen' by Clive Pig. But even a local label seemed too much like a proper record label to us, and so Dave Foster decided we should put together a compilation cassette of local bands (including us, of course, along with The Toys, The Alcoves, Clive Pig and The Innocent Vicars) and release it ourselves.

The demystification of the record-making process was a very current idea, with groups like Scritti Politti sharing information on how to go about literally Doing It Yourself, without recourse even to an indie label. A local fanzine called *99%* (started by Richard Norris, who would go on to form The Grid) was as much an information booklet as anything else, and gave step-by-step breakdowns as to how to put together and distribute your own cassette or single, along with advice about how to organise your own gigs. ('Get a list of the local halls for hire. If you are planning a gig in St Albans, write to the Director of Leisure and Legal Services . . . ') With all this kind of thinking around us, making our own tapes and then selling them ourselves seemed a logical thing to do. The tape put together by Dave was called *Local Produce*, and was priced at £1.50. We sold it through J and J Records in Hatfield, and Rough Trade, and when we ran out of copies to sell, I went with Ade to a tape-copying facility up in London to get more done.

While we may have felt at one remove from the institutions of the London music scene, they were by no means impregnable, and by virtue of our own industriousness we were able to make use of what they had to offer without sacrificing any of our independence. It was a mindset that was enormously empowering, at least in the beginning, and would continue to inspire all our decisions for the next few years. Only when the obvious limitations of scale, in terms of what you could achieve, became apparent did this ideology begin to crack. But it would be some time before any of us harboured ambitions to sell more than a few hundred copies of anything we produced.

As for the Stern Bops, we were nearing the end. Throughout early 1980 we did a few more gigs – playing in a pub with The Alcoves, at my school sixth-form party and (our biggest gig!) at St Albans College, supporting rockabilly band Whirlwind. That was the first occasion I remember experiencing proper stage nerves, possibly because it was the first time I got anywhere near a proper stage. Photos of the evening show me looking apparently cool and detached, with a heavy dark Cathy McGowan-style fringe, a turquoise Pringle jumper and tight black drainpipes, but in fact my hands were shaking so much I could barely hold my guitar or form a chord shape. It was thrilling to be onstage, but I didn't breathe properly until we got off again.

We may have carried on playing gigs like this for some time, though I think looking back we were not overly burdened with the desire to achieve anything in particular. But we could not have foreseen the sudden and somewhat brutal event that would precipitate our demise.

On 18 July 1980 we were due to play a gig in Harpenden, and for a little while preceding this gig a rival local band called the Manic Jabs had been threatening to have a go at us somehow. There was intense rivalry and bitchiness within the local scene at the time, which was sometimes exacerbated by divisions between bands from the boys' school and bands from other schools. In a nutshell, the Manic Jabs regarded Stern Bops as posh boys, while they themselves were rough boys from the town. If at this point it all sounds a bit Enid Blyton, it was about to get a bit Irvine Welsh. On the day of our gig in Harpenden they visited a local butcher's shop, and came down to the gig armed with suspicious-looking carrier bags.

Halfway through our set, they appeared down at the front of the stage and started throwing something at us. I remember being hit, I didn't know by what. It was heavyish, but soft, not a bottle or anything like that. It flopped to the floor and I looked down and saw something pale and bloody. I stopped dead in my tracks, having no idea what it was but realising it was something genuinely nasty. We stopped playing, as you would, and some fighting broke out, during which Ade got a bit roughed up, and eventually the police were called.

We'd all had a look by now at what was lying on the stage floor.

Pigs' ears. They'd been throwing pigs' ears at us.

Blimey. This was a step on from gobbing at the band, I thought. It was all a bit too *Carrie* for my liking. I mean, pigs' ears. Come on.

I never played another gig with the Stern Bops, though they carried on without me for a while. I can't remember that anything as dramatic as me 'quitting the band' ever officially happened. Instead, on 12 August 1980, my friend Gina Hartman came round to my house and we recorded, in my bedroom, a song called 'Getting Away From It All' for another compilation cassette. Gina was a friend from school who was famous for having made a screen-printed Joy Division canvas bag, in which she used to carry her books to school each day. We liked the same records, and the idea of being in a band. That was all it took. My diary makes no mention of our plans until the day of this first recording, so there is no build-up, or indication of what led to this decisive step away from the Stern Bops and back towards my friends from school, though possibly being pelted with animal body parts was influential.

The song for this new project features me playing two inter-twining lines on the guitar, reflecting the fact that I was now listening to The Durutti Column as well as The Undertones, though Vini Reilly's guitar-playing skills would for ever be out of my grasp. Gina was on vocals (she remembers telling me that she could sing like Pauline Murray out of Penetration, who was one of our heroines) and we had a tiny little drum machine that sounded rather like an automated biscuit tin. And the lyrics to this utterly fey piece of wimp-pop? Well, they describe people getting caught up in a terrorist bombing while on a package holiday in Spain, inspired by my reading about just such attacks, which had been carried out by ETA on Spanish tourist resorts since 1979. You can see how this approach was always going to confuse people, can't you?

In a nice casual aside, my diary remarks: 'PS– we're called the Marine Girls.'

We hear they're having fun
In the continental sun
It's so action-packed
With everything their lives at home lack

Can this be real?
Yes, it's all part of the deal

At the railway stations
Explosive situations
Nothing to spoil our fun
But underneath the Spanish sun

This isn't what we bought
A holiday resort

The weather's great
There's only one complaint
All the hills are haunted
This isn't what we wanted
We didn't want to see Spain fall
All we wanted was to get away, get away from it all

This isn't what we bought
A holiday resort
We wanted relaxation
Don't like this situation
Can't stand another day
We want to get away, get away, get away from it all

'Getting Away From It All', 1980

GIRL GROUP

The Marine Girls began as just me and Gina in my bed-room, playing the wafer-thin little songs I had written. We played quietly – after all, it was only my guitar and a drum machine – and Gina sang quietly, and I still didn't really like being overheard. In September our friend Jane Fox joined the band on bass. Jane recalls now the fabulously casual manner in which she was recruited. 'Tracey just said, "Why don't you join? What do you want to play?"'

Although me and Gina were the original members, we were by no means best friends, and it was my friendship with Jane that was at the heart of the band. At school I had drifted away from the girls I used to go to gigs with, and made a con-scious decision that I would try to get to know Jane. Despite being a music fan, she had never been part of that early crowd, and she seemed slightly separate from any of the cliques or gangs. Her reputation was that of being The Nicest Girl At School, usually to be found in the art room, paint-spattered or ink-stained from some current all-absorbing project. She was

independent-minded but very well liked by pupils and teachers, and became Head Girl with a personal manifesto of
wanting to abolish school uniform. Unusually for the time she
had parents who were divorced, and she lived half the time
with her mum and half with her dad. The more I got to know
her the more I realised she was a lovely person to be friends
with – cool, in that she was arty and listened to John Peel, but
more importantly, warm and kind.

Once she joined, we were a bit more like a band. Three
members, two instruments. Despite all of us having a solid
grounding in recent punk and post-punk groups, we had
apparently not bought into the convention that bands needed
a drummer – and we would never in fact acquire one. What
became our trademark, and a statement of our nonconformism,
started from the simple practicality that we didn't know a girl
who had a drum kit – and we had by now decided we would
be a girl group. All the other bands we knew were either
groups of boys, or groups of boys with a token girl, but we had
an inkling that the only way to be in charge was to do it without the boys.

When Gina missed a rehearsal one day, Jane's sister Alice
stood in on vocals – and so we became four. Alice was two
years younger than us and so only fifteen years old, and she
sang with a kind of deadpan blankness, an affectless cool, that
was in direct contrast to the often emotional lyrics written by
me and, later, by Jane. Her delivery gave us a harder edge
than we might otherwise have had and made us sound defiantly indie. Jane, meanwhile, developed an approach to
playing the bass that was absolutely unique and a signature
element of the sound of the band. Having no drummer
meant that the bassline wasn't part of a rhythm section –
there was no rhythm section! – so instead Jane played complex melodic lines, often interwoven with the vocal melody,

or what I was playing on guitar. It was quirky, without straining to be.

By this time I was writing songs on a daily basis. Much of what I would have poured into my diary was diverted into my lyrics instead, and every event of note was recorded and replayed in song. By November we had a list of about eight songs, including our best one so far called 'Hate The Girl'. An almost direct steal from Delta 5's 'You', it's all shouty vocals, jerky funk bassline and staccato guitar bursts, with lyrics about hating a girl who was trying to get off with your boyfriend. A friend of Gina's in Hertford asked us to record it for a local compilation album called *Rupert Preaching At a Picnic*, and after that point the Marine Girls got moving pretty quickly.

I borrowed a four-track tape recorder from Ade and spent an evening working out how to use it. This simple fact will cause hilarity to anyone who knows me now, and who will appreciate that in terms of technological understanding and ability to master recording equipment, that evening probably marks the high point of my career. I have never progressed any further beyond working out how to use that four-track. In fact, it was probably downhill from there.

Still, I didn't know then that technology was a bewildering and daunting thing. I had worked out how to press Record on each separate channel and we were away. The following evening we recorded ten songs, intending to put out our own cassette. In other words we were RECORDING OUR FIRST ALBUM, some three months after forming – a feat attempted so far by none of our contemporaries, all of whom had restricted their ambitions to tracks on compilations or the odd single here and there, an EP at most. God knows where this audacity came from, though perhaps, being girls, there was a sense of having something to prove. Nonetheless, while it's true that this was the era of do-it-yourself dynamism, and there were now more fanzines and independent record releases than you could possibly keep up with, we were still only seventeen years old, at school and living with our mums and dads. We were as industrious and self-motivated as any conservative parents could ever have wished for, and it simply never occurred to us that there was any reason not to do these things, or anything that could stop us.

The inside cover of my diary for 1981 reflects the fact that for the first time my own musical activities were more important to me than anyone else's. Instead of the usual pictures of other bands, there is a Marine Girls sticker and a small clipping from the *NME* advertising a gig we will play much later in the year, at the Moonlight Club in London. My resolution for the New Year is to 'put less trivia' in my diary. Somewhere along the way I seemed to be getting more serious. Or maybe just growing up, and pretending to be more serious.

The ten songs we had recorded in December, with another two added later, made up the cassette called *A Day By the Sea* – of which we got fifty copies made for £36. We paid for this ourselves, pooling any cash we earned from my Saturday job in the village toy shop, and Jane's serving 'intergalactic burgers' at the space-themed restaurant The Module in Welwyn Department Store.

J and J Records in Hatfield agreed to sell a few copies, and we put a little ad in the back of the *NME* advertising the fact that you could order a copy by sending a postal order to my home address. The day after this ad appeared I got my first order, and then two more the next day. When a few days later I got a letter from a tape distribution company wanting some tapes, I didn't have enough left to fulfil their request. A week after this I got a letter from someone in Germany wanting to play the cassette on his radio show, and in the same post a set of interview questions for me to answer from a Dutch fanzine. You may have noticed that we had never played outside my bedroom at this point, so it's debatable as to whether we could truly be said to exist as an actual band yet, but we were certainly getting noticed.

Listening again to that first tape, *A Day By the Sea*, I'm amazed at how incredibly primitive it is. It's perhaps not surprising that it should sound so completely lo-fi – after all, it's not as if we had the means or the technique to make it sound otherwise. But even so, I can't help thinking as I listen to it, 'How on earth did we get away with it?' It has all the sophistication of a class of Year Five children let loose in the music room to express themselves. There's a moment at the start of one song when the volume leaps to such an extent that if you are listening on headphones, as I am now, you have to snatch them off quickly or lose your eardrums. The level settles a few seconds later, presumably as I found the relevant control knob.

But at the same time, I can see its merits too. The songs have charm, and are as melodic and engaging as the playing is haphazard and unpredictable. And the simplicity of the sound gives the whole thing a directness and spontaneity that's impossible to dislike. Mostly Gina on vocals, I sing only two songs, and the four of us share backing vocals. There's bass on only about six tracks, the rest are just electric guitar and vocals. No drums, of course, and no percussion either. The influences are plain to see, and reflect the fact that we were all listening to Young Marble Giants, Delta 5, the Au Pairs and The Modettes. At least, those were the influences we had any hope of attempting to sound like. Jane and Gina were, at the time, probably more devoted to Joy Division, but emulating the sound of a doom-laden, post-punk Manc art-rock band was never going to be easy.

The sweetness is there, and is so in-your-face that it's easy to miss some of the lyrical content. 'Getting Away From It All', for example, with its terror-bomb lyrics, and the final song, simply called 'Marine Girls', which is pure feminist invective but sung as a kind of nursery rhyme: 'Trying so hard, trying to be, what every girl should be / Meek and mild, good with children / Not too bright and no opinions / Kind and pretty, sweet and willing, finds every party thrilling'. The dripping sarcasm of these lyrics was not subtle, and showed that we were growing up now, and getting very fed up with the limitations of femininity, or at least the version of it that seemed to be on offer to us.

There's a random element to how bands develop, which goes against the idea that there has to be some unifying plan or manifesto giving rise to the band's sound and identity. Often, it's more that there are chance meetings with people who turn out to be important. And when you're young and moving in somewhat limited circles, it's not as though you have a world of choice. The people you meet are just the people you happen to meet, and the rest all follows.

If you'd considered what sort of person might be appropriate to help the Marine Girls make some progress with their recording, I'm not sure you would have settled on Pat Bermingham, but there you go – he was the one we met. He was a dub-reggae fan with a motorbike and a mobile recording studio, which he sometimes set up in his garden shed in Ilford. Later on, this location would always provoke hilarity from journalists, who liked nothing better than basing whole articles around the fact that some of our early recordings, which went on to sell in reasonable quantities, were recorded in a garden shed! Right next to the trowels and the weedkiller! Not so much garage rock, as shed rock!

Pat had recorded us when we did a song for yet another

local compilation, and he liked us and we liked him, so when he suggested that he record us we happily agreed. It may have been an incongruous pairing but, as is often the way, its very unpredictability introduced a certain magical element to the story.

Pat's original and startling plan was to do a C60 tape with our songs on one side and dub versions of them on the other side. The dub part of the plan sadly never came to fruition, but between March and May 1981 we went over to his shed and recorded the songs that would make up *Beach Party*, six of which were simply rerecorded versions of songs from *A Day By the Sea*. Patrick had his own label – didn't everyone? – called In Phaze, and so the plan was that he would put out the cassette this time, instead of us doing it entirely ourselves. A year or so later, when we befriended the Television Personalities, it was released as an actual vinyl LP on their Whaam! label, and so it is what most people regard as our first album.

In terms of musical sophistication, it's not a great leap forward from *A Day By the Sea*, though there is more of a sense of there being someone at the controls, and Pat's production is great, bringing a real dubby sense of space and emptiness and a willingness to turn the echo up to eleven whenever possible. It's a very sparse record – still just guitar and bass, with a little bit of percussion – but it's not acoustic-sounding, in that the guitar is all electric, and with Pat's treatment of both guitar and vocals the overall sound is more metallic than woody. Musically it's still a minimalist post-punk blend of ska-pop, funk-pop and classic Shangri-Las-style girl-group pop, plus a sprinkling of the defiantly non-rock Postcard Records sound which we had absorbed from Orange Juice and Aztec Camera.

If this all sounds great to you, then I should perhaps just own up and admit that the record is not without its flaws, and

I would be lying if I said it was an instant hit, universally loved. It's much more the case that from this point on, when people started noticing us, opinion was completely divided. We were the kind of band that some listeners fell instantly in love with, treasuring our quirks and rough edges, feeling a personal affinity and connection with the kind of people we seemed to be. But we were never the kind of band that appealed to the muso brigade, who wanted someone to admire for their slick professionalism. For all those who got it, there were surely many others who didn't, and never would. An overview of my musical output on TrouserPress.com has this to say about *Beach Party*: 'The Marine Girls' minimalist debut is a sorry attempt at writing and performing offbeat romantic pop. Between Thorn's hapless guitar-playing ... and the quartet's two inept singers ... *Beach Party* is a winceable soirée worth missing.' That just about sums up the case for the prosecution, really. If the shambolic sincerity of it left you cold, then all that remained was a kind of amateurish hopelessness.

The case for the defence, however, would hinge on the uniqueness of what we were doing, despite all those influences I've mentioned. Unlike the other local bands we'd started out with – Stern Bops and The Toys, and so on – we sounded utterly unlike your average local garage band, and while we may have been less competent than some of our peers, we were definitely more original. Something intangible happened when we got together, and we ended up producing music which was more than the sum of its parts, and which sounded emotional as well as intelligent, vulnerable as well as brave and somehow mysterious, as though even we ourselves weren't quite sure where it was coming from. We owed a debt to Jonathan Richman and The Modern Lovers, and to Patrik Fitzgerald, for showing us that you could be raw and challenging without ever making much noise. And, as with all things that are something of a specialised taste, for those who did get it, or who could at least see past some of the obvious failings, it was the beginning of a very deep attachment.

As more people started to notice us, though, so something began to change for me: I began to get more attention as a singer. I still thought of myself primarily as a band member – singing, playing guitar and writing songs. Stuart Moxham of Young Marble Giants had said of their singer, Alison Statton: 'Alison's not a singer! She's someone who sings.' That was how I saw myself too, but now other people were beginning to see things differently. In March 1981 the Marine Girls did our first gig, at Balls Park College in Hertford, and a week later we got our first review in a Hertford fanzine which said: 'They all have nice voices and use them well, especially Tracey.' And, symbolically, the day I left school, 26 June, was the day we got our first review for *Beach Party* in the *Hertford Independent Press*, describing the cassette as 'something rich and strange and unforgettable', and saying that I had 'a voice with a future – rich, controlled and soulful'.

I was flattered, and excited too. Having been too scared to sing with the Stern Bops, I had now taken a few steps forward and let people hear what I sounded like. And they liked it. I was beginning to realise that singing could possibly bring me something ultimately more satisfying than just playing the guitar. The shyness that inhibited me and made it problematic for me to be the singer was, ironically, the very thing that made me need it so much. Shy not just onstage but in everyday life, I never found it easy to be emotionally expressive or overt. Things would often remain unsaid; a lot went on below the surface. I was never demanding, or dramatic, instead presenting to the world a reserved, controlled demeanour, which was really a front for a lot of unexpressed interior turmoil.

But singing, I found, was a way of expressing it. Not only

via the words you sang, but also through the physical act of
making a sound with your voice. I wasn't able to be the kind
of shouty singer I had longed to be, but discovered instead that
I made a sound that was unquestionably emotional, heartfelt,
sincere, and which connected with people and moved them.
Surprised them too, in that it seemed to reveal to them a side
of my personality they hadn't suspected. It was an outlet, a
direct conduit from the interior 'me' to the outside world, and
it was proving to be more fulfilling and held out more potential for me than my 'hapless guitar-playing' ever would.

In July, Gina, the other founding member with me, decided to
leave the band. Although we didn't know it at the time, she
had been forced to quit by her parents who, disapproving of
her being in a group, had simply refused to let her go to
rehearsals any more. Heartbroken, she was nonetheless too

proud to admit to us that she'd effectively been grounded, and so announced her departure as her own decision. And in that self-obsessed manner common to all teenagers, where your own problems seem almost life-threatening, while those of even your closest friends barely attract your passing attention, we other Marine Girls had merely shrugged our shoulders and taken at face value her excuse that she had got bored with being in a band. Only some twenty-five years later would we finally discover the truth, a little too late to make any meaningful amends.

Her departure, though, left Alice, not me, as the main singer. I was beginning to think this wasn't ideal, and that it was awkward writing songs and then having to discuss which of us would sing them. I couldn't say so, but more and more I wanted to sing my own songs, and yet the democracy of the band meant I sometimes had to hand them over to Alice. It was a completely buried issue, never brought out into the open, and so as these things do, it simmered and festered and would ultimately become the weak point along which the band would fracture.

But for now it seemed impossible to bring up any grievances or problems, because we were on something of a roll and coming to the attention of more and more people. Rough Trade agreed to take fifty copies of *Beach Party*, saying that they planned to send twenty-five of them to America! In June, Jane and I went up to Rough Trade ourselves to sell them some more copies, continuing to operate in a completely DIY fashion. John Peel had started playing tracks from the cassette on his show, and inevitably we had been noticed by someone from a real, proper indie label – Mike Alway from Cherry Red – and were unwittingly approaching the end of our period of total independence.

Honey wants possession of my heart
Wants to know the secret of my dreams
Doesn't understand my treachery
I know I'll love him for ever
Or until I find another boy

La la la la la la la
La la la la la la la la la
La la la la la la la

Honey wants the sole keys to my love
Wants to know the reasons why I'm feeling blue
Doesn't understand me when I say
I love him every day
Or at least until this feeling goes away

La la la la la la la
La la la la la la la la la
La la la la la la la

Honey holds his breath and waits to see me
Can't trust me when his back is turned
He locks the door, I steal the key
But honey knows I never lie
And I'll be his until this feeling dies

La la la la la la la
La la la la la la la la la
La la la la la la la

'Honey', from *Beach Party*, 1981

SIGN HERE

I knew exactly who the cool indie labels were. I could have listed them for you. Rough Trade, and Postcard, and Factory, and Zoo ... But a name that wouldn't have been on that list was Cherry Red Records, and it wasn't even because I sneeringly dismissed them as uncool – it was just that I'd never even heard of them. At the time they were a non-label; they didn't count.

Cherry Red had been started by Iain McNay in 1977, and was run for a time out of his house in Wimbledon. Iain's involvement in music pre-dated the punk era and the label, though admirably independent in spirit and motivation, lacked any coherent or credible image, and by 1981 seemed disconnected from the vibrant post-punk scene. In an attempt to rectify this situation, Mike Alway was recruited as A & R man, specifically to sign new artists to the label.

One of the most engaging characters in the music business, Mike Alway was a true pop maverick. It's too clichéd to describe him as a typical English eccentric, although that is certainly part of his make-up. But how to sum him up? For a start, he didn't *look* like anyone else did at the time. He would wear smartly polished leather shoes and crisp, if frayed, cotton shirts and had his hair cut in a sort of Richard III-style bob. He didn't eat like anyone else, either, existing on an apparently food-free diet of coffee and cigarettes, and his particular passions were not the same as anyone else's: you would find him enthusing on the one hand about Brentford FC and on the other about Quentin Crisp, or Ennio Morricone, or Quicksilver Messenger Service. His combination of tastes and influences was so singular as to make him a unique figure, transcending the stereotype. Although, when the Marine Girls first met him, it seemed to us in our naivety that he represented something slightly ominous called 'the music industry', we could not have known at the time how lucky we were to have encountered someone so original and so sympathetic to artists. Up until the point when he joined Cherry Red, he had been running a club in Richmond called Snoopy's, where he had promoted gigs by, among others, The Low Countries – or The Artist Soon To Be Known As Ben Watt. The new job at Cherry Red presented itself as something of a challenge, and he says himself: 'I was seized by the idea that Cherry Red prior to my arrival was a terrible label, full of singing milkmen and things … which I was determined to get up there with Factory and Rough Trade and 4AD and Mute.'

Mike first heard of the Marine Girls via a fanzine, and remembers getting in touch with Pat Bermingham for a copy of *Beach Party*. 'I was a little envious of the fact that Geoff [Travis, head of Rough Trade] had The Raincoats,' he says. He was in fact on the lookout for a similar kind of alternative girl group, and along came the Marine Girls.

Good friends with Ben Watt by this stage, he remembers them listening together to the tape of *Beach Party* and being struck by my singing: 'I remember playing it to Ben, and we just realised that in your voice, it was, you know, it was like going to Hackney Marshes and finding the new Pelé ... d'you know what I mean? It was like, "He's good. He's a bit better than you would normally expect to find on a Sunday morning at eleven o'clock," and we were aware that it was something that was going to transcend indie.'

Through August and September of 1981, having just left school, we started having meetings with Mike to discuss signing to Cherry Red Records, and with Theo Chalmers of their publishing department to talk about a publishing deal. If you'd asked me what a publishing deal was I wouldn't have had a clue, but I don't think we admitted to that level of ignorance in front of anyone. We went up to Rough Trade a couple of times to discuss a possible publishing contract, Rough Trade being a kind of mecca to us at this point. Gina had made friends with Nikki Sudden from Swell Maps, and we used to go to the Rough Trade shop in Notting Hill to meet up with him sometimes, hanging around, offering to fold flyers and stuff them in envelopes. Anything just to *be there*, at the heart of the scene we idolised. Geoff Travis remembers us all coming up one day with a birthday cake for Dan Treacy of the Television Personalities, and having a kind of impromptu party in the back room.

But Theo at Cherry Red must have been quite persistent, and persuasive, and by September we were close to a deal. My diary says that on 22 September a contract from Theo arrives, 'thick and confusing and very official-looking'.

During that summer, we played our first gigs in London. We rehearsed hard for these gigs, and would tape the rehearsals to listen back to, though because we had had no schooling in arranging or performing music, we had very little idea how to correct the obvious failings and would often simply repeat the same mistakes over and over till the rehearsal ended. Jane's dad worked for the Lea Valley water board, and allowed us to rehearse after school at their social club, setting up on the foot-high stage, while he watched us from the back of the room and let us have an orange juice from behind the bar.

The very first London gig was on 27 August at the Moonlight Club in West Hampstead, and felt like something of a triumph. We'd been to the club to see people like Swell Maps and Maximum Joy and Pigbag, and now here we were ourselves, on a bill with Cherry Red label-mates Felt, and The Reflections, featuring original *Sniffin' Glue* punk guru Mark Perry. Many from the old St Albans scene turned out to see us – Ade Clarke, Huw Davies, Richard Norris – and if I'd looked out into the crowd that night I would have seen several people who would turn out to be important to me – people like Lester Noel and Dave Haslam – though fortunately none of them witnessed me throwing up from stage fright just before we went on. Lawrence from Felt was the one who sympathised with me for this moment of sudden panic when I was overwhelmed by a fear I hadn't experienced before, but which was only a foretaste of things to come. I hadn't suspected that I would feel this bad, and it was a horrible shock.

I was, after all, thrilled to be playing this gig. It was an enormous achievement, and I felt incredibly proud – as the only local girl group, we had beaten the boys at their own game and got a London gig before any of them. There was an element of defiance involved in all of it: if the boys had always thought that they were the ones who really understood the music scene, we had proved to them that we could take it and make of it something of our own, and gain a wider kudos than any of them. So although I was terrified to go on, so terrified that I was physically sick, it was the defiance that won through. I was defying not just those who thought perhaps that girls couldn't really do this, but also my own inhibitions, the awful, crippling shyness and reserve that threatened to derail me. I was damned if I was going to let it get the better of me, and so I rinsed my mouth out, wiped the sweat off my forehead and went onstage. Proud, excited, terrified, determined.

Also in the crowd watching that night was Ben Watt, who was due to play at the club himself the following night.

In September, we played three gigs at the Basement in Covent Garden – Richard Norris remembers coming to see us and being very impressed that we were playing in London now, thinking, 'Yeah, this is proper' – and after one of them we were interviewed for the first time by someone from the national music press, Mick Sinclair from *Sounds*. The article didn't come out till the December, and was one of those annoying pieces where every line contains a humorous maritime reference – partly our own fault, I suppose, given that the *Beach Party* cassette came with 'Catch the Cod' stickers, and we had songs called 'The Lure Of The Rockpools' and '20,000 Leagues Under The Sea'.

'Mick Sinclair dons his scuba gear to meet the Marine Girls', quips the headline, and it goes on from there. 'The seafaring threesome admit to a dislike of recording, and would much rather promote Marine Girl mania (it *will* come) via the live media.' (Eh?) It ends with a somewhat unprovoked outburst of feistiness from me: 'I'm worried that *Sounds* readers will think we're sweet little things. We're *not* sweet little things, and we *don't* make sweet little records, OK?' OK.

This was the tone of much of the attention we received, from both press and public, and you can see how well it went down with us. On the one hand men and boys seemed to revere us and on the other, patronise us. It's often stated by men in the music business that they formed bands in order to

SAT 19 SEPT 7:30PM
LEMON KITTENS
THE MARINE GIRLS
12 CUBIC FEET
SPUTNIKS A GOGO

tickets £1·50 The Basement,
29 Shelton St. London WC2.
nearest tube Covent Gdn.

meet girls, and I've admitted that I was motivated at the beginning by the hope that there was a link between being in a band and getting a boyfriend who was in a band. But we found out in the Marine Girls that the atmosphere that surrounded us was sexually complicated and confusing, and there was certainly no easy or clear connection between our being in a band and attracting boys.

I was no longer going out with Ade, and neither Gina nor Alice had a boyfriend at the time. Jane sort of had a boyfriend but not really. Local boys in other bands would flirt with us a bit, then run away. And for girlfriends, they'd often choose girls who weren't in bands, and would never be in bands, but just wanted boys in bands to be their boyfriends.

I was utterly pissed off at being made to feel that it was inappropriate and unfeminine to be spiky and opinionated, an attitude I struggled with particularly at home, but which I then also encountered in many of the boys I met, who, I realised, could be as reactionary as my parents when it came to their opinions about girls. It drove me mad to discover that the kind of female docility which I'd hoped had died out in about 1958 could still be appealing to boys who seemed otherwise to be part of the same generation as me. I was probably a bit slow on the uptake, but I had assumed that the qualities I found attractive in boys – being clever and spirited and having a good record collection and being in a band – would work in reverse, but I was starting to wake up to the fact that, of course, many boys found those things threatening and unattractive in a girl. Just like my mum had said they would. Which made it even more annoying.

Meanwhile, I was hopelessly in love with someone who was either not interested at all, a little bit interested, or very interested but too inept to do anything about it; I never really knew.

Until I reread my old diaries recently, I had truly forgotten how monotonously wretched I became for a few months in 1981. I only mention it at all now because the whole sorry business inspired me to write a few good songs, and maybe even brought about a shift in my songwriting that marked the true beginning of everything I've done since.

In June 1981, for instance, I write that we had a Marine Girls rehearsal at which we practised the song 'On My Mind' for the first time, which I had only just written. Perhaps my most genuinely heartfelt song at that point, it was a real step on from the kind of generic teenage boy/girl lyrics I had been writing, and made a first move into the territory of grown-up emotional pain. It still sounds like a pop song written in pop language, but it is confessional and intimate, as many of my songs would be from then on.

As for the one-sided love affair, it dragged on through the summer. I tried getting off with someone else in front of him to provoke a reaction (there was none). After another irritating semi-flirtation I wrote a new song, 'Don't Come Back', which adopts the opposite stance from 'On My Mind'; where that first song had been all indulgent suffering, 'Don't Come Back' was my attempt at defiance. Marine Girls singer Alice, who was only sixteen at the time, enquired astutely: 'How can "On My Mind" and "Don't Come Back" both be about the same person?' Ah, but she was too young to understand. Even I was too young to understand that what I was having to put up with was just a bit of emotional fuckwittery. If only I'd known.

And even that's an unfair accusation. He was only a boy, seventeen years old, totally unprepared to face a world of girls. I'm fifty now, and I have a boy of my own. Every day I watch the sixth-form boys mooch out of the gates of the school over the road. Lanky, awkward, sucking on fags and cans of Tango, they loiter outside our house, sometimes leaning on the car, then leaping shamefacedly out of the way if one of us approaches. On sunny days they lie down in the road, just assuming the fact that it's a cul-de-sac means that no cars will ever reach speeds that will in any way threaten them. They look as if it hasn't yet occurred to them that anything will *ever* in any way threaten them. They look innocent, naive, more or less hopeless, barely more than children. My heart goes out to them, and in retrospect, to the boy their age whom I blamed and raged at and sulked over, when probably he had not an inkling of what was going on inside my complicated girl head. And what *was* going on was a complete mess.

After the second of our gigs at the Basement, at which the boy was in the audience, I wrote that I was feeling so bad that 'at the end all I wanted to do was smash a window'. The twenty-sixth of September was my nineteenth birthday and the Marine Girls played at the Basement again, after which a whole crowd of us went to an all-nighter at the Scala cinema to watch some camp horror films. It should have been a great birthday celebration, but when I got home this is what I wrote in my diary, a quote from Jack Kerouac: 'Strange melancholy forebodings were in him, and a heaviness of heart, a dark sense of loss and dull ruin, as though he had grown old at nineteen.' I was nineteen myself, and obviously feeling heaviness of heart and melancholy forebodings.

Even now, reading that quote, I can recall something of the disconnected emptiness I was feeling – admittedly not uncommon feelings for a nineteen-year-old, but nonetheless painful for that. Possibly, without realising it, I was also in a state of anxiety about the changes that were about to occur in my life. I was leaving home only a week after my birthday and going up to Hull University to study English. Despite all the music, the DIY industriousness and the gathering attention we were getting, it never occurred to me not to go to university. Being in a band wasn't a *job*, it was just ... being in a band. It was what you did. I'd still have to have a proper job at some point, and given that I had no idea what I wanted that to be, I was happy to put the decision off for three years.

And despite the apparent teenage rebellion, I had never completely turned my back on schoolwork, although by the time of my A levels it was really only English literature that was holding my interest. For years I had been precociously reading Camus and Sartre, along with George Orwell, Sylvia Plath, Kerouac and D. H. Lawrence, and the opportunity to carry on reading them for three years while I thought about related possible careers – journalism? teaching? 'something in the media'? – was too good an opportunity to turn down. In those days, it was a readily available opportunity. My A-level results were scarcely brilliant by any standards – an A for English, which I was proud of, but then only a C for history and a disappointing E for economics – but were still good enough to get me into Hull. Not my first choice, admittedly; I'd been rejected by the University of East Anglia after a disastrous interview where I suddenly couldn't think of anything insightful to say about *1984*, but the course at Hull had the distinct advantage of beginning with twentieth-century literature, instead of the study of *Beowulf*, and that appealed to me, so the choice was made. I'd be leaving home and going up to Hull.

My last night at home was spent out at a party, and afterwards I sat up talking to *him* till 4.30 a.m. That was the last time I ever spoke to him at any length. A brief and futile episode, but at the time it seemed to go on for ever. And I can laugh about it now, but at the time it was terrible.

And so, in the midst of what should have been a brilliant and exciting time, I was as unhappy as I have ever been. It was 2 October 1981. The next day I would leave Brookmans Park and home, and go up to Hull, and meet Ben.

You got me feeling so happy
(Feeling so sad)
Only smile now when you're with me
(She's got it bad)
I look around for someone new
(Wasting her time)
'Cause no one can compete with you
(And that's a bad sign)

My friends I don't hear what they say
(Talking to you)
My heart's a million miles away
(What can we do?)
And I don't know whether to laugh or cry
(Please don't ask me)
But I know I've kissed my heart goodbye
(Well, that's easy)

(We tell her she's wasting her time
But still she finds)
You're on my mind
On my mind

And every day is just another
(Day without you)
And I don't know why I bother
(Thinking about you)
I see you should I run and hide?
Well, I get home and slam the door and shut the
        world outside

(We tell her she's wasting her time
But still she finds)
You're on my mind
On my mind
On my mind

'On My Mind', 1981

PART TWO

PART TWO

PLAIN SAILING

It's 3 October 1981, and along with thousands of other soon-to-be-students from across the country, I am leaving home to go to university. I'm the first of my family to do this, and so it's a significant and symbolic event for all of us. I pack my clothes and guitar (but no amp) and stereo and record collection into the back of my dad's car and we drive up to Hull, where I am going to be sharing a room with a complete stranger in a small terraced house in Cranbrook Avenue. When we arrive at the student house I meet my new room-mate, Tina, who has been carefully selected for me on account of the fact that we both put 'Music' in the hobbies section of our UCCA form. Musically we're very compatible: Tina plays the trumpet in a brass band. She has arrived earlier than me, and has already bagged the bed farthest from the window, and, more alarmingly, has tacked up a kind of little curtain across one of her bookshelves, behind which, I later discover, she has arranged her toiletries. My parents help me unload my stuff and we say our goodbyes, and within about an hour I realise I am not going to be able to stand this.

Cranbrook Avenue is just on the edge of campus, and is a long terrace of houses that have been taken over by the university, lending it a *Prisoner*-like air of uniformity. I look out of the bedroom window and can see the university buildings just across a windswept car park. Only a five-minute walk away is the union bar. 'I'll head over there,' I think, 'and see if I can spot anyone I know.' A couple of other girls from school have come up to Hull, so in the bar I scan the room for familiar faces, but can see no one. I start queuing for a drink when an announcement comes ringing out over the tannoy system: 'If Tracey of the Marine Girls is in the building, will she please come to reception.' Now I'd be lying if I implied that this was a complete shock – I had already been told earlier in the summer by Mike Alway that a label-mate of mine on Cherry Red, a solo artist called Ben Watt, was going to Hull at the same time, though I barely took it in at all. Mike had pointed out Ben's photo on the wall at the Cherry Red offices, but again I took no notice, and he also gave me a copy of Ben's first single, 'Cant', and I still took no notice. Hearing this message broadcast, I realise it is probably Ben trying to track me down, and he suddenly seems like a possible kindred spirit in this hellish place full of prats in rugby shirts and girls who hide their Tampax behind flowery curtains. I make my way up the stairs to reception and there he is, leaning against a pillar.

After all these years, can I still picture him standing there, and recapture my first glimpse of him?

I can't, exactly. The memory is there, but slightly out of reach, or blurred, a first impression buried underneath so many later impressions. He had short, close-cropped hair, but what was he wearing? Levi's probably. A white shirt? Or possibly an Oxfam overcoat? Maybe his little blue canvas James Dean-style shoes. But there was something striking about his face, something exotic. He wasn't entirely English-looking. I immediately guessed there were genes from somewhere else, and later found out that they were Romany Gypsy. Above all, he seemed unfamiliar.

'D'you know who I am?'

'I think you're probably Ben Watt.'

'That's right. Have you got your guitar with you?'

I have, of course, though not literally. I have by now learned to leave it behind when I go out in the evening. We go back down to the bar and have a couple of drinks, and share some thoughts about records and students, until eventually Ben suggests we go back to his house. It turns out that he has also been allocated a shared room in a student house, only three doors away from mine in Cranbrook Avenue, so we walk back there together. It's only October but it's already freezing, and an icy wind blows across the exposed car park, as it will do for the rest of the winter. I'm wearing a thin anorak, 1950s-style rolled-up jeans and bare feet inside my pumps. He teases me about how ridiculously underdressed I am – as he will do for the rest of the winter. I've known him for about an hour, and already he doesn't seem so unfamiliar. We get to his house and go up to his room.

Bear in mind that Ben only arrived that afternoon, and so has been here for exactly the same amount of time as me, that is, about five hours. But already his room has been completely transformed, and looks nothing like mine. His desk, the piece of furniture theoretically so central to a student's bedroom, if not their very existence, has been put safely out of the way on top of the wardrobe. In its place is a huge trunk, on top of which sits Ben's record deck, with two enormous speakers on either side. I've never seen speakers that big before: I hadn't realised they were an option for the home listener. The entire wall above his bed is papered with photos and posters, stuck edge to edge with no wall showing between – pictures of bands, film posters and a large black-and-white photo of his girlfriend. I know why I am here, and so I waste no time and immediately start looking through his record collection, where I find my two current favourite albums – Vic Godard and The Durutti Column.

A pivotal moment in any relationship, I described the impact in an interview years later: 'I thought, this is incredible, complete soulmates. But in retrospect, when I now think of all the other records which were in his collection, I don't have any of them. He was a big fan of Joy Division, and he also liked people like Kevin Coyne and John Martyn ... music I knew nothing about.'

That is all about to change, though, for Ben rolls a joint, puts on John Martyn's *Solid Air* and my mind, as they say, is opened.

I had never met anyone quite like Ben before. He was on the one hand simply posher than anyone I was used to, while at the same time less conventional and suburban through having grown up in a bohemian household. His dad had been a jazz musician and big-band leader, his mother an actress-turned-journalist and he was the fifth child in the house, the other four being half-brothers and a half-sister from his mother's first marriage. Though three months younger than me, he had somehow managed to cram in a year off between school and university, during which time he had worked as a groundsman at a sports club, mowing lawns and marking out pitches. He seemed older than me, infinitely more self-confident and assured (which he wasn't), and at first, after he interrupted a lecturer to correct a mistake the poor man had just made in his introduction to Beckett, I mistook him for an intellectual (which he certainly wasn't). The displacement of the desk by the record player in his room should have alerted me to that fact, but it took me a while to realise that all he cared about was music, and it wasn't until I noticed he was choosing his courses purely on the basis of which ones required the least reading that I finally let go of my initial misapprehension that he was cleverer than me.

So we would never share a passion for reading long Victorian novels, but at least he liked Vic Godard. As for the rest of his record collection, well, it reflected the fact that punk itself had largely passed him by. There were no Sex Pistols or Clash records. The band who really first inspired him was Joy Division, followed by other archetypal post-punks like Magazine, Wire, This Heat. Along with these bands Ben had records by people I had barely even heard of: Eno, Kevin Coyne, Robert Wyatt and Captain Beefheart. In 1977 Johnny Rotten had famously broadcast a show on Capital Radio where he played his eclectic record collection. Many of the records he had played were also in Ben's collection, alongside Public Image Ltd's *Metal Box*. Then there were things like Neil Young's *Decade*, and John Martyn's Island albums, *Solid Air* and *One World*, all records Ben loved for their emptiness and sonic open spaces. A sprinkling of soul – Stevie Wonder, George Benson, Chic, Earth Wind and Fire. And jazz, of course, via his dad – Roland Kirk, Bill Evans, Clifford Brown. Not much pop, though. No Undertones, Buzzcocks or Orange Juice. Ben had more albums than me, but fewer singles. I thought that might need addressing.

He had played guitar in a couple of bands during 1979 and 1980. First, the startlingly named Fléau Moderne (French, apparently, for 'modern scourge'), who dressed in grey sweat-shirts and digital watches to look like David Byrne, except for the lead singer who was allowed to get away with wearing make-up and red trousers. They played one triumphant gig in front of an audience of two hundred and fifty at a church hall in Twickenham, at the end of which the drummer performed the customary salute of throwing his drumsticks into the crowd, only to have one thrown back and catch him in the eye as he left the stage. The local rivalry inspired by this gig was such that another nearby school formed a band called Macabre.

In 1980 Ben met Mike Alway at Snoopy's, the club in Richmond where Mike promoted gigs, and asked if he could do a solo slot there one night.

'Sure,' said Mike, 'what do you sound like?'

'I sound like The Durutti Column with songs,' said Ben, and on the strength of this Mike offered him a slot supporting the then unknown Thompson Twins, in ten days' time. At this point Ben had never played a solo live set, or recorded anything, or in fact even written any songs. Surely this was audacity gone mad? But remember, the DIY ethos, still firmly entrenched, suggested that you could and should do anything you wanted, so he simply went home, wrote ten songs in ten days and did the gig. Performing under the name of The Low Countries (possibly to avoid identification, should it all go horribly wrong) he stood up with an electric guitar, a cassette player playing pre-recorded drum-machine patterns and sang desolate, atmospheric songs with titles like 'Communion', 'A Darkness So Deep', and 'Ice'. It wasn't hard to spot the Joy Division influence, and it all sounds about as far removed from the Marine Girls as you could possibly imagine. But the common strand came from the philosophy of the moment, which embraced more or less anything as long as it wasn't hoary old rock music. Both of us were making quiet, minimalist music but within the context of rock-gig venues, where playing at low volume was in itself a confrontational thing to do. Music journalist Simon Reynolds quotes Stuart Moxham of Young Marble Giants replying to a heckler, who demanded some rock 'n' roll, with the words: 'Anyone can do that. They're doing it all over town. But we want to do this.'

And so when Ben and I met, we clutched at the little we had in common in our music, realising immediately how much we had in common in our attitudes. The lyrics to Subway Sect's 'A Different Story' (the B-side of 'Ambition', another of the few records we shared), were defiant and wilful, and they became our manifesto.

> We oppose all rock and roll
> It's held you for so long you can't refuse
> It's too much to lose

We both bought into that completely, albeit from different angles – he from the avant-garde corner, opposing the idiocy of rock; me from the popster's corner, feeling an instinctive affinity with the pure simplicity of pop.

The other thing we had in common, of course, was that by late 1981 we were both signed to Cherry Red. Ben and Mike Alway had become friends, after those gigs at Snoopy's, and Mike remembers being convinced of Ben's potential even before it was apparent to others around them: 'Ben struck me as someone who was probably out of time stylistically. That was not to say his time had gone, but that it might be about to come. I was very impressed by his hunger, and when Cherry Red came along he was one of the early signings. I can remember not arguing with Iain about it, but certainly being asked if it was wise. The days of everybody quoting Nick Drake were still in the future.'

Mike had duly signed Ben as a solo artist, and released one single, 'Cant', before Ben left to go up to Hull, where, as Mike predicted, he would meet me.

Knowing us both, Mike anticipated the effect that Ben's record collection might have on me: 'We understood that the things Ben and I were listening to – Kevin Coyne and Can and people – were not things that in any way we were going to attempt to foist on you ... We were afraid you'd be frightened away.' Having two of his artists thrown together in this way, though, inevitably led his A & R brain into thoughts of a possible collaboration, but he decided to bide his time. For all of, oh, six weeks.

On 19 November, with the usual complete lack of preamble that would be considered entirely implausible in a novel, my diary announces: 'Mike Alway wants me and Ben to do a single together. A-side will probably be Ben's new song, B-side "On My Mind" and "Night And Day". We want to call ourselves Everything But The Girl.'

Meetings arranged, they say, never work out
I say we've proved them wrong without doubt
I can't remember now just what we said
Though I never could have guessed what lay ahead
As I ran towards you up the stairs
Did a voice in my ear cry beware?

Even now I'm surprised to recall
Such a short time it took me to fall
Pretending that my heart still lay elsewhere
When in truth I had long ceased to care
For one I thought I'd never replace
Till in my heart you left him no space

You say you wonder what was it I saw
I say, oh, I don't recall any more
My first impressions have been left behind
Replaced now by feelings of more lasting kind

Sure that you know but you never can tell
When I think I understand you so well
Shakes me that you are a constant surprise
Or so you appear in my eyes

Tempting to think now it will all be plain sailing
Old enough now to know there's no such thing

'Plain Sailing', from *A Distant Shore*, 1982

POPSTAR TRACE

After that first evening in Ben's room, we spent most of our waking hours together. After playing *Solid Air* to me, he turned up a couple of nights later on my doorstep with a bottle of wine and a Bill Evans record and that was that, really.

He was living only three doors away, and was doing virtually the same course as me, so we went to lectures together, ate together and sat in the union bar together slagging everyone off. There didn't appear to be anyone else in the whole place who might have any of the same records we did, and we were at the age when that seemed to matter more than anything else. Or maybe we were just the kind of people to whom that mattered more than anything else. United in feeling isolated, we decided that the contrary elements of our very different personalities and tastes were exactly what we liked about each other.

I loved Ben's dynamism and motivation, the irreverent sense of humour he had inherited from his dad, and I envied the freedom he seemed to have enjoyed at home and in his relationship with his parents. On the day we both arrived at Hull, he too had been driven up by his dad, but his journey was somewhat different to mine, with the two of them speeding across the Humber Bridge, windows down, Count Basie blasting from the speakers, passing a joint back and forth. Earlier on on the evening we first met, Ben had already tried to make friends with someone else over in the bar, and they had gone back to Ben's room to listen to records. Possibly unaccustomed to smoking dope, the poor bloke had promptly been sick and gone home to bed. So Ben had come back to the bar and found me.

All this perhaps makes him sound a bit scary. And it's true; I think he could be. But it became apparent to me very quickly that all of that self-confidence went barely skin-deep.

The influence we had on each other was mutual, and soon I was listening to John Martyn while he was borrowing my Postcard singles. The Vic Godard record we had in common was his brilliant album *What's the Matter Boy?*, and it became a starting point for us. Before coming to Hull, I had used to go with Jane of the Marine Girls to Club Left, which was a residency Vic and Subway Sect had set up on Thursday nights at the Whisky A Go Go on Wardour Street. Now they were doing a tour, and so Ben and I went to Manchester to see Vic's recreation of a kind of swing-era jazz joint. What Vic Godard was doing was confrontational and punky in the same way Young Marble Giants' quietness had been. He would tour with Bauhaus and The Birthday Party, getting bottled off in Liverpool, and writes of this period that: 'We were wedged between Bauhaus and The Birthday Party ... wearing our tuxedos and smiles in a sea of gothic black leather and mascara', describing the whole experience as 'the most satisfying rebellion I have ever been a part of'.

For a while Ben and I toyed with the idea of trying to start a club in Hull, in the image of Club Left – somewhere people would dress up, albeit in thrift-shop clothes, drink spirits not beer, smoke Park Drive not Benson & Hedges and listen to Blossom Dearie, Scritti Politti and Nico. Looking around us at the sea of cagoules and non-haircuts which seemed to be the regulation Hull student look, we didn't think there'd be many takers. Instead, we spent much of that first term getting drunk, watching *Brideshead Revisited* and hatching a plan to take over the world with our stark jazz minimalism.

Hull was not in any sense a trendy university, and it attracted neither the flamboyant high-fliers of Oxford or Cambridge, nor the urban hipsters who, quite sensibly, were drawn to Manchester or Liverpool or Sheffield – cities where there was actually a music scene and where bands regularly came and played. Larkin's poem about Hull described the building of the Humber Bridge as 'this stride into our solitude', but it was a stride that very few bands ever bothered to take. Hull's geographical remoteness – despite the bridge – and its lack of any rock glamour to speak of meant that we were forever left off the tour circuit. In all the time I was there I can remember going to see Haircut 100, The Polecats and, er, that's it.

One result of this situation was that Ben and I began to evolve in a musical isolation that was both good and bad for us, and like some bizarre Darwinian experiment we gradually became more and more like ourselves and less and less like anyone else, anywhere else. The seeds of our separation from the main developments in pop music through the 1980s can perhaps be traced in part back to this separation, our sense of being set apart; that 'you and me against the world' attitude which was finally spelled out on *Idlewild* in 1988 but was there, really, from the moment we met.

In the Christmas holidays at the end of that first term, I was reunited with the Marine Girls and we did a couple of gigs. I also went over to Pat Bermingham's studio in the shed with some songs I had written in Hull and recorded them on my own. Ben and I went into the studio together for the first time, and recorded the three songs that would make up the 'Night And Day' single. Doing a Cole Porter cover was a statement of intent, allying ourselves with Vic Godard's slightly controversial attempt to resurrect jazz, and we also did a version of the Marine Girls' 'On My Mind' and a new song Ben had written. It was my first time in an actual recording studio, Alvic Studios in West Kensington, but I don't remember being particularly excited about that. I was more focused on the fact that it meant I got to spend time with Ben, even away from Hull. This holiday marked the beginning of a complicated period of trying to be in two bands at the same time, as well as being a solo artist, while attempting to get a university degree. The logistical difficulties of all this were only compounded by the competing loyalties involved: I had a new gang now and it was me and Ben, not me and the Marine Girls. My friendship with Jane, which had been so intense only a few months earlier, was now stretched thin by the distance between us – she had gone to art college in Brighton – and by the fact that we were both meeting new people. Ben and I may have recorded those three songs in a fairly casual manner, certainly with no view to the fact that we were a band, or at the beginning of a long career, but it was a pivotal moment, an axis on which something tilted and would never be the same again.

On hearing the tracks Ben and I had just recorded together, Mike Alway put it to us that the Cole Porter cover, 'Night And Day', which we had planned as a B-side, should actually be the single. We agreed to this decision, went back up to Hull and suddenly started to become celebrities.

In February, the Marine Girls did their first ever John Peel session, and then the first Marine Girls single 'On My Mind' was made Single of the Week in the *NME*, earning me the nickname 'Popstar Trace' up at Hull. It was a lovely review that summed up exactly what I wanted the Marine Girls to be: '"On My Mind" is a lovesick lament that lies midway between The Shangri-Las and Nico's Velvet Underground'.

For the next few months we seemed to be in the music press every other week, and as Mike Alway, who was handling our publicity at the time, remembers: 'It would be eleven o'clock on a Sunday morning and I'd be on my twenty-fifth cup of coffee and I'd just be thinking, "This is easy." And it was easy.'

In March, the Marine Girls did a *Melody Maker* interview which would end up as the front-cover article. There we are in the photos in our second-hand chic – Jane wearing a 1950s print dress, Alice looking punky in drainpipe jeans and brothel creepers and me in my mum's old 1960s anorak and a grey sweatshirt. Reading the piece, it's clear to see the cracks appearing in the band, one unresolved issue being our changing attitudes towards our own musicianship, or lack of it. I was starting to be bored by the limitations set by that idealisation of amateurism that we were taken to represent.

Mike Alway summed it up charmingly when he said to me recently that we were 'unintentionally atonal', and while that may have been a good starting point, it didn't seem to me to be a road you could travel down for ever. From a feminist perspective, too, I was beginning to feel that it was pandering to an audience's patronising expectations of female musicians to remain at this shambolic level, and that we'd be making more of a point if we improved. Jane and Alice didn't fully agree with this, and instead were more concerned about the music being too professional or overproduced in a slick, commercial way. We were by no means alone in having this argument, either. By now, the post-punk consensus about avoiding the mainstream and deconstructing the pop song was splintering, and some of those who had been at the very core of this scene – most notably Scritti Politti – were formulating a whole new concept based around making gorgeous, lush pop records and infiltrating the pop marketplace. For the first time since, well, since before punk, credible groups started to talk about wanting to have hits, and were championing the quest to create the perfect pop moment. In this climate, there was a danger that the semi-skilled approach might just start to look wilfully dated and Luddite. Even, God forbid, less committed, in that it might seem as if you simply didn't care enough, as if you were a mere pop dilettante.

In April, we went to Birmingham to appear at a couple of arts events being staged by our friend Dave Haslam. He called them Extravaganzas, and combined bands playing with screen-ings of films and performances of plays. His diary descriptions of the couple of days we spent there capture what we were like at the time.

Went to meet the Marine Girls at Digbeth bus station. They arrived about four-ish with guitars in solid little battered brown cases. Tracey is the oldest and most musical and the quietest, Jane is by far the most enthusiastic and Alice is the singer, and she was wearing a big flying jacket with fur neck and collars and leopardskin shoes. When we got home I tried to feed them but they weren't bothered, and so we walked up to Boots for throat lozenges . . .

The Marine Girls went on earlier than planned but did really well. Alice hit objects and sang and Jane sat down in the front row when Tracey and Alice duetted 'Fever' which was stunning . . . After the play we cleared up a little and then the [Marine Girls] and Chris and two of his friends went and got the bus into town for Lesley and Libby's party at Holy City Zoo. I danced with Jane and talked to Pete Wylie a lot of the time, he's a very funny man. Introduced him to Guy but not to the Marine Girls. He said pop groups meeting each other in clubs was "gross".'

Dave's diary encapsulates how young we were, and how small our frame of reference.

Up earlier than usual and had a cooked breakfast and took the Marine Girls into town. Went to Inferno Records, then Virgin and spotted Marine Girls posters here and there. Spent ages trying to buy a stamp for Tracey. In HMV the man there put their LP on when he saw them, he was very excited and said he was coming to the gig. Then we went buying sweets in the Bull Ring and Alice was excited because she'd been studying the Bull Ring in her geography lessons.

Still studying the architectural landmarks of urban Britain for school projects, we were at the same time being splashed over the front cover of *Melody Maker*. A week later there was a Marine Girls interview in the *NME*, and a couple of weeks after that an interview with Ben in *Melody Maker* (he had released a solo twelve-inch EP in April called 'Summer Into Winter', with Robert Wyatt guesting on piano and vocals). This was followed by an *NME* interview with Eveything But The Girl . . . and so it went on.

Mike was right. It did just seem so easy. We wrote songs and made records, and got into the music papers more or less every week. Even writing the songs themselves was basically easy. With the certainty of youth, I felt sure that the things I liked –

the books I read, the music I respected – were simply the correct things to like, and the list of my influences was something I could proudly display to anyone. The lyrics I wrote now were almost exclusively personal, and given that every second of my life seemed so vivid and rich with detail and event, there was no shortage of subject matter. The smallest, most 'trivial' things could provide inspiration or an opportunity for reflection. I had no worries about whether or not these stories were too private to be of interest to an audience; I never really even considered any particular audience. I felt entirely connected to the time and place in which I was writing the songs, and so believed that those around me would feel the same as me and would understand them. Like every other new band who find themselves taken up by the press, we took the attention for granted, having no idea how precious it was, how hard to come by and how impossible to recapture once lost.

What our fellow students thought about it all I'm not entirely sure. We were still trying to fit everything in around university, so during term-time we did what all the other students did; it's just we were marginally famous. There was the little Popstar Trace quip, but aside from that, in a typically English way, most people dealt with it by not referring to it. We were neither unduly feted nor shunned – it simply wasn't mentioned.

As our first year at Hull ended, the first Everything But The Girl single, 'Night And Day', was released, to good reviews in the *NME*, *Sounds*, *Melody Maker* and *Smash Hits*, where reviewer Neil Tennant wrote that it was 'an outstanding new cover of this classic song ... Tracey Thorn is the young, smokey voice against the picked electric guitar of Ben Watt. I've got this under my skin.' It was also reviewed on Radio 1's *Roundtable* by Elvis Costello and Martin Fry of ABC, who both loved it and threatened to steal the show's copy afterwards. I have an old cutting from *Melody Maker* with the week's indie chart, showing 'Night And Day' at number one, and the Marine Girls 'On My Mind' at number 9.

Ben and I came down to London for the summer and were promptly interviewed by the *NME* again, this time for their feature piece 'Portrait of the Artist as a Consumer'. More lists. Heroes, favourite songs, films and books. Ben's included Paul Weller, Bill Evans, Orson Welles, Bob Dylan 1961–64 (you have to be specific about these things); *The Third Man*, *Mephisto*, *Henderson the Rain King* by Saul Bellow, *Frankenstein* by Mary Shelley; 'Just like Gold' by Aztec Camera and 'So Strange' by Kevin Coyne. My heroines were Billie Holiday, Lesley Woods, Siouxsie, Nico and Astrud Gilberto. My favourite songs were by Marvin Gaye, Scritti Politti, Vic Godard and Stan Getz, while my favourite films included *Badlands* and *Assault on Precinct 13*. One of my favourite books was still Kerouac's *On the Road*.

In August, Cherry Red released my solo album – or mini-album, as it's only about twenty minutes long – *A Distant Shore*. It was really a handful of songs I'd written during the winter of 1981, intending them to be Marine Girls songs, but which were so intensely personal that I knew I had to sing them myself. I went and recorded them in Pat's shed, the whole recording session taking me no more than two or three days, and I think costing the grand total of £167. I sent the tracks to Mike Alway as demos, not sure in my own mind what they were for or who was going to perform them, but he was adamant they be released just as they were.

The resulting record is even more minimalist than the Marine Girls – just me and my guitar and a bit of Pat's reverb. By the time it came out in the summer of 1982, Ben and I had worked things out between us, and after a period of pretending to be friends, were now living together in a flat in Hull's

Pearson Park. But the period *A Distant Shore* records and the mood it captures is one of uncertainty and vulnerability. The first song, 'Small Town Girl', sums up the whole story, in that it's a song about trying not to fall in love – 'keep your love and I'll keep mine' – and blankly owns up to the fact that my self-esteem was at an all-time low: 'Still so much a part of me is my past disgrace / And you might say you don't care / But how could you when you weren't even there?'

I felt I had made a fool of myself back home, falling in love with someone who wasn't available, or wasn't interested, even though, in truth, probably no one had even noticed and the humiliation was all in my own mind. But I was damned if I was going to let it happen again, and so Ben and I had been through a slightly tortuous few months of advancing towards each other, then backing off; beginning a relationship, then ending it. It had been difficult, but also quite inspiring, and led to the creation of something that was raw and truthful and that struck a chord with a lot of listeners at the same stage of life as we were.

The record was again well received by the music press. (This whole period was really one long honeymoon.) The *NME* said the songs revealed 'a simple skill that hasn't been apparent in the pop chart, save the odd Undertones single, since the heyday of Pete Shelley and the Buzzcocks'. I treasured that, of course. *Sounds* described it as 'stunning in its very simplicity', while *Melody Maker* said: 'It's the most extreme thing Tracey has done so far. This is a demanding record to listen to, both emotionally and intellectually.'

I was glad people had noticed the extremity in it. The growing concern we had at the time was that the quiet, minimalist thing could easily be misinterpreted as easy listening, and we would soon begin to be defensive about this issue. In a solo interview I did with *Sounds* in October, I say of *A Distant*

Shore: 'People say they relax to it, but I can't relax to it at all. I play it and it puts me on edge! The music is relaxing, but the lyrics certainly aren't. I'd hate it to be thought of as background music.'

Those dreaded words, background music and easy listening. They were out of the bag now, and we were just at the beginning of an argument that we would continue to have, on and off, for years.

I know you're down again and you see nothing but
        rain
You put your friends through hell
And that's why we get along so well
You see, I always was your girl
It always will be
You and me against the world

We know the years can give
Romance to the street where we once lived
You wondered why no one called
Between you and me we scared them all
You see, I always was your girl
It always has been
You and me against the world

Maybe we're wrong and the world is right
But don't tell me that tonight
Self-assured and abusing guests
That's the way I like you best
You see, I always was your girl
It always will be
You and me against the world

'I Always Was Your Girl', from *Idlewild*, 1988

I know you're down again, and you're looking for
it
You put your friends through hell,
And that's why we're acting so well
You see, between us your girl
Is always with the
You and me against the world

We know life were we can give
Romance to the stars where we think that
You wondered why no one called
Between you and me we can go on them th
You see, I always was your girl
Is always has been
You and me against the world

Maybe we're wrong, and the world isn't a
But don't tell me that I might
Self-assured and knowing it sets
That's the way I like you best
You see, I always was your girl
Is always will be
So You and me against the world

Always was your girl (from *Lunatic*, 1981)

THAT'S ENTERTAINMENT

In December 1982, The Jam played their last ever concert, at Brighton Conference Centre, before Paul Weller split up the band who were by now, apparently, inhibiting his desire to experiment in different musical directions. The band were huge at the time, certainly the most successful group to have emerged during the punk era, and when 'Beat Surrender' went to number one in December 1982, it was their fourth number-one single since 'Going Underground' in 1980. Paul Weller was still only twenty-four, but was a heroic figure to many of us, managing to bridge the worlds of credible and commercial pop, with a Midas-like touch to his songwriting. During late 1982 we had heard that Paul liked the Everything But The Girl single 'Night And Day', and was possibly interested in producing us. We still didn't really have any long-term plans to become a proper band, so we weren't sure what to do with this suggestion, but we were flattered and star-struck.

Ben and I were now planning to do our first gig together, at the ICA in London, as part of their annual Rock Week. The night was being organised by *Jamming!* magazine and we were going to be playing in between King, with their paint-spattered DMs, and Pete Wylie's Wah! Heat. Shortly before the gig, word came through to us from Paul Weller's 'people' that Paul might be interested in playing. As Ben put it in an interview with the *NME*: 'He asked if he could, er, jam with us.'

We were up in Hull at the time, in our student flat with no phone, and so in order to try and plan the thing it was arranged that Paul would call us at the phone box at the end of the road. A time was arranged for him to call, and the two of us huddled inside the cream-coloured phone box, waiting for it to ring, like something out of a 1960s spy movie. When the phone did actually ring, and Ben picked it up to actually find Paul Weller at the other end, we couldn't help boggling at each other, both of us gawping and pointing silently at the receiver, even as Ben tried to carry on a conversation, as if this were the most normal thing in the world and something that happened to us every day.

As yet, Ben and I didn't really have many songs, so we arranged to meet up with Paul down in London to rehearse a few cover versions. We only managed to get together for one day, Ben and I both completely in awe, nothing up to this point having prepared us for the likelihood that we would suddenly be encountering one of our musical heroes, face to face, in a rehearsal studio. And that he would be excited about the idea of coming onstage with us to perform covers of jazz standards. But it didn't go seamlessly, and at the end of that day things were a little vague, and up until the very last minute we were uncertain as to whether Paul would actually turn up or bail out.

On the day of the gig word leaked that he might be appearing, but no one was sure. Ben and I arrived at the ICA early and spent an anxious couple of hours wondering what would happen. We were relieved when he suddenly appeared backstage. I remember him peeping round the door of our dressing room, where we were getting ready for the gig.

'What are you gonna be wearing?' he asked.

'Um, well, this ...' we said, pointing at the second-hand clothes we had on. I had chosen another slightly shabby 1950s print dress, and Ben was doing a kind of Jacques Brel look in a white shirt, jeans and a corduroy cap.

'OK,' he said, 'but, you know, it's a gig. Maybe you should, like, dress up a bit.'

He didn't seem too impressed.

He himself was wearing a blue cotton shirt with pale polka dots, narrow grey Sta-Prest trousers with a razor-sharp crease down the front, white socks and black bowling shoes. His hair was immaculate – spiky on the top but sculpted around in front of his ears. Every inch the über-mod. In the photos I have of the night, I can see now that he was right, of course. We look a bit rubbish, and he looks fantastic.

Ben and I went onstage, and started out with our own version of 'On My Mind', the Marine Girls song, that we had recorded. Then we did an old song called 'Nevertheless', and a song of Ben's, 'Waiting Like Mad'. The element of uncertainty and expectation in the crowd added a frisson of excitement to our set, and when halfway through Paul wandered onstage, to no real introduction from us, there was a definite moment of thrilled disbelief. As I said in John Reed's Weller biography: 'The whole audience collectively fainted.'

I have a bootleg tape of the night, bought years later from a stall at Camden Market from a guy who couldn't believe it was me buying it. You can hear the gasps as people realise who has just walked on. A few whoops. Then I say, 'This is a *really* old song' (cheeky), and we play The Jam's 'English Rose', which we had just recorded for the *NME*'s *Racket Packet* cassette. Ben and Paul play interweaving guitar parts, and at the end is Paul's unmistakable, gruff 'Thank you' into the mic. Next we do 'Night And Day', where Paul plays a guitar solo, and then a version of 'Fever', with each of us taking a verse on vocals. Paul sounds great, singing with that trademark tightly coiled energy and gritted-teeth soulfulness, and in many ways the contrast between us could not be more striking. There we are, the two arch-minimalists and anti-performers, with Paul beside us offering us an understated lesson in how to 'give it a bit more'.

Unusually, both for us and for Paul, there is some humour involved: when we go on to sing 'The Girl From Ipanema' you can hear very clearly that both Paul and I are trying not to laugh as we sing the line, 'When she passes, each one she passes goes aaahhh'. The very notion of Paul Weller singing this song at this point in his career is so unlikely, there's a ripple of laughter from the audience, which we both seem to share in, and it's a very human and likeable moment.

And then that's it, it's the end of the set. The crowd cheer and stamp and we come back for one more, but we don't actually have one more, so we just do 'Fever' again. We leave the stage to more applause. Then an American girl standing next to the guy making the bootleg tape says, 'What were they called again?'

'Everything But The Girl,' he replies.

'Excuse me?'

'Everything BUT The Girl,' he repeats, a little irritated this time. And the tape clicks off.

The reviews of the night were great, with big photos in the *NME*, *Sounds* and *Melody Maker*. *Record Mirror* hilariously notes that the touts outside were charging a tenner for three-pound tickets. This was, of course, before the first Style Council album had been recorded, and no one was anticipating Paul's sudden transformation into a sleek jazz sophisticate. It was his

first appearance onstage since he'd last been seen with The Jam. We went back to Hull barely believing it had happened.

Paul, however, kept in touch, with a view to us appearing on the album he was starting to record. His enthusiasm was incredibly infectious, though his thought processes could be hard to keep up with. Letters and tapes would arrive, demos of songs he wanted me to sing, complete with handwritten lyrics scrawled on bits of paper. I would get into one song, and start learning it, only for another to arrive a few weeks later with an accompanying letter announcing a complete change of plan.

At first I was keen on 'Headstart For Happiness', but then a letter arrived saying, 'I'm not sure about "Headstart" any more, but I have a new song which I'd really like you both to play on (it's a two-part harmony, very close harmonies, and it could be great for Tracey's voice . . .) It's called "Run Away With Me".' I don't remember even hearing that one, but then a tape of a song called 'Ghosts Of Dachau' landed on the doormat, followed soon after by the song we eventually settled on, 'The Paris Match'.

It wasn't until November 1983 that we finally got together to record it at Paul's Solid Bond Studios down in London. We did a very slow, torch-song version of the track, with Ben on guitar and me singing. It certainly sounds moody and languid, and captures an atmosphere of sort of exhausted desire. But I've found it hard to shake the feeling that we just did the song too slow, and remembering *how* it was recorded has always tainted the experience of listening to it. Paul wanted me to sing and re-sing the vocal many times, which I simply wasn't used to. I've always been something of a one-take girl, and I get bored and tired very quickly. For some reason I remember Paul being unhappy with the way I was pronouncing the word 'fire', so I sang it over and over again, trying to vary it each time, although it sounded the same to me however I sang it.

That sounds churlish, but it was just that we had different approaches to the whole process of recording. And perhaps even then there was a sense of Paul battling with the concept of what he was trying to do. That Style Council album, *Café Bleu*, struck many people as being the sound of a square peg trying to force its way into a round hole, and while I quite liked that tension between his dynamics and this newer, cooler context, for many people it was just too confusing. It was that Vic Godard conundrum again – how could a bunch of ex-punks be getting into jazz? Was it all just a silly fad?

But part of the impetus behind the jazz infatuation was a growing boredom with the deliberately lowly and amateurish element of the old indie DIY ethic. As the 1980s got under way, a new fascination with pop's glamour was beginning. The Style Council flirted with images of luxury, continentalism and sophistication, and we too were beginning to crave something more than the defiantly small-scale ambitions of the indie scene. As Simon Reynolds writes: 'Post-punk's refusal to swoon or risk intoxication quickly became oppressive and self-dessicating. And demystification kinda took the mystery out of everything.'

Working with Paul had meant a brush with something outside of our self-referential indie world. The gold discs in the corridor of his Solid Bond Studios were a testament to a different, higher level of achievement. We began to peek through a door which had started to open. We didn't know what was behind that door, and up until now we hadn't even wondered. But now we'd had a glimpse, and it was intriguing and a little bit tempting.

DEATH OF A GIRL GROUP

The ICA gig with Paul Weller was, most probably, the beginning of the end for the Marine Girls, symbolising the gulf that was growing between us, which was more than just geographical or even musical. It was there in that *Melody Maker* interview, where Jane and I expressed our differing attitudes towards our musical amateurism. It was to do with ambition, fame and success: all those filthy concepts which punk had briefly swept under the carpet, but which were back now, if they ever really went away. We didn't want the same things, so it was hard to see how we could carry on being in the same band.

In September of 1982 the Marine Girls had recorded our second album, *Lazy Ways*, at Cold Storage Studios in Brixton. It was produced, in the most hands-off manner imaginable, by Stuart Moxham of Young Marble Giants, who did little other than sit around and let us get on with it. Despite the addition of a producer and an actual recording studio, in many ways it doesn't sound as good as *Beach Party*, which had been recorded in a garden shed.

I had bought a new semi-acoustic guitar and Jane had bought an acoustic bass, and we had absorbed a more jazzy influence. Sonically the record is more mellow than *Beach Party*, and somewhere along the way a bit of the punky spirit seems to have been lost. This might not have mattered if there had been a leap forward in other directions, but as that TrouserPress.com piece, which was so rude about *Beach Party*, comments, much of the album still falls on 'the wrong side of competence', though we are acknowledged to have made 'an overall improvement in songwriting' and my 'jazzy playing is vastly improved'. But it suffers from being neither as spiky and quirky as *Beach Party*, nor as extreme and stripped bare as *A Distant Shore*.

When it came out in March 1983 it was mostly well received, although interestingly one of our long-time supporters, Mick Sinclair at *Sounds*, expressed some reservations: '... their much fabled "innocence" acts as an imaginary barrier, preventing them striking ahead into a style that is assertive and mature ... while so much [of this LP] is good, so little is brilliant'. He was hopeful for us: 'I still await great things', echoing Penny Kiley's comments in *Melody Maker* that 'it's obviously a transitional record, pointing to a future that could be interesting, though what form it will take is as yet unclear'.

There was an unspoken problem between us all at the time, and it was to do with singing. I'd moved on a long way since those days of singing from inside the wardrobe, and since working with Ben and making my solo album I had been growing in confidence and self-belief. It had occurred to me by now that I wasn't really cut out to be a guitar player, but perhaps I did have a future as a singer. The trouble was, in the Marine Girls I wasn't really the singer, Alice was. It was impossible for me to say that I wanted to change that, because then what would Alice's role be? And without her, what would the

Marine Girls be? Like any band which has two almost diametrically opposed lead singers, we tended to polarise audience opinion, often having quite separate but equally devoted fans. Penny Kiley in her review of *Lazy Ways* said of Alice: 'If her voice lacks the passionate intensity that's made Tracey Thorn so popular, it has a wit of expression that allows her to be sad or sensuous, playful or relaxed, wistful or defiant.'

Defiant indeed. It was onstage that Alice fully came into her own, being less shy than either me or Jane. When we played at London University in February 1983, someone made the mistake of lobbing a glass at the stage. Adrian Thrills wrote in his review: 'Any cynics in this audience were left in no doubt about a more caustic, cutting edge ... the offender was immediately offered the chance to have it out onstage but politely declined.' That was Alice – vertical peroxide hair standing a full six inches above her head, leather miniskirt and boots, beckoning the audience up for a fight.

We soldiered on, doing a gig at Kingston Poly (where another review said that 'the Girls' sweetness is the type that suggests they'd break your arm before you broke their heart'), a Capital Radio session, another Peel session and a gig at the Lyceum supporting our heroes Orange Juice. On that day we arrived at the Lyceum, the largest venue we'd played yet, carrying our guitars, our bag of percussion and our extremely small amps, at about six o'clock in the evening. Which seemed reasonable to us. Orange Juice's crew and management were in a fury.

'Where the hell have you been?' they shouted. 'What time d'you call this to turn up for a soundcheck?'

'Er, what's a soundcheck?' we asked. We genuinely hadn't had one before, and had no idea you were supposed to be there in the afternoon, check the levels of everything, then go away again and come back for the gig. Only the intervention

of Edwyn Collins prevented us being thrown off the bill in disgrace. We meekly lugged our amps up on to the stage, plugged in and soundchecked in two minutes flat and were allowed to stay and do the gig.

But it was all just a matter of time, and in August everything came to a head when we went up to do a gig in Glasgow at a club called Night Moves. My memories of the night are hazy now. It did not go well: some guys in front of the stage started spitting, and I walked offstage, ending the gig. That in itself might not have been such a disaster, but backstage an argument broke out between us. We quarrelled about whether it was right or wrong to abandon a gig that was going badly, though that wasn't what we were really arguing about, of course. Alice's boyfriend got involved – I seem to remember he had even somehow been onstage with us, and that had in itself been a source of anger for me, that he had invited himself into

the band. Some harsh things were said, and by the end of the
evening the Marine Girls were no more.

Do we all remember the past in an edited version, choosing to
recall versions of events which suit us? Forgetting things we
said, or didn't say, which reflect less well on us than we would
like? And even if we compare notes with others who took part
in those events, do we end up with the complete truth, or
simply a disjointed set of different points of view?

For twenty years or so I'd carried around with me my version of how and why the Marine Girls split up, and as time
passed I forgot some significant details and embellished others,
and played and replayed certain scenes in my mind till I had a
scenario that suited me and that I could live with. It revolved
around the backstage row after that Glasgow gig, and it painted
me as more or less the innocent party. Meanwhile Jane and
Alice each had their own interpretation of what had happened.
If we'd stayed in closer contact, or been twenty years older and
able to talk about difficult emotions like jealousy and resent-
ment, friendship and betrayal, we could have made an attempt
to see things from each other's point of view. Instead, as is the
way with these things, we drifted apart after that gig in
Glasgow, and our slightly different takes on that last evening
hardened into something approaching complete contradiction.

For some years I bore a vague grudge about having been
made to feel that I was the one who carelessly let the Marine
Girls die. Jane and Alice harboured alternative grievances.
Occasionally we were each called upon to give our version of
the Marine Girls story, usually to anoraky fanzine writers, and
because we had never spoken about the way the band ended,
our versions differed and so the grievances deepened.

In 2005, when I started thinking about writing this book,
I finally met up with Jane and Alice, and Gina, for the first

time in over twenty years, and we laid everything out on the table. It was a reunion of sorts, though unlike other band reunions it didn't involve us picking up any instruments or getting anywhere near a stage. It was enough to be in the same room again; that was something. There was a conversation about the ending of the band, which started politely, got a little heated and then ended politely, and it seemed as though we had all said our piece and made our peace. But in truth, I think that all that happened was we got a few things off our chest, then went home with our opinions intact. We're grown-ups now, of course, so we can be civil about it all, at least to each other's faces, but there are some rifts that will never be healed, and there are things that it seems cannot be forgiven. But this is how bands break up, isn't it? There's not much that's new or unique in this story. It's rock's oldest cliché, the one where the phrase 'musical differences' seeks to cover up any number of personality clashes and petty quarrels. Marine Girls ended badly, and to be honest we've never really recovered, but that takes nothing away from what we had, and what we were, and what we did.

We used to get up onstage in front of mostly male crowds who'd come to see a rock gig, and we'd quietly but defiantly play our heartfelt songs about boys we loved and despised, with strange, mysterious references to the sea that created an almost magical sense of other-worldliness. We hand-built our own little universe, and when audiences were allowed a glimpse of it, often they were entranced. I'll never be sure where we got the courage or the imagination to be quite so much ourselves and so unashamedly unconventional, but we were radical in being unlike anyone else around, and brave to defy audience expectations of what we should be doing.

But whatever happened, and even if we'd never done that disastrous gig in Glasgow, or fallen out over what direction we should take, the Marine Girls were one of those bands who could only ever have lasted for a couple of albums. However messily we handled it, there is a kind of perfection in our having split up just when we did, leaving a legacy of a more or less uncompromised version of indie pop.

The two albums we made went on to sell something in the region of fifty thousand copies each, which is extraordinary when you think that the first one began its life in my bedroom and was completed in a shed. And while we might have expected to be forgotten fairly quickly, in fact the opposite happened, and in that curious, late-night obsessive world of the internet we have become a somewhat seminal post-punk DIY band, more revered now than we ever were at the time. Those who loved us did so deeply and enduringly, and Jane, Alice and Gina all have great stories of suddenly being recognised at unexpected moments down the years, as someone discovers they were in the Marine Girls and reveals themselves to be a fan.

The unlikely nature of this enduring aftershock of ours was brought home to me some fourteen years after our split, when I was appearing on *Later . . . with Jools Holland*, performing with Massive Attack. Also on the show that night was Courtney Love with her band Hole.

Widely regarded at the time as something of a loose cannon, she was the focus of all attention in the studio that day, and when the bands gathered on their respective sets for the filming there was a sense that all eyes were on her, mine included. Just before the cameras started rolling she looked across to our stage, put down her guitar and strode across the empty central area to crouch down next to me where I was sitting. 'Hey,' she said, 'you're Tracey from the Marine Girls! Kurt and I were both huge fans of your band.' (Kurt was not long dead at this point.) 'Y'know, my band, Hole, we do a cover of one of your songs, called "In Love".'

More or less speechless, I managed to mumble something polite in return, before she strode back and the show began.

Fast-forward to May 2010, a full *twenty-seven* years after the demise of the Marine Girls. I was back on *Later . . . with Jools Holland*, this time performing as a solo artist. Also appearing on the show were the current incarnation of all things hip and New York, LCD Soundsystem. I was sitting at the side of their stage, watching them set up to do their song, when a member of the band looked up and saw me, made his way over to where I was sitting and said – yeah, you guessed it – 'I just *have* to tell you, I have always been such a huge fan of the Marine Girls.'

It's become a recurring theme, but at the time of the Courtney Love confession I'm not sure I entirely believed her story. It was one of those bizarre showbiz encounters that happen from time to time, where things are said and you're never quite sure how much of it is true. What I pieced together later was that it was a distant old friend of ours called Calvin Johnson who had carried our legacy to Portland, Oregon, first by forming a band almost entirely in our image, called Beat Happening (whose records he had sent me during the 1980s) and then by starting the label Sub Pop which ultimately signed Nirvana. He had played *Beach Party* to Kurt and Courtney, along with things like The Raincoats and Kleenex.

The whole unlikely story only finally became real for me when Kurt Cobain's *Journals* were published in 2002 and I was able to see for myself, in his own handwriting, our appearance in his many lists of favourite bands. There are the Marine Girls on page 128 and page 241, while on page 77, in a list of his all-time favourite songs, are two of mine, 'Honey' and 'In Love'. Most incredibly, on page 271 *Beach Party* is listed as one of Nirvana's Top Fifty albums, along with the Sex Pistols, The Clash and Public Enemy.

Something has come between me and the world that
        I knew
What I thought would last is falling apart
In the face of something new
How can I explain that I had no choice?
The sound of the waves fills her ears
And drowns out my voice
And I'm just too far away for her to believe what I
        say
She couldn't hear me
And she wouldn't listen anyway

How can I write a letter, the post is so slow
If I'm to disappoint her then that's something she
        ought to know
I can just hear her voice fall as I wait here alone
How can so much harm be done by just two minutes
Spent on the phone
You say that things will get better
But she would hate me if I let her
And she reads so much in every word that I say

I thought that being apart would just bring us some
        variety
But after some time it seems clear that she's changed
In a different way from me
And I would like to shout at someone but no one's to
        blame
It's just her, it's just me, and everything that is just not
        the same

Sometimes I would turn back the clock
And recapture all that we've lost
But I couldn't give up all that we have today

'The Spice Of Life', from *Eden*, 1984

STUDENT UNION

During 1983, a steady stream of journalists made their way up from London to the bedsit I shared with Ben in Hull. The thing they loved most of all was describing the conditions in which we lived. This is from *Hot Press*:

> Midway, the gas fire gutters and dips low.
>
> 'Have you got a ten pee, Trace?'
>
> Trace hasn't. So I dig deep.
>
> 'This is dreadful. Every time someone comes to interview us, we wind up getting ten pences off them!'
>
> This exchange occurs in a dishevelled ground-floor flat in the unfashionable end of Hull's bedsitterland. The bell-push tag reads BEN WATT & TRACEY THORN; it's in newsprint lettering cut out of some article about them.

And this is from *Sounds*:

> The flat, which he shares with fellow songstress Tracey Thorn, is vast and cold, littered with records and books. As

we huddle round the rampant gas fire for life-supporting warmth, a brief glance around the room reveals a wall adorned with press clippings, the odd photo and a couple of guitars.

This is from *Melody Maker*:

Huddled round a gas fire eating crumpets and toast . . .

Look, what is all this? Didn't they have gas fires down in London? I know, I know, it's just all so romantic, isn't it, and that cutting on our bell-push proves that we were as aware of this as the next man.

The flat they describe was a shrine to everything we loved, papered with photos of everyone from Siouxsie to Virginia Woolf, and we stoically refused to go down to London to do interviews. Instead, we thoroughly enjoyed making them come to us and shiver round our gas fire, letting the meter run out. Oooh, we were well on our way to becoming honorary Northerners.

Life in Hull was looking up a bit, as a new club had opened called Desolation Row, and in May we played live there.

'Shyest duo's Hull debut', announced the review in the local paper, going on to describe the club as the sort of place where you could hear 'twenty minutes of Peter Tosh, followed by the Doors, and Smokey Robinson and the Miracles'.

We'd also done a gig with Weekend at Ronnie Scott's down in London earlier in March, *The Times* reporting that 'the avant-garde rock kids' had had 'a novel idea: let's turn Ronnie Scott's into a jazz club!' In all the press, the audience's clothes were reviewed as assiduously as the music: 'all flecked jackets and baggy jeans, deep-chested charcoal v-necks and crew cuts modified like art-class studies', said *The Times*, while *Sounds*

commented that 'crowds of foaming trendsetters mixed with mere mortals'.

Paul Weller came to see us, and many more came to see him, and the whole atmosphere reeked of a 'scene', which really we were more than happy to leave behind, fleeing back to Hull.

If there was a New Jazz movement we felt only partly connected to it, in that it seemed to be as much a clothes scene as a music scene. In his book about the history of modern street fashion, *The Way We Wore*, Robert Elms brilliantly chronicles the competing styles of the period, pointing out that a group like Blue Rondo à la Turk 'had formed, primarily, to display their wardrobes to the world'.

Ostensibly, we had much in common with the style crew currently congregating in Soho, but living in Hull most of the time meant that we were a million miles away from what was happening and were carving out our own, somewhat warped, version of cool. We hoped that people would notice that, while we did covers of jazz standards like 'Nevertheless' and 'Night And Day' at the Ronnie Scott's gig, we also did Echo and the Bunnymen's 'Read It In Books', and that they would understand why. We were basically 'a little bit indie, a little bit bossa nova', and while we knew lots of people who were either one or the other, not many were trying to be both. In our musical tastes we were eclectic without even knowing there was a word for it, and our choice of cover versions ranged far and wide, from the Velvet Underground to Paul Weller to Cole Porter. It was all about trying to piece together a kind of lineage of classic, simple songwriting, no matter where or when those songs had been written.

But however interesting a search it may have been, we couldn't just go on for ever building up a repertoire of unexpected cover versions. If Everything But The Girl was going to become anything more, then we needed to start writing our own songs.

Question: Is it a good idea to start a band with your boyfriend/girlfriend?

Possibly not, but that's what I was about to commit to doing. Ben had released his solo album *North Marine Drive* by now, and I was planning to record a follow-up to *A Distant Shore* and we were each still holding fast to an element of independence from the other. Despite sharing this glamorous Hull bedsit, we very rarely sat huddled round the sputtering gas fire trying to write songs together. Instead, I tried to find moments of solitude in which to work. I still disliked being overheard while working on songs as much as I had when I'd lived at home, and would wait for Ben to go out before I'd pick up a guitar and start trying out ideas. Perhaps even then the creative difficulties involved in living and working together were something of a hindrance. I was writing songs quite often about Ben, and about the relationship we were building, and to sit and do that in front of him was a step too far.

The other thing was that I had discovered feminism, and through my reading of Germaine Greer, Betty Friedan and Kate Millett, I was finding a theoretical framework for many of the instinctive grievances I'd had since I was a teenager. A lot of what I was reading was helpful, but some of it created as many problems in my mind as it solved. For instance, it was obviously Good and Feminist of me to have been in an all-girl band (or all-woman, as I now felt obliged to say), and being a solo female artist was OK too. But was it the right decision to be in a band with my boyfriend? In fact, was it even cool to *have* a boyfriend? Was monogamy inevitably awful and oppressive? Should I really try to be a lesbian? These were serious concerns within feminism at that time, and I agonised over many things I wanted to do, worrying about whether they were the right things to want to do.

In the end, there was no clear moment when we made a firm decision to become a permanent band together; it was a choice which simply emerged from the realities of the situation. I was struggling to write songs fast enough, and at the same time Ben was working on his own songs, and it got to the point where we had about four each, and it suddenly occurred to us that if we pooled the songs we had, there'd be nearly an album's worth! Our commitment to the idea of Everything But The Girl as a full-time band was about as profound as that. For God's sake, if we'd known we were going to carry on for years we would have come up with a better name.

And if I worried about whether or not it was sufficiently right-on to form a band with your boyfriend, I could also point to the fact that the very *shape* of our new group seemed like the most up-to-date current model. The boy/girl duo was more modern, more unconventional in rock terms, than any other band format, and so we joined the ranks of Yazoo, Eurythmics and The Cocteau Twins, sticking two defiant fingers up at the notion of the four-piece male rock group.

But whatever the shape or make-up or gender balance of a group, there are always going to be issues about power and control. I was a strong-willed, opinionated individual, and I was at the end of a period of frustration, feeling that I'd had to compromise while I was in the Marine Girls. Ben was used to working solo and having his own way completely, without any need to compromise. There were things about each other that we both needed – it was clear that my real strength was singing, and Ben was a better guitar player than I'd ever be – but how democratic were things going to be? Would our relationship take precedence over our work, and if we had a row, would we still be able to do a gig? Who'd be in charge, and have the final say? And the big, ultimate question – what would happen if we stopped being a couple? Would we still be a group? That question was answered in 1983, when we very nearly split up. (Answer: NO! We would not still be a group.)

But at the time I was only twenty-one years old, so I didn't really have the answers to any of these questions, and I'm not even sure that I asked them. They were issues which would sit there, usually in the background, for years and years, not always easy to discuss.

Meanwhile, we simply carried on regardless, and set about recording an album together. Next question: Did we need a producer? Between us so far we'd only had two producer experiences, and they had both resulted from asking an artist we admired to produce us, rather than employing anyone who had any experience or talent at producing. So in the Marine Girls we'd been 'produced' by Stuart Moxham from our beloved Young Marble Giants, while Ben had his first single 'Cant' produced by Kevin Coyne. Disastrously, Ben had booked the studio for this latter piece of recording on what turned out to be the day of the FA Cup Final. To his credit, Kevin had turned up anyway, only to spend the entire session listening to the radio commentary of the match via an earphone in one ear. As Ben attempted to record his track, a plaintive acoustic little number, he found himself staring through the glass panel of the vocal booth at Kevin, who in the control room was punching the air and mouthing the word 'GOAL!!'

But now Geoff Travis introduced us to the concept of the actual producer, someone who might conceivably add something to the recording process. The name that came up was Robin Millar, another of those music-biz mavericks we admired, who genuinely liked music and musicians. His philosophy of making records was simply to try to let a band capture exactly what it was they intended, and as such he was a kind of anti-producer in the same way that we were anti-performers. He describes us at the time as 'formulating this bizarre, *bizarre* hybrid of jazz, and at the same time still influenced by people like the Buzzcocks', which shows a very good grasp of what we were wanting to do, and proves that he saw the difference between us and Sade, whose *Diamond Life* album he was producing at the same time.

Sade and her band were in and out of the same studio, Power Plant in Willesden, while we were recording *Eden*, and while being very nice people, they were all intimidatingly gorgeous and fashionable and just absolutely not indie. They seemed wholeheartedly to embrace and embody the New Jazz cool soul aesthetic in a way that was so pure and simple as to be easily translatable into pop terms. *Diamond Life* was patently NOT a bizarre hybrid. (Which is why it won the Brit Best Album Award that year, while we sat at home in a rented flat, watching the whole ceremony on a rented telly.)

Our album *Eden*, on the other hand, was a much stranger record. We had by now come up with a fairly clear-cut musical manifesto, consisting of a somewhat esoteric set of ground rules which informed the recording sessions. We were defining ourselves as much in terms of what we were anti as what we were in favour of. What we liked about the small-combo, 1950s-style jazz that we were inspired by was the precision of the playing, the no-fuss, no-frills approach, which we saw as being the antithesis to rock's excesses. In the austerity of the jazz trio we saw a continuation of the purity of punk.

So there were basic rules about what was and wasn't allowed to appear on *Eden*, and to be honest I think probably only Ben and I understood what on earth they were.

On drums was Catweazle lookalike Charles Hayward, who had played in one of Ben's favourite avant-garde post-punk groups, This Heat, and he had to adhere to Rule Number One: no snare drum, which was too rockist. Only rimshot was allowed.

Rule Number Two: no electric bass guitar; had to be double bass instead.

Simon Booth from Weekend was on guitar, and had to abide by Rule Number Three: no acoustic guitars, as they meant Folk Music. He was allowed to play electric or semi-acoustic guitars only.

There was some Hammond organ, which we saw as being very 1960s, and therefore cool, but—

Rule Number Four: no piano, which meant ghastly 1970s rock ballads.

Rule Number Five: no backing vocals – too glossy, too high-production, potentially vacuous.

Though *Eden* was finished in the autumn of 1983, it wouldn't be released until June 1984, nearly a whole year later – an unthinkable time gap in the world I'd been used to, where songs had been recorded in the morning and practically in the shops by teatime. It was a delay which contributed to some of the problems the record faced on its release, and it was caused by a drama which would prove to be my introduction to the machinations of the real music business.

Mike Alway had left Cherry Red, and turned to Geoff Travis at Rough Trade with the concept of setting up a new label – an indie which would be financed by a major, potentially harnessing all the merits of an indie label but with greater financial backing and support.

He described to me recently what his dreams for the label had been. They read almost as a blueprint for his whole aesthetic ideal: 'I thought . . . [it's going to have] a cosmopolitan feel, it's gonna be very international, it's gonna take us away from rock music . . . superior . . . timeless . . . just a little retro, but largely futuristic.' The label was to be Blanco y Negro, and Mike wanted us to join him there, but unfortunately Ben and I had both made the textbook teenage music-biz error of signing draconian and binding contracts with Cherry Red, which would take some escaping from. It would be almost a year before we could extricate ourselves from Cherry Red and rejoin Mike. All this time our debut album was languishing on the office shelves, unreleased and unheard.

And there was still another year to do at Hull University, so after recording *Eden*, and being unable to release it, we quietly returned to student life. We'd moved out of the famed bedsit on Pearson Park and into a top-floor flat on Salisbury Street, with an attic room reached by climbing up a ladder and a loo shared with the flat next door. For a while I concentrated much more on studying and less on music, building up towards my finals in June 1984. For me, there had never been any question of abandoning university; I was absorbed in my studies there. I fell in love with William Blake, and wrote the longest essay my tutor had ever seen on the subject, and through a Women in Literature course I learned even more about feminism and, like many female students before and since, became immersed in the world of the Brontës and Sylvia Plath and 'lost' classics such as *The Yellow Wallpaper*. I'd got no nearer to making a decision about where all this studying was leading, and hadn't really confronted the job question. Was I ever given any careers advice? I have no memory of such a thing. The decision was being made for me, it seemed, almost behind my back, as music began to break free of its role in my life as Just A Hobby and to make claims for itself as A Career. I never really asked myself whether it was what I wanted, or whether it was the life I was cut out for. Part of me enjoyed the limelight, but another part, possibly a larger part, was happier in the library.

Finally, in May 1984, just before my exams started, the first single from our album, 'Each And Every One', was released on Blanco y Negro. Any group should be full of dreams and aspirations for their first single, but in truth I think my attention was more focused on my work in Hull. Ben's heart, though, was set on the progress of the single, which seemed about to be a hit. A proper Top Forty hit, not the indie charts we were so used to. If Ben was dreaming of imminent stardom, I was more fired up by the fact that I was now predicted to get a first, and I was damned if I was going to let a record get in the way of that. I broke out in an itchy and irritating rash all over my hands, caused by stress, the doctor said, but what was causing the stress? Was it the pressure of exams, or the pressure of a hit single? Or the pressure of having both at once, and not being sure which was more important?

On 4 June 1984, at nine-thirty in the morning, we sat the last exam of our finals – Seventeenth-century Literature. 'Each And Every One' was number 28 in the charts. We finished the exam, got straight on a train down to London and were in the recording studio by the afternoon, finishing off a new B-side.

Bye-bye student life, hello ... Well, what, exactly?

I had no idea.

Here is the street and here is the door
Same as it was before
And up the stairs and on the wall
Was Doisneau's kiss
And Terry Hall
And Siouxsie Sioux and Edwyn too
And Bobby D in '63
And everything I knew was good
And like it was just understood

And now I need that feeling
I'm reaching for that feeling
Hands up to the ceiling

'Hands Up To The Ceiling', from
Out of the Woods, 2007

LET'S GET SERIOUS

For a long time there was a popular story about Everything But The Girl, which provided the opening question to many of our interviews, and it ran like this: despite having a Top Thirty hit, the band refused to go on *Top of the Pops* because they were sitting their exams at university! Aaah, bless.

Like most of these kinds of stories, it isn't true. There never was a phone call asking us to appear on that week's *Top of the Pops*, to which we replied, 'No, I'm sorry, however much we would love to come to London and be filmed lip-synching to our current single for the nation's biggest pop show, we are unable to do so as we will be taking our Birth of the Modern Novel paper.' So, no, it's not quite a true story.

But then again, it is exactly the sort of thing we would have done. And not because of our exams, but because of politics. I violently disapproved of *Top of the Pops*, which I regarded as being too mainstream, too commercial and, what's more, probably sexist (there was a period when they had a set featuring women in CAGES dancing at the side of the stage, and that, for me, led to a complete veto). Our career may have been heading at full speed towards the mainstream pop world, but I had in no way made my peace with what that meant, and so while we were making quite commercial-sounding music, we were at the same time trying to uphold the stand taken by The Clash, who had also famously refused the show. I think what we actually said to our record company was, 'We won't do *Top of the Pops* even if they ask us!' And then, guess what? We weren't asked. I wonder why.

'Each And Every One' did well anyway, spending seven weeks in the chart. Besides not doing *Top of the Pops*, we did very little else to help its progress, having as yet no sense at all that there was such a thing as a promotional schedule to follow. So instead of staying in London, poised and ready to appear on any TV show offered, or do a phone-in radio interview, or just be 'on call' for whatever might arise, we went on holiday. It may have looked to our record company as if we were deliberately sticking two fingers up at the idea of promotion, but it didn't seem that way to us. After all, we'd just finished our finals at uni, and we felt we deserved a break, and we had a cheque in our pocket from Paul Weller, so we did what any thrustingly ambitious young pop group would do and jetted off to Lesbos for a fortnight. Long before mobile phones or email, this meant that we were effectively uncontactable for two weeks, while our record company were working on our hit single. As they tried their best to keep it on the airwaves and in the shops, we lazed on a beach and pottered contentedly around the archaeological ruins.

Deliberately flouting the rules? I just don't think we knew there were any.

Finally the album, *Eden*, was released, and on the back of the hit single it entered the charts and was to spend twenty-two weeks there, getting to number 14 at its peak. This was commercial success at a level way beyond what I had achieved until now. The honeymoon period with the press, though, was coming to an inevitable end and, while I have copies of good reviews from *Sounds*, *Time Out*, the *Guardian* and *The Times*, there is a noticeable gap where the *NME* and *Melody Maker* reviews of *Eden* should be, leading me to the conclusion that they were unfavourable. Those who didn't like what we were doing had marshalled themselves by now and launched an attack, and it was mostly based on the recurring accusations that we were soppy wimps, wallowing in easy-listening bland-ness, making jazz-tinged soft-rock background music for bedwetters. I think that about sums it up – have I forgotten anything?

Those who did like *Eden* defended it at least in part by making reference to the lyrics – drawing attention to the grit-tiness of some of the stories being told, the kind of kitchen-sink drama quality of the subject matter. '*Eden* is wordplay in motion,' wrote Dave Henderson at *Sounds*, 'like some 60s armchair theatre, graphically illustrated in black and white, exploring the emotions and expressions of everyday people.' *City Limits* commented that: 'The ballads are sad vistas of wasted lives ... And the drippiness quotient? Absolutely nil.' Adrian Thrills would write about us later in the year at the *NME*, describing us as 'new realists', along with Billy Bragg and the Redskins.

That was all great, and showed that many people, as well as just enjoying the music, had understood what we meant and the context into which we fitted. But we took very badly the criticisms from other sections of the press, and began to give dreadful interviews in which we came across as defensive, dog-matic, humourless and aggressive. Those who came to meet us found two people who were ready for a scrap before the tape machine was even turned on. I remember once hearing Peter

Ustinov say of film actor-director Charles Laughton that he was 'somebody who was hanging around waiting to be offended', and that just about sums up what Ben and I were like in 1984. Woe betide any unfortunate journalist who made a lazy remark about politics or New Jazz. I exploded with indignation and stormed out of one interview when the journalist uttered the words 'easy listening', and I remember that much of the time I seemed to delight in being almost pathologically opposed to the most trivial things.

Dave Henderson talked to us for *Sounds* (and remember, he had actually liked *Eden*!) and found us exhausted and irritable: 'Other journalists, too, feel the rougher edge of the EBTG tongue, following their inability to grasp just what the duo are about.'

Adrian Thrills was sympathetic to our rantings about not being easy listening and not having sold out, but even he worried for us: 'EBTG have an admirably rigorous approach to the marketing process, and are reluctant to take part in anything that conflicts with their punk-rooted ideals. Whether such idealism stands up to commercial pressures remains to be seen.' Eleanor Levy at *Record Mirror* wrote that 'Tracey Thorn and Ben Watt ... have a reputation for being perhaps a little unfriendly [to journalists] ... ' though she admitted we were 'hardly the enfants terribles I'd expected'. By the time Graham K. Smith came to talk to us for the same magazine later in the year, our reputation was secure – the headline read 'Difficult, Us?' – and Smith pointed out that 'they both appear more concerned with using their new-found position to impart opinions, rather than honing their budding abilities as songwriters and makers of records ... they possess a fear of misquotation that is quite out of proportion with the tenuous position they hold in today's pop palaver.'

Dave Henderson had seen to the heart of the problem,

which lay in the apparent gap between the actual sound of the music we made and our intentions in making it. 'If they were Test Dept, they could probably beat their critics into submission, but their far more subtle approach requires a much more sophisticated ear to discern between innuendo, implication and intention.' In the musical melting pot that constituted early post-punk, everything had been allowed for a while and it was acknowledged that many bands, though sounding nothing like each other, shared a common pool of inspiration and intent. But that didn't really last long, and soon a kind of rock orthodoxy reasserted itself, especially within the music press, and our musical experiments began to be seen by some as being reactionary rather than progressive. The result was that I felt misunderstood, out of place, and responded by trying to display in interviews the spikiness and attitude which wasn't immediately apparent in the music. But sounding like Astrud Gilberto while coming on like Gang of Four was always going to be a problematic approach.

It didn't help either that we were becoming more successful, so we would have arguments about 'selling out', and about what was and wasn't permissible in terms of pop promotion. We refused, for instance, to release a second single from *Eden*, believing that that was ripping off the fans, and having no sense that a single was merely a marketing device to gain airplay and sell an album. I felt that was making a very strong point – but did anyone even notice? Did they hell. You didn't get crowds coming to our defence with, 'Well, you can say what you like about old EBTG, but at least they don't release four singles off an album.'

Many of the old punk attitudes about the music business were beginning to fade away during the 1980s, and some felt that those debates were simply over. I was left clinging to the wreckage of an ideology that others had abandoned, like some old drunk in a pub carrying on an argument long after every-one else has given up and gone home. Pop hadn't yet entered the phase of ironic postmodernism which now holds sway over the whole show, but even so, we perhaps hung on to a seri-ousness about it longer than some of our contemporaries. There's a quote from journalist Ian Penman, talking about the post-punk era and saying, 'Post-punk was post-everything, really ... except, oddly, sincerity. Everyone was brittle with it.' In 1984, and for a while afterwards, we still were, and it didn't make for easy reading.

Not only had attitudes changed, many of the original bands who had inspired me had split up by 1984 – the Buzzcocks had called it a day as early as 1981, along with The Specials and Delta 5. The Undertones and the Au Pairs had split up in 1983, Gang of Four and The Raincoats in 1984 and even Orange Juice were on their last legs, having been dropped by Polydor at the end of the same year, and would finally play their last gig in January 1985 (ironically at a miners' benefit, where we were also on the bill). If 1984 was the point when post-punk was officially 'over', it was unfortunate that it was just then that we released our first album. We were in the uncomfortable position of being the products of an era and a musical movement that was winding down before we got our chance to make ourselves heard, and for most of the rest of the 1980s nothing would really fill that void left after punk and post-punk dissipated into the ether. From now on, it seemed, we were just an individual group, alongside all sorts of other fairly disparate individual groups, with no sense of belonging to any kind of collective moment in pop history. That wouldn't really change until the late-1980s rave scene, but acid house would in itself prove to be more troubling than helpful to those of us who pre-dated it by such a long way.

Though we have often been described as an '80s band', I

still feel in many ways that I was a fairly typical child of the 1970s. Punk may have claimed that it hated hippies above everything else, and I certainly remember joining in with that claim, but really my ideological mindset had more in common with the political and ethical movements of the 1970s than with what came afterwards. I'd grown up in an era of collective thinking, of 'movements'. I was full of political and moral certainties, and the wave of feminism that had taught me so much was a very uncompromising one. It was purist, and could drift into being puritanical, but for better or worse it had formed much of my way of thinking, and it was a mindset that had seemed the norm if you were part of 'alternative' culture. But that was all starting to change. For now, there was simply a sense that we were on our own, as were our contemporaries – individual bands in an age that revered the individual above all thoughts of collective identity. If the 1980s saw an attempt to undermine and belittle the notion that there was any such thing as 'society', then it was perhaps no accident that the feeling we had of every band being an island took hold at the same time.

If you ever feel the time to drop me a loving line
Maybe you should just think twice
I don't wait around on your advice
You tell me I can go this far, but no more
Try to show me heaven and then slam the door
You offer shelter at a price much too dear
And your kind of love's the kind that soon disappears

So don't brag how you have changed
And everything's been rearranged
I thought all that was over and done
But I still get the same from each and every one
Being kind is just a way to keep me under your thumb
And I can cry because that's something we've always
　　　done
You tell me I'm free of the past now and all those lies
Then offer me the same thing in a different guise

'Each And Every One', from *Eden*, 1984

THE BOY WITH THE THORN IN HIS SIDE

A lmost a year had passed between the recording and the release of *Eden*, which added to some of the awkwardness we experienced on its release. Aside from our increasing politicisation during 1983 and 1984, something else had happened which left us out of step with ourselves – we had discovered, and fallen in love with, The Smiths.

I remember Mike Alway playing me their first single, 'Hand In Glove', in the summer of 1983. My first thought was that I wasn't sure. It was a bit alarmingly like a rock record, wasn't it? Though probably not rock*ist*, and therefore OK. The singer sounded quite defiantly masculine. And the sleeve – well, the sleeve, with its adoring gaze at a male nude, looked very sexual and obviously gay, so what was going on there?

As that year progressed, you couldn't help noticing The Smiths more and more. When Geoff Travis came to visit us up in Hull he gave us an early pre-release copy of their first album, and the penny dropped. They were simply unlike anyone else. Pretty soon I was besotted, and during November 1983 started following them around on tour. Wearing the little brown badges given to us by Geoff, which in tiny writing said things like 'Handsome' and 'Don't Ask Me About The Smiths', we went to several gigs on what was their first proper UK tour, seeing them at Leicester Poly, The Haçienda in Manchester, and Westfield College and the Electric Ballroom in London.

The gigs were fantastic, ecstatic celebrations. Morrissey, skinny, shirtless and energised, seemed to be both throwing

himself on the mercy of the crowd and utterly dominating us. It was as exciting as any punk gig, but with a total absence of unwanted aggression – instead of snarling at us, Morrissey would flatter us. 'Thank you, you're very charming, very charming,' he'd say, or change a lyric slightly to see if we'd notice: 'No, I've never had a job because I'm – too handsome!' (We did notice, of course.) The Smiths at this point were funny, and moving, and sexy, and that was a new and unfamiliar combination.

I loved Morrissey with a devotion which outweighed anything I'd felt for a rock singer before, and which I now blush to recall. It wasn't that I wanted to sleep with him (well, no, I did actually, but that seemed unlikely to happen, what with one thing and another). It was more that I wanted to BE him. I know I wasn't alone in feeling this, though I suspect most of the others who felt this way were probably boys. For an androgynous girl like me, Morrissey was an intoxicating new kind of role model – camp in many ways, but also surprisingly butch. He reminded me more of a male version of the female singers I liked – Patti Smith or Siouxsie – than any previous male rock star. His onstage performance style inspired mine for a good couple of years – a *Melody Maker* review from 1985 reads: 'Tonight Tracey might have played it like the girl with the Morrissey at her side', while this one is from *Sounds*: 'Thorn continues to stifle her desire to impersonate Morrissey, arms threatening to lose control of themselves.'

Of course, it wasn't unheard of for female rock fans to want to emulate the guys onstage – after all, Patti Smith herself had claimed that when she saw the Rolling Stones she knew she wanted to be Keith Richards, and adopted much of his iconic look. But in doing so she was buying into his unfettered rebellious masculinity, and the status it offered, as an escape from the limitations of femininity. It surely says something about the more fluid gender-identity politics of the early 1980s that I aspired to look like a flamboyantly oversensitive and self-dramatising gay man.

My appearance was changing by 1983 anyway – I'd had the black curls chopped off in reaction to seeing one too many photos of myself in the press looking doe-eyed and ringletty, and my hair was now long and spiky on the top and shaved all round the back and sides, inspired also in part by Terry Hall's current look. I'd started wearing a Sex Pistols T-shirt and big boots, deliberately trying to look as *unlike* the music we were making as possible, in order to undermine people's preconceptions. The Morrissey influence merely completed the new style. Baggy, ill-fitting tops. Cardigans. Beads. And flowers, flowers everywhere.

In March 1984, The Smiths had played at Hull University. Ben and I managed to get backstage and hang out with them by virtue of being minor recording stars ourselves, but I can only remember being tongue-tied and overwhelmed. We started writing to Morrissey, fan letters really, but on the pretext that we were all equals, sort of, although that's not what we felt. Thrillingly, he wrote back, addressing us from that point on as The Kittens, and was very complimentary about our music. We took heart from this, and pinned the postcards to the wall. Already they were influencing our new songs – among them, one which would end up on the B-side of 'Each And Every One'. 'Never Could Have Been Worse' is absolutely pure Smiths, a heartfelt homage to 'Reel Around The Fountain' or 'Wonderful Woman', and shows quite clearly where we were going next. The trouble was, at that point *Eden* wasn't even out yet, and we'd already moved on. Hence the awkward interviews after it was released. The business of promoting a record that was a year old, and sometimes defending it against

criticisms we were beginning to see some truth in, was uncomfortable to say the least, and left us in the middle of a full-scale
identity crisis. We were desperate to start recording again as
soon as possible, to prove that we had less to do with New Jazz
and more in common with Morrissey and Marr.

In my own mind, it didn't feel like that big a deal. Maybe we
didn't SOUND much like The Smiths, but that wasn't the
point, really, was it? There was obvious common ground in
that love of melody, and the purity and directness of approach,
and a lyrical fascination with the kind of bleak romance of the
everyday, the mundane and the humdrum. Morrissey's passion
for British 1960s black-and-white films and the kitchen-sink
dramas of Shelagh Delaney echoed my own obsession with
exploiting the emotional drama in the lives of ordinary people.
In the slogan of the times, which still seemed quite fresh as a
theoretical idea, I definitely believed that 'the personal was
political', and that by telling stories about individuals – often
women in familiar 'domestic' settings – you could make a
political point about women's lives. With this in mind, only
four weeks after the release of *Eden*, we released our next
single, 'Mine', a song I'd recently written which doesn't appear
on that album and which had been recorded in an enthusiastic hurry as we tried to move forward. The track itself was a
somewhat mournful ballad with gritty lyrics about a single
mother, and the gender politics involved in surnames.
Surprisingly, given all these commercial elements, it failed to
follow 'Each And Every One' into the charts, stalling at
number 58. In July we appeared on a TV show called *Earsay*
performing the song, and also on was Morrissey doing an
interview. He sent us a postcard later that week saying that
'Mine' had made the show blossom.

When our next single, 'Native Land', which even featured

Johnny Marr on harmonica, came out in September, it didn't trouble the charts at all, merely scraping in at number 73. We'd committed the cardinal sin of changing before people were ready for it, and left an audience who'd only just discovered us wondering what they'd done wrong to be so quickly abandoned.

Not that I much cared about lack of chart success at this point – I was happy that as a band we'd caught up with ourselves, and whether a wider public wanted it or not we were making the music we wanted to make. And, all told, it hadn't been a disastrous year, more an eventful one, where things had taken off in a perhaps unexpected direction. The end-of-year readers' poll in the *NME* had The Smiths as Best Group, and Morrissey and Marr as Best Songwriters, but there we were at number 10 in Best New Act. 'Each And Every One' was the 24th Best Single, *Eden* was 17th Best LP and I was number 4 in the Best Female Singer category. *Eden* was even voted to have had the 15th Best Dressed Sleeve. All this was much better than we might have hoped for, and suggested we had been premature in becoming so defensive.

Even more amazingly, when they asked the poll winners for their own lists of favourites, Morrissey chose me as his Best Female Singer. Paul Weller did, too, also citing *Eden* as Best Album, and Ben and me as Best Songwriters. Weller and Morrissey might not have had much time for each other, but here they were, two heroes of mine, selecting me as their favourite singer of the year! In some ways, they represented the two strands which had been apparent in the records we'd made so far, strands which to some people seemed to be polar opposites – that tug of war between the indie roots on the one hand (Lyrics are important! Skill is not!) and the soul-jazz roots on the other (Fuck all that – let's dance!).

The same dichotomy was apparent when the unlikely

triumvirate of Morrissey, George Michael and Tony Blackburn discussed *Eden* on a TV talk show. Tony Blackburn had been playing 'Each And Every One' incessantly on his radio show because it had soul, but admitted that the rest of the record made him realise that he didn't really like albums. George Michael too liked the single, but owned up to the fact that his favourite song of mine was 'Plain Sailing', while Morrissey complained that he *hated* the single 'Each And Every One' because it was sort of ghastly and jazzy, but loved other tracks on the album, such as 'Another Bridge'.

There were two sides to our music, then, and in simplistic terms they represented me on one side and Ben on the other. I'd come from the more indie background, while Ben grew up knowing about jazz. So it may have seemed clear who was bringing what to the table, although a closer look would always reveal it to be more complicated than this. But still, some listeners would always see a clear divide between the two strands, and which one was more important depended entirely on where you stood.

Blown in on winds of mischance
He would stay but that's not his way
What escape for her, she swims in the dark
In too deep, but still waves, 'I'm OK,
And I don't need his name, thank you
Mine fits me nicely and mine will do
Yeah, mine will do'

Unsteady footsteps, can't walk alone yet
He sends a postcard, he says he's in debt
Now she's treading water
Got a back room to let
Curses in the backyard, neighbours on the doorstep
'You must give the child a name sometime'
'Well, you mean his and what's wrong with mine?
Yeah, what's wrong with mine?'

Sometimes she could kill him
And sometimes this house gets too small
She drives him to distraction
To see if he will fall
And if the truth were told
Which it never is
With a family like that, who needs enemies
She'd be better on her own
You sink her like a stone

'Mine', 1984

ALL YOU WANTED

In 1984 I'd never been 'on tour' before. Neither had Ben. I'd done gigs with the Marine Girls, here and there, one at a time, and Ben and I had done a couple of what would now be called 'acoustic' shows, just the two of us. But touring seemed to be something that other bands did. Proper bands. Bands with careers. But now here we were, with a booking agent and a tour manager and a set of printed and bound itineraries telling us where we were going to be every moment of every day for the next four weeks. A whole team of people had been hired – roadies, monitor engineers, lighting riggers – who were temporarily part of our entire existence, but who otherwise had nothing to do with us at all. We'd never met them before, and would possibly never see them again after the tour was over.

In order to play live, we'd assembled a band: Phil Moxham from Young Marble Giants on bass, June Miles-Kingston from the Mo-dettes and Fun Boy Three on drums and Neil Scott on guitar, who'd auditioned after an ad was placed in the

NME. It was important to me that there was at least one other woman in the band, and I tried to make that a rule for the first few years, though later it lapsed, and there would be long trips across America where I was the only woman on the tour bus.

On this first tour, we were playing mostly universities, and The Haçienda in Manchester, where the promoter was Mike Pickering, future resident DJ there and founding member of M People. The tour was something of a revelation, and I had to learn pretty quickly about the routine of travelling and soundchecks and support acts and onstage times, and all the paraphernalia of life on the road. I was like a kid just let out of school.

At the first hotel, I ran out into the corridor shouting, 'June! I've got a PHONE in my room!' I'd barely travelled anywhere before, and certainly had no experience of hotels. It all seemed very glamorous, though at that point the hotels were anything but. Arriving late at one overnight stop we banged on the locked front door, managing to rouse a surly night porter who scowled through the glass at us. 'What time d'you call this to be arriving?' he barked at us. 'You're not coming in at this hour.'

'But we're the band, you've got to let us in. We're Everything But The Girl!'

'I don't care if you're the Dave Clark bloody Five, you're not coming in.'

The first gig was at Aberystwyth University. I stepped out onstage in front of a crowd of students. The noise they made in the hall was quite overpowering before we'd even started. In the Marine Girls we had confronted this dilemma by simply playing quietly and forcing the crowd to shut up. This time, with a band consisting of bass and drums and two guitarists, the plan was to make some actual noise, create some excitement in

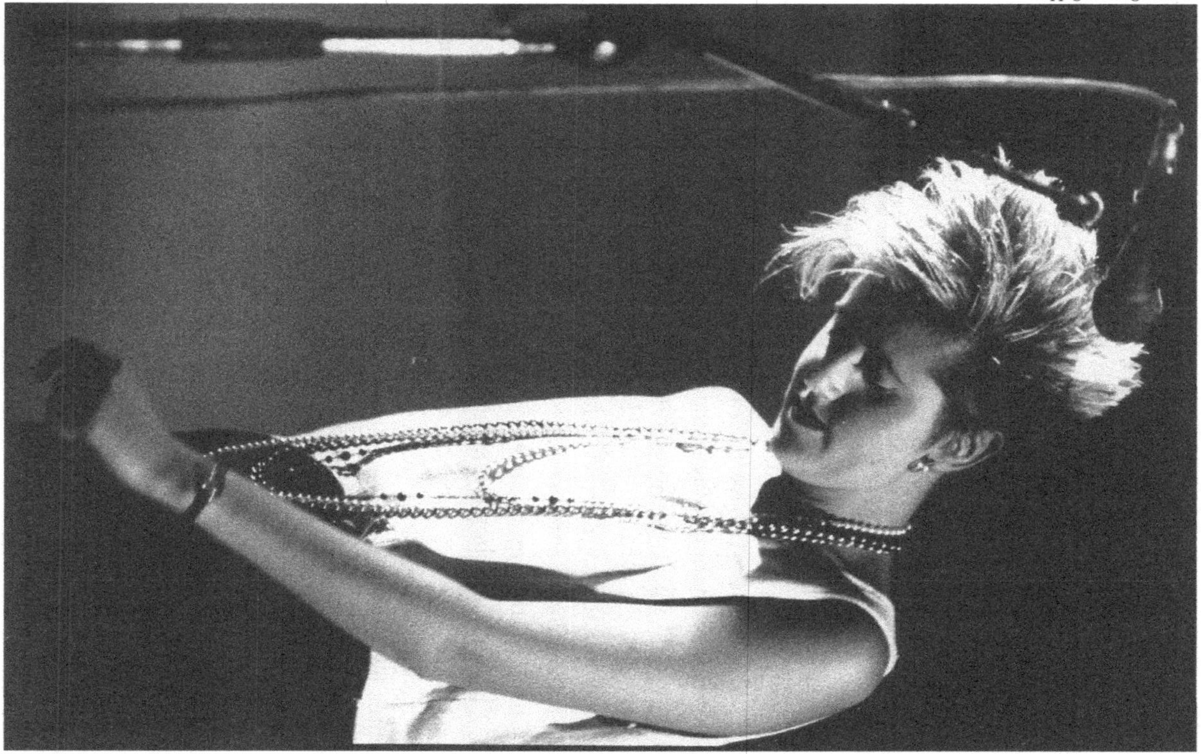

the room and be more than just the hushed supper-club act some accused us of being. I took a deep breath and decided to sing as loud as I could, and prove that I could dominate an audience, that I was no wallflower, but a Strong Frontwoman. The plan worked brilliantly for about five songs, then I lost my voice. What had started as an apparently confident and assertive vocal suddenly dwindled into a nervous, tight-throated croak and then vanished altogether. Seizing control of the situation, Ben stepped forward and sang a couple of his lead-vocal songs, while I chucked back glass after glass of water, tried to relax, and got back the ability to make a bit of a sound from out of my mouth. Chastened, I sang the rest of the set more gently, realising that I'd have to learn about pacing myself and not giving everything away in the first five minutes, before I'd even warmed up. It was something I'd seen happen to Liz Fraser, when she'd played at The Haçienda with The Cocteau Twins and fled the stage in tears when her voice deserted her. At least I'd managed not to do that – I hadn't cried, and I *had* managed to finish the gig, but it was a baptism of fire.

Back at the hotel, June said to me that I ought to drink hot milk and honey onstage, so the next night I had someone backstage provide me with some throughout the set. It seemed to help, and from that point on I became dependent on hot drinks with honey onstage, though the milk would soon be replaced by tea. I would get into the habit of always having a thermos, which I'd carry on with me and place on the drum riser, pouring myself little cups throughout a gig, as if I'd set up in a lay-by for a picnic and all that was missing were the sandwiches. The thermos became my onstage prop, or more to the point, my crutch. So much so that, years later, a gig promoter would have made for me my own tiny silver flight case, into the thick foam lining of which was cut the perfect outline of the flask. Too embarrassed ever to use it for that purpose, I removed the lining and used it as an on-tour make-up case.

But I soon got used to the rituals and routines of life on tour, and also began to realise that, like much of the pop-star life, it could be a strangely infantilising experience. It's easy to imagine that pop groups have an enviable amount of freedom, and I suppose they do in many ways, but on a day-to-day level the job can be subtly disempowering. From the moment you get a manager, they become the adult, playing the role of Mummy or Daddy, while you are at liberty to be, childlike, the artist. On tour you have a tour manager, who organises every waking moment of your day. You are told what time to be down in the hotel foyer each morning in order to get on the bus, what time you will be collected for the soundcheck, what time you are onstage. You are given 'per diems' – an amount of money each day that should keep you alive, i.e. buy you a day's worth of food and other necessities. At the gig venue, your evening meal is cooked for you backstage and you all eat together around a big table. Lasagne and chips. Apple crumble, with custard in a stainless-steel jug. School dinner.

And when you're not on tour, there is still a sense of other people doing all the boring bits for you. The record company will book a car to take you to be interviewed, or to an airport. At the airport, if you are going abroad for a day or two to do press and promotion, a representative from the record company will go with you *to look after you*. Because how else will you get on a plane, take a taxi from the airport and manage to check into a hotel?

So yes, it's infantilising, but also addictive. Turning up to a video shoot, you will be ushered into a dressing room with a clothes rail hung with outfits to choose from. Sitting down, your hair will be pinned back and you can close your eyes for an hour while someone else puts your make-up on. And then the stylist will help you into the best outfit, and then finally, *finally*, you might be called upon to go out and pretend to sing. Then a break, and someone will fetch your lunch. You can see why celebrities turn into arseholes, even if they're not to begin with.

The days seem on the surface to be luxurious and lazy, but in the middle of it all you can feel powerless, useless and without choice. If the room you're in is too hot or cold, for instance, you can't do anything about it, like finding the heating control and turning it up or down – you have to ask someone to fix it, you have to complain. Immediately, you're a diva. If there's no food you actually want to eat, or the clothes really don't suit you, again you can't do much about it, except complain. Again. Diva.

Technically you are your own boss, and yet much of the time you're not, and the hardest thing is working out how to continue being normal. Not too starry, not too humble, not a bossyboots, or a pushover. There is a tightrope to be walked, an awful lot of balancing to be done.

By now Ben and I were living down in London, in a rented flat in a mews in Belsize Park. I had duly got my first from Hull University, but having collected it, had straight away moved to London and abandoned all my vague ideas about carrying on to do a PhD. That would have to wait; there was a music career here which seemed to be mine for the taking, and it would have seemed reckless to turn it down.

Morrissey and Marr were living in London now too, and Ben started hanging out with Johnny a bit, going guitar-shopping with him and enviously watching while Johnny spent some of his new-found wealth on beautiful classic guitars which Ben could still only dream of.

By 1985 we had made a new album, *Love Not Money*, much

more of a pop-rock record this time, with the band of June, Phil and Neil. I tried to deal with the singing problems that had emerged through touring by having some lessons, with renowned Singing Teacher To The Stars Tona de Brett. She got me doing classical la-la-la-LA-la-la-la-type exercises, which I would have to sing in an entirely different voice to the one I used for my songs – a fairly high 'head' voice as opposed to my usual lower tone – which always made me wonder how helpful it was. She told me that she had also taught Liz Fraser, and that one of the things she was trying to encourage Liz to do was to wear more make-up onstage. Singing along to the warm-up tapes, I began to get the feeling that the message they were subliminally sending me was that I was singing 'wrong', that in fact all pop-singing was, in effect, more or less 'wrong', in that it comes from somewhere different to the classical voice, from the throat rather than from the chest. It's what makes the pop voice difficult to sustain, and, yes, does create all sorts of problems, but ultimately it's what makes people sound the way they do, and to confront it fully is to throw the baby out with the bathwater. I took an executive decision, and during the recording of *Love Not Money* I would go into the office upstairs at Power Plant before recording any vocals, stick on a Pretenders album and spend half an hour singing along at full volume with Chrissie Hynde. And that made me feel a lot better in every possible way.

When the new album came out, Morrissey remained supportive, and sent us a postcard thanking us for the copy we'd sent him and mentioning 'Shoot Me Down' as his favourite track.

He invited us for tea at his flat in Kensington, but at the last minute I had to cancel, suffering from flu. Another postcard arrived, suggesting that I had chucked him in favour of going to the Wag Club. We rearranged the tea date, and duly turned up outside his flat at the appointed time – only to find him not in, or hiding somewhere! Perhaps, it began to occur to us, Morrissey could be a little unpredictable. We remained devoted, but slightly wary. And though the relationship was still violently unbalanced in terms of status, this was beginning to change as we ourselves were becoming more of a mainstream success.

As would become the pattern, we failed again to have a hit single to promote the record, but the album still did well, charting at number 10 and selling 100,000 copies. Selling 100,000 records means you get a gold disc, those trophies so beloved of the ageing rock star with acres of Cotswolds wall space to fill. The discs themselves were huge, framed artefacts – a piece of twelve-inch vinyl sprayed either gold or silver according to how many you'd sold – but here's the hilarious bit: it wouldn't necessarily be your own actual record that had been sprayed gold – just any old piece of vinyl. You would know, for instance, that your album had five tracks on side one, but there it was, a piece of 'gold' vinyl, with seven clearly separated sets of grooves on that side. You might have earned the prize for selling an admirable number of copies of a fairly quirky, uncommercial British pop record, but there on your wall you might well have a framed and gilded copy of *The Number of the Beast* by Iron Maiden.

Ever since the release of *Eden*, we had been becoming increasingly well known across Europe, and especially in Italy. In March 1985 we went out to do a tour of Italy – playing in Bari, Naples, Rome, Bologna, Florence, Milan and Padua – and experienced for the first time a taste of genuine pop-star treatment. Just before we arrived, my photo appeared on the front page of the newspaper *Il Giorno*, alongside pictures of John McEnroe and the Pope. The headline read, '*Arriva la più bella voce del pop inglese*' – The most beautiful voice in English pop arrives!

We were surprised to find ourselves playing in enormous tents, apparently perfectly regular venues for concerts in Italy. The sound swirled around inside the cavernous spaces, and I found it impossible to hear myself or to sing in tune. Added to this was the fact that the audiences had come hoping to hear *il jazz-pop inglese*, with Brazilian percussionists and a horn section, and instead found a very British guitar band. The review in *Il Giorno*, which I think needs no translation, describes us as sounding '*come una pub band*'.

It should have been a disaster, but such was the heat of the moment, all was forgiven (at least until the next time we toured in Italy, when reduced audience numbers revealed that we had in fact done some damage). Expectations had been so high that no one wanted to admit to disappointment, and so we performed in an atmosphere of near-hysterical adulation, and fled each gig in a bus chased by fans shouting our names and thumping on the sides. After one show, we had to wait on the bus for one member of the band, who had met a girl earlier in the evening and sloped off somewhere with her. The crowd around the bus started pushing it and shouting; there were faces pressed against the glass, ugly and distorted. We felt they didn't know what on earth they wanted from us, or what they might do next. We were becoming nervous when finally our errant band member returned, sheepishly apologising and furtively brushing mud from his knees.

On a day off, Ben and I went for a stroll around Florence and found ourselves being pursued by a shouting mob of teenagers, whose numbers swelled on each street corner as they picked up passers-by. We sped up, trying to escape, but they kept up with us. It was like the Keystone Kops meets an episode of *The Monkees*. Halfway across the Ponte Vecchio, they got close enough that we could hear their voices.

'Hey! Matt Bianco! Matt Bianco!' they were shouting.

This was too much. We stopped in our tracks and wheeled about to face them. With forty kids bearing down on him, Ben stood his ground and shouted, 'We are NOT fucking Matt Bianco.'

Already I was realising that being a pop star, even a minor one, could be a strangely schizophrenic existence, veering from ego-boosting episodes of public acclaim and recognition to, well, the exact opposite, in a very short space of time. An element of almost ritualised humiliation seemed to be part of the process, and outside the enclosed and self-referential world of the *NME* and the indie scene there were often bizarre and hilarious juxtapositions. We appeared on a Dutch TV show where the other musical guest was Father Abraham and the Smurfs. A while later, we were in Rome doing a TV show, where our fellow guests were Charles Aznavour and a troupe of Spanish dancers on stilts. I began to think it was going to take some effort to maintain a normal sense of self-esteem, neither unhealthily high nor too low.

Since I'd left Hull a year ago, my life had changed enormously, and what had been a small-scale, part-time endeavour was now very definitely a career. I had learned about the schedules involved in making records – that singles were supposed to be released four weeks before the album, for instance, as a kind of fanfare. This was news to me: it hadn't happened like that at the indie level. There were videos to be made too, and they, like singles, were supposed to be promotional tools rather than interesting works of art. We made our first three (for 'Each And Every One', 'Mine' and 'Native Land') with the director John Maybury, who came from an art film background and would go on to work with Derek Jarman and direct the biopic of Francis Bacon, *Love Is the Devil*. 'Each And Every One' is a simple black-and-white film of us playing the song, but I was unused to having a camera in my face all day and chose to ignore it, staring fervently at the floor for the duration of the song.

The video for 'Mine' was filmed in a stupefyingly hot studio, where my make-up melted and had to be reapplied throughout the day, till by the evening it was inches thick on my face and made me look like Jackie Stallone. Then a bright light shining from behind me made my ears go red and translucent on film, so I had to have thick gaffer tape plastered over the backs of them. Yes, I did feel very glamorous, thank you for asking.

By the time we came to make the video for the first single from *Love Not Money*, called 'When All's Well', it was suggested that we consider working with someone who actually made pop videos for a living. Tim Pope was chosen, who'd had great success with his witty and wacky videos for The Cure. The lyric to the song goes: 'When all's well, my love is like cathedral bells', and so here's what his idea for the video was. 'Tracey will be performing the song inside an enormous cross-section of an upturned *bell*, while Ben will be down a *well*.'

Yes, I know. But the idea went down a storm in the record-company offices, and at great expense a film set was duly constructed, with the bell and the well as required. What could we do but turn up and obey instructions? If in the finished version we look a little uncertain as to what on earth we're doing, I ask you to search your conscience and tell me if you could have done any better.

Do you want to get on in this cowering country now?
Do you want to get on, get on
Or would you be happy just to get by?
The small thoughts of a small-town girl
Grew up and wanted to change the world
Will heaven echo back my plea
Or cast it as a curse on me?

Do you want to get on in this beautiful country girl?
Listen hard to what the big folks say
And you'll believe anything
If you believe what they say of this world
From the orchard to the foundry
From farms to the city night
Everyone cracks if the price is right
Ideals soon begin to fail
God must know by now
This love is not for sale

'This Love (Not For Sale)', from
Love Not Money, 1985

POLITICS ASIDE

Coming of age as I did, as a music fan in the late 1970s, meant that your politics were pretty much inevitably left wing. It was a time of marches and rallies, benefit gigs, slogan badges. At the age of sixteen I went from knowing nothing about politics to being a marching, chanting, fully paid-up lefty in the space of about six months. I probably wasn't entirely clear at the time how Rock Against Racism or the Anti-Nazi League had started, but there were some events that had swiftly passed into rock's political mythology. Hadn't Eric Clapton said something unpredictably awful about supporting Enoch Powell? And wasn't there some business with David Bowie and a clumsy Nazi salute, or was it just a wave to the camera? I didn't know the full details, but you'd have to have been extremely dim at the time not to sense which way the wind was blowing. Many of the groups I liked – Gang of Four, Scritti Politti, the Mekons, Delta 5, the Au Pairs – were explicitly left wing, and through their songs and interviews introduced me to concepts and political theories which I was often simply too young and inexperienced to comprehend fully. Nonetheless, I agreed with every word.

This politicisation seemed to be the norm, and would continue to seem so well into the 1980s. Even as musical styles changed, and many of the old punk battles were left behind, for those of my age the ideals of the late 1970s remained a driving force. We weren't to know it, but years of being in a political wilderness lay ahead of us. Mixing pop with politics would become increasingly difficult, and even seem irrelevant to a later generation, our level of commitment appearing to them to be somewhat quaint and hysterical.

In the mid-1980s, though, the battle lines were still clearly drawn. I found my diary for 1985 and, true to form, there are the stickers on the inside cover to sum up the year. Dig Deep For The Miners; Meat Is Murder. It may have been Thatcher's decade, with vacuous social climbers such as Duran Duran sometimes held up to represent the whole period, but it didn't feel like that at the time. While the lovely Durannies revelled in their own dim-wittedness – 'There are plenty of bands catering for people who want to hear about how bad life is . . . We're not interested in that . . . One of the perks of this job is getting rich,' said Simon le Bon – those of us who still remembered punk held firm to the belief that the purchasing of yachts had NOT been our sole reason for deciding to form a band. John Harris writes in *The Last Party* that throughout the 1980s there was a strong political counterculture, and that although the edifice of Tory propaganda may have seemed impregnable, 'ranged against all this were both those who had been excluded from the Thatcherite dream, and an ever-present constituency of refuseniks'.

I often feel that I barely recognise 'The 1980s' as a decade, in the form that it is now remembered and repackaged for glib TV programmes. I would later see the decade reviled, and then revived, but in a manner that bore almost no relation to the years I had lived through. Events which many of us had shied away from, or sneered at, or at least had reservations about, from the Royal Wedding to Live Aid, have now become the unchallenged and unchallengeable iconic moments of the period. It's not possible to say that you watched not a second of the wedding, and that you were dismissive of Live Aid, without sounding like a complete killjoy outsider, but many of us simply lived an entirely different set of experiences, which seem to have gone unrecorded and unwritten about, so that it's as though they never happened. Scenes which I never witnessed in my life – yuppies chugging champagne in City wine bars, toffs dancing in puffball skirts to Duran Duran – have now become the universal TV shorthand used to locate and define the era.

In place of the supposed ambition and Greed is Good ethos, within the world of the alternative band we still adhered somewhat piously to the altruism of the benefit gig. In the mid-1980s we had our own causes, and the benefit gigs were many and various. In 1984 I had sung vocals on a track called 'Venceremos' with Simon Booth's Working Week, in support of Chilean opposition to the Pinochet regime. In January 1985 we appeared at a benefit gig for Nicaragua, and later that same month we played with Orange Juice and Aztec Camera at a benefit for the striking miners.

Mostly, it's true to say, it was the usual suspects who turned out for all the causes, though we once appeared at a miner's benefit at the Royal Festival Hall on the same bill as Wham!, who appalled the ideologically sound audience by committing the cardinal sin of miming. Inexperienced in the mindset and prejudices of the politically right-on, they may have believed that turning up for free in support of striking miners was proof enough of their authenticity, but that night they discovered how easy it was to earn the disapproval of your comrades on the left.

We got a name for being part of this lefty wing of pop, along with Paul Weller, Billy Bragg, and so on, and at the time we were all fired up with the belief that it was perfectly reasonable to try and infiltrate the pop marketplace with leftist politics. When I was interviewed by *Smash Hits* in 1985 and asked what was the last book I read, my answer was *The British in Northern Ireland: The Case for Withdrawal*. In *Smash Hits*!

Red Wedge was officially launched in November 1985, and was an attempt to fuse all of this somewhat disparate political activity into the one supposedly common cause of ousting the Thatcher government and getting Labour elected. Neil Kinnock was trying to modernise the Labour Party, following the landslide defeat of the 1983 election, and realised that one strand of this process would be to try to reconnect with the youth vote, and to marshall some of that highly motivated activism which was clearly prevalent among young rock fans. Red Wedge was intended to be more than just an earlier version of Blair's Cool Britannia marketing ploy, and the organisation was actually given its own office at Labour Party HQ on Walworth Road in south-east London. There were no cocktail parties, but there were fully minuted meetings, at which strategy and theory were discussed and argued, sometimes, it must be said, by people who might have been more secure in their opinions on guitar amps.

It was well intentioned and earnest, in keeping with the spirit of the times, and was the product both of the idealism which still permeated political thinking and the desperation which many of us felt in the face of the apparently unstoppable dominance of the right. There was a Red Wedge tour in January 1986, and a long-held, much-discussed plan to release a Red Wedge album, which never came to anything, and everything culminated in the activity around the 1987 election, during which we played at several gigs aimed at winning specific seats.

How prosaic our ambitions seem now, by comparison to today's pop stars and their lofty pronouncements. Far from trying to end global poverty with one wave of a hand, we were simply trying to get a local official elected to a safe seat in Leicestershire. And even that was beyond us. Backstage at that particular gig, Glenys Kinnock loaned me her little red rose badge to wear as I went out onstage, but her token of good luck landed on stony ground. The complete failure of the movement to have any impact on what turned out to be yet another humiliating Labour defeat was totally demoralising, and Red Wedge disbanded in 1988.

But in all that time, nothing I experienced could rival, for sheer strangeness and for highlighting the possibly irreconcilable differences between pop and politics, a meeting Ben and I were invited to along with Geoff Travis and Simon Booth. It was nothing to do with Red Wedge, but was the product of a moment of inspiration from someone – who, for God's sake? – who suggested that what was really needed was ... A Song for Labour! Choosing a current hit with a relevant lyric must have seemed, in those purist days, a little too much like advertising, so instead it was announced that entries should be sent in on cassette and a meeting would be held to listen to them and choose the winner. Like a kind of socialist Eurovision Song Contest.

We duly turned up, along with Simon and Geoff and several others, and there, representing the top brass of the Labour Party, was Eric Heffer, Old Labour personified. It's hard to remember now, in these post-Blair days, what proper old-style lefties were sometimes like, and how properly out of date they

seemed to our younger generation. Heffer was a hugely masculine presence from the moment he entered the room,
glowering with ego, female minions scampering behind him.
I began to bridle at his immediate and unquestioning dominance of the proceedings, and sure enough, as we started
listening to the catastrophically hopeless offerings, no one else's
comments got much of a look-in. After a somewhat generi-
cally apocalyptic reggae number, Heffer looked completely
bamboozled but floored all of us with his declaration that: 'We
certainly don't want that kind of country and western thing.'
Was he being humorous? I really don't think so. The idea that
we would approach this with any degree of irony did not seem
to be an option, and keeping a straight face was becoming difficult. Finally, after we had all listened to a seemingly endless
collection of really extraordinarily incompetent songs, he flew
into a sudden, though possibly not unexpected, temper.

'LIVERPOOL!' he bellowed, apropos of nothing.

'That's where the only bloody good pop music comes from,
and ever has come from! I want to hear all the entries from
Liverpool!'

The room fell silent, no one sure whether this was a)
entirely serious, or b) open for discussion. It was intolerable.
He had completely hijacked the whole thing, and having
thought in our innocence that we had been invited in order to
make competent musical suggestions and be listened to, we
were outraged by this chauvinistic high-handedness. I'd been
biting my tongue for the best part of an hour, but this was
really too much. I stood up and yelled back at him, 'All right
then, and while we're at it, I want to hear all the entries by
WOMEN!'

Momentarily taken aback, he peered at me in mild irrita-
tion, as if one of the ladies had suggested he try a different kind
of biscuit. Who on earth was this strange-looking girl, and

who'd invited her here, and what the hell was she on about? There was a brief stand-off, then he drew breath and pulled himself up to his full height, chest puffed out authoritatively, and announced the compromise that only served to prove how irrelevant and time-wasting the whole thing was: 'Fine – the motion is passed. We will hear everyone from Liverpool, and all the women!'

Who would be born into a man's man's man's world?
But what do children care
For grown-ups' despair?
A house can hold both boy and girl.
But every mother's son grows up
And daughters imitate
And the burden of a careworn world
Is his to bear
Hers to wait

As the open world of a tomboy girl
Closes on a growing wife
From a childhood clear
Through teenage years
That always seem to be more
Trouble than strife

From the hot dark of night
To the cold light of day
From the cradle to wife to grave
Unless I stand in the way
As the open world of a tomboy girl
Closes in with growing strife
For my own sake I'll comfort take
In the knowledge that I'd never make a wife

You hear them talk of women's ways with hatred
And it cuts me like a knife
Poor men, so much to bear
The children and the trouble and strife

The open world of a tomboy girl
Is the best of life
From a childhood clear
You end up here
In trouble and strife

'Trouble And Strife', from *Love Not Money*, 1985

the open world, the journey and
in the open air.
an exhilarating place,
felt and uplifting
toughest and more

The Valley of Fear, from Love Not Money, 1992

FLYING OVER RUSSIA

Even before Red Wedge had got started, we found out that earning a political reputation could bring unexpected results when, in the middle of 1985, we were invited to go and play in Moscow. Initially we were somewhat flummoxed. After all, it was a bit like the kind of thing my dad might have said: 'All right, if you want to be a bloody communist, why don't you all bugger off to Moscow!' We weren't sure that Moscow was where we wanted to be at all, but it seemed like too interesting an opportunity to pass up.

In July 1985, Moscow was hosting the 12th Festival of Youth and Students. 'I've never heard of that,' you may be thinking. 'What on earth was it?' Your guess is as good as mine, quite frankly. All I know is that there were 'delegates' from all around the world, representatives from youth groups, unions and political organisations, all there to have meetings and discussions and workshops and rallies. From each country there were also musical delegates, to perform at what was supposed to be a huge, week-long party. I may be wrong, but I think that the job of selecting Britain's musical representatives had fallen to All Trade Booking, the live-music wing of Rough Trade. And in their wisdom they selected Everything But The Girl and our natural musical allies, reggae band Misty in Roots.

Also on the trip with us was Sean O'Hagan from the *NME*, and I'm indebted to the piece he later wrote in the paper for any clear recollections of the trip at all. To say the experience was a strange one would be an almost criminal understatement.

Mikhail Gorbachev had only been in power for four months, and it was too early for his glasnost policy to have yielded any significant or noticeable changes. The country may have been poised on the brink of sweeping and radical reforms, but to our eyes it still seemed to be operating in an almost parodically oppressive manner.

For a start, Moscow seemed to have been cleared of all its inhabitants under the age of forty – anyone, in fact, who may have been interested in witnessing the appearance of some Western pop or reggae groups. There were dark rumours swirling around the city concerning the apparently forcible relocation of all its young people during this two-week period. Having believed, in our naivety, that we were coming to make some kind of symbolic connection with communist youth, we were confronted with the full, dreary daily reality of living in the Soviet Union. Nothing unexpected, or threatening, or even FUN! should be allowed to take place, if at all possible. We had been determined to bring back reports of a thriving society with which to deflect the 'Evil Empire' cliché current in the West in the mid-1980s, but blimey, they didn't make it easy. If the authorities had actually been in league with Ronald Reagan they couldn't have done much more to undermine our idealistic faith in the possibility that the Soviet Union was A Good Thing.

The whole trip was more or less a joke. We played gigs to rooms full of middle-aged party officials, went on sightseeing trips with clearly censored and near-mute translator-guides, were followed round our hotel and in the streets by anonymous-looking, green-suited men and were fed an enervating diet of watery cabbage. I'm not making this up. It was probably a mistake to have gone vegetarian just before we went (bloody Morrissey), but even so, the food on offer seemed almost comically frugal. Could it really be true that in a modern communist society there was nothing to buy in the shops, and nothing to do, and nothing good to eat? Well, er, yes, apparently.

In his piece for the *NME*, Sean described the incongruity of some of the gigs we played – the first one being in the Hermitage Gardens.

> In the end, against all the odds, it sounded just fine and a little bit of history was made. Halfway through Everything But The Girl's set, the British contingent in the audience leave their seats and start dancing, to the astonishment of the staid, but appreciative, Russians present. The security guards scratch their heads, Ben and Tracey exchange a relieved grin and Nick Hobbs, who knows about these things, claims that this is the first time an audience in Russia has danced in the aisles . . .

But it was downhill after this show. The next 'gig' we played was at the Olympic Village complex, up in the Moscow hills, where we performed alongside a German pomp-rock group called Enno and a Russian group, Zemliana (People Who Inhabit The Earth!). In between the band performances, two men sat on the stage and had a debate about 'music and the state'. Then we played at the Sovin Centre. Before we went onstage a magician performed, in top hat and tails, pulling doves out of thin air. Then a woman in a pink evening gown came on to introduce us, her long speech in Russian referring to two famous names of English pop: John Rotten and Tracey Thorn.

We all got extremely drunk every night, as did the entire population, apparently, because there was simply nothing else to do; and when even that palled, we set up our equipment in the foyer of the Hotel Cosmos one night and played an impromptu gig for anyone around. As it turned out, it was the best show of the whole trip, the only one remotely resembling what you might call a gig, with people smoking and drinking and actually enjoying themselves.

The last show was supposed to be a triumphant appearance in front of 12,000 people in Gorky Park, and we hoped it would make up for the preceding non-events. But it was not to be. Our set seemed to start out all right, and for once the equipment was of quite good quality and the audience could actually hear us at normal volume. Then fate dealt a cruel hand as the heavens opened and a torrential downpour began to soak the PA, which had been set up right at the front of the stage, unprotected by the overhead canopy. We'd only done four songs when we were told that we would have to leave the stage immediately or risk electrocution. It was a bitter blow.

That final failure was emblematic, really, of the yawning gulf between East and West at the time; the unpreparedness of the Russian organisers for the realities of staging the kind of pop events with which they simply had no familiarity. And our own unpreparedness for the true state of what was in reality a crumbling, hollow edifice of a society. We hadn't anticipated that, and didn't really know what to do with the information.

All in all, it was a dispiriting experience. Sure, there were some rowdy nights in the foyer of the Hotel Cosmos, and we

discovered more varieties of vodka than we had hitherto suspected might exist, though getting hold of this vodka wasn't
straightforward, as it had to be purchased during the day from
a semi-secret location – a US hotel, was it? – and involved
some complicated currency transactions, all of which seemed
fantastical and farcical.

One of our party visited the famous GUM department
store, hoping to choose a hat to take home as a souvenir, and
made the discovery that there really was just the one hat to
choose from. Ben and I learned that it was illegal to share a
hotel room if you were unmarried, but got away with it
anyway, half expecting each night to be dragged from our bed
and arrested. Was it possible that our illicit relationship could
send us to the gulag? Were there still gulags? We didn't know;
we joked about these things, with no real concept of how serious any of it was, or how serious we should be about it. I felt
anxious much of the time, while also feeling embarrassed
about the anxiety. As if I was stereotyping an entire nation –
more than one entire nation, in fact – even though it was
behaving fairly stereotypically.

But the general feeling was one of discomfort. We were out
of our element, and out of sorts. It was too much like a
parody – someone genuinely did ask if they could buy Ben's
Levi's – and also unreal, like going back in time, or through the
looking glass. A Russian sound engineer told me I sounded
like Patti Smith, and we had our photo taken in Red Square
with Misty in Roots, plus an Aeroflot pilot and his young son
who simply wandered over and asked if they could join in. But
these events, in their strangeness, took on a hallucinatory and
vaguely threatening quality, like being in a dream over which
you had no control and in which you could find no familiar
landmarks.

The highlight of the trip, and the one moment when true

human contact was made, was when we visited the flat of legendary Russian rock critic Art Troitsky, whose mother fed us garlic potatoes, salad, pickled cucumber and Glenfiddich whisky. We probably weren't supposed to be there; it was all a bit hush-hush, again in a way we weren't sure whether or not to take entirely seriously, but their hospitality was genuine and heart-warming, and crossed all the boundaries.

But we were glad to get home in the end, and guilty at feeling so glad.

Sean O'Hagan wrote his piece for the *NME* when we returned, and it ended up as the front-cover story, with a Soviet propaganda-style cartoon of me and Ben looking like Lenin and his girlfriend, the implication being that we were still flying the flag for the good old USSR.

'What was it like?' everyone wanted to know.

The only honest answer was that it had been very interesting and everything.

But God, you wouldn't want to LIVE there.

31 August 1985   45p   US$1.95 (by air)   ISSN 0028 6362

NEW MUSICAL EXPRESS
NME

RED ALERT!

EVERYTHING BUT THE GIRL
AND MISTY IN MOSCOW

WITH SEAN O'HAGAN

& NICK CAVE ▪ SQUEEZE ▪ MAX ROACH ▪ SCIENTISTS

Look down over people smiling
Waving handkerchiefs to the sky
Clouds hang over hills and mountains
Moscow airport says goodbye
Behind the Iron Curtain, across the Berlin Wall
No news, no word can reach us
There's no one there at all

I'm flying over Russia
Looking where no man can go
I'm flying over Russia
Looking down on Russian snow

Through the frosty window
Looking at the guards below
Just how happy are they?
That's something I'll never know
Now the hills and valleys
Give way to icy plains
I see the rising smoke
From the eastern border trains

I'm flying over Russia
Looking where no man can go
I'm flying over Russia
Looking down on Russian snow

But we don't know
And the Russian snow
It never shows
What only Russians know

I wonder do you believe
The lies that you're sold
I wonder do you ever
Dream of being free
They tell us you have to
Do what you're told
Well, so do we

'Flying Over Russia', from *Beach Party*, 1981

IT'S THE NEW THING

I t's January 1986, and the ICA are organising another Rock Week. This time, instead of being asked to perform, Ben and I are invited to book the bands for one of the nights, and this is who we choose: our favourite band from Hull, Diskobolisk; Irish band Microdisney, who write strikingly melodic songs only to have them roared at the audience by the slightly terrifying Cathal Coughlan; and Primal Scream. Yes, that's right, Primal Scream. At this point, they are not the louche rock 'n' roll hedonists that you know and love. They are basically Bobby Gillespie in his immediately post-Jesus and Mary Chain days, playing shimmery 1960s Velvet Underground pop. Bobby, standing up to play the drums and looking as though he's just absconded from Andy Warhol's Factory, taking all the outfits with him. He's wearing skinny black leather trousers, which no one has worn for years, and he can only get away with this because he has apparently no hips. From the neck up he is all floppy fringe and dark glasses.

What the band represent is an idealised notion of a perfect

pop sound, and it consists of a classic Spector drumbeat, a wall of chainsaw guitars, a tambourine and then on top, where Ronnie Spector's voice should be, Bobby Gillespie's utterly wet and weedy singing. It's fabulous in its self-delusion: you can almost will yourself into believing, as Bobby apparently does, that he sounds like all three of The Shangri-Las, when in fact he just sounds, and looks, like they'd eat him for breakfast.

I'm standing watching them with my best friend Lindy Morrison, the drummer with The Go-Betweens.

'He's GORGEOUS!' she shrieks in my ear. 'Such a BOY!'

I know what she means. He seems so young and frail and vulnerable. We feel almost protective towards him. Clearly he's never going to be able to survive out there in the world, and not many people are ever going to get into this band.

Ha ha ha.

There was a new tendency, from the Jesus and Mary Chain onwards, to reference the past in citing musical influences, which simply hadn't been the case during the punk and post-punk years. Simon Reynolds talks of the Mary Chain pioneering what he calls 'record-collection rock', where the influences were worn so blatantly on the sleeve that you felt you were being invited to admire the reference points as much as the actual records being made. The crop of 'Creation bands' were constantly namechecking bands from the 1960s, and seemingly drew on the same list of influences: the Byrds, Love, the Velvet Underground.

I wasn't immune to this tendency, and was myself beginning to look backwards, partly in the hunt for new musical inspiration and partly in a search for female role models. The indie scene was boy-heavy at this stage, more so than when I had started out. Back then, even if there hadn't been many local girl bands, there were plenty of examples within the post-punk world to encourage and inspire, from Poly Styrene and Siouxsie through to The Raincoats and Delta 5. I tried looking beyond the confines of alternative music, but I couldn't find many women in the mainstream who seemed even to come from the same planet as me. I needed to widen the search. Homing in on the non-rock aspects of the 1960s, I cited women like Dusty Springfield and The Shangri-Las, opting for the camper end of pop production where a swooning, melodramatic hyper-emotionalism could be found. I began at this point to envisage myself as a kind of classic torch singer – not a failed rock singer, but a successful version of another tradition entirely, the female pop diva.

I was also becoming entranced by the history of Hollywood, a place where women had both dominated and, in many instances, been crushed. The life stories of people such as Marilyn Monroe and Frances Farmer seemed to offer startlingly vivid encapsulations of the fates that could befall women who aimed high, who played by the rules or broke the rules, and whose options were limited. I had my hair cut in a black bob in homage to the rebellious Louise Brooks, and felt at this point that there were more women outside rock than inside it who I identified with, or whose stories excited me.

The exception to this was Lindy Morrison, the drummer with The Go-Betweens, who had become my closest friend. Ben and I saw a lot of both Robert Forster and Lindy, who shared our situation of being a couple in a band, and we spent a lot of time talking music with them and with the whole crowd of Australians who seemed to have invaded London to take advantage of the indie music scene. In many ways, these Aussies were more rock 'n' roll than us – our friend Peter Walsh from The Apartments once said of certain members of this scene that they were the kind of people 'whose idea of fun is to arrive in a cab and go home in an ambulance' – but Lindy and Robert were a great couple. Robert was tall, handsome and taciturn. Nose in a book all day long. A flamboyant dresser who, when we all visited a local village fete one Saturday during a holiday in Sussex, rummaged through the jumble stall and found a long flowing cape, which he bought and put on there and then, to the astonishment of the assembled villagers. He wore it throughout the rest of the holiday, as evidenced by a photo I still have of him wearing said cape and sitting cross-legged under a tree in an English garden on an English summer's day. The episode was soon immortalised in his song 'Bow Down', with the lyric: 'You live with a prince / You live with a cape / You see things my memoirs won't say'.

And as for Lindy, well, she was a sheer force of nature, an Amazonian blonde ten years older than me, unshockable, confrontational and loud. She was a great role model to me – super-intelligent and well read, and unquestioningly feminist in her views. Being the only female member of a rock group, she moved in even more exclusively masculine circles than I did, and we took great comfort in sharing with each other the tribulations of being a woman in this world, often feeling like the men were just talking among themselves about the whole business.

The Go-Betweens carried the distinction of being seemingly the best-reviewed band of all time. Never had any of us seen such consistent adoration poured forth in the music press. It was almost beyond a joke. What wasn't a joke was the depressing lack of correlation between the band's reviews and their record sales. We sat around discussing this endlessly. For some reason we now felt under pressure to have hit singles, to compete in the pop marketplace, rather than exist somewhere else entirely. In the early 1980s this kind of ambition had seemed new and positive, and was born of a genuine belief that those of us from the post-punk generation were poised to take over the charts and reinvent the rules of pop music.

But that takeover hadn't happened, and instead we were all left somewhat adrift, without a clear alternative home to inhabit and still battering at the doors of the charts, doors which, much of the time, remained resolutely shut. What started as optimism hardened into a kind of despairing cynicism, and was a pernicious mindset which did none of us any good in the long run.

Along with this new gang we were also absorbing a new set of influences. Our watchwords of the moment were Spector, The Shangri-Las and the album *Dusty in Memphis*. Peter Walsh from The Apartments moved into our flat for a while, and introduced us to his old Charlie Rich records. A kind of supper-club sleaze crept into the brew, and again the thinking was resolutely anti-rock 'n' roll. And with all this in mind, in March of 1986 we started recording our third album, *Baby, the Stars Shine Bright*.

The making of it reflected the fact that the way Ben and I made records was beginning to settle into a pattern, in which we fulfilled quite different roles and contributed different amounts at different stages of the process. The songwriting was shared, and for this record I wrote lots of lyrics about fame and its destructive qualities, and how it had burned various iconic women. Once my songs were finished, I took a back seat. It was a while now since I had played much guitar on record, and for this album there wasn't going to be a lot of guitar anyway. Ben knuckled down and wrote an album's worth of huge pop string arrangements, spending hours constructing elaborate settings for the songs, while I went up to the Everyman Cinema in the afternoons to watch *Sunset Boulevard*, *Mildred Pierce* and *In a Lonely Place*. For the recording, we went into

Abbey Road Studios with a whole orchestra and backing singers, and I imagined this was the way Dusty had recorded. Producer Mike Hedges, who would later go on to work with the Manic Street Preachers, was brought in to do a full Big Production number on it, and it was a million miles from the Marine Girls in a shed in a way that was both thrilling and scary.

It was a grand gesture of a record. Slightly manic in both intent and delivery, it is both a wonderful thing and absolutely barking. Geoff Travis, who was now our A & R man since Mike Alway had left Blanco y Negro, came in to the studio to listen to one of the first finished mixes, and at the end he turned to us and said politely, 'Well, it's very good, but is there possibly a little *too* much going on in there?'

We spluttered defensively and had a bit of a row about it. After all, as far as we were concerned, that was the whole point:

to make a big-sounding record for once, inspired by an era of pop melodrama, the antithesis of our previous understatements. We were tired of being accused of tastefulness; we wanted to be vulgar.

A couple of years after the making of *Baby, the Stars Shine Bright*, we did an interview with David Quantick for the *NME* where he cheerfully describes the album as having been 'completely insane', and we fairly cheerfully agree. It surprised people, but then we were already falling into the habit of doing that. They hadn't expected *Love Not Money* after *Eden*, and now they certainly didn't expect this. I was proud of that; proud that we were finding ways to break out of the boxes you inevitably get put into, and that we had the guts to defy categorisation even at the risk of losing a guaranteed audience.

In fact, the album was a reasonable success, despite having no real connection to any current pop sound, and the first single 'Come On Home' was very nearly a hit, being played incessantly on Radio 1 for a couple of weeks but getting stuck at number 45. Given that by now we were concerned about such things, this was disappointing. We would have liked a hit, and it would have eased things a bit at the record company, who were probably starting to worry. We certainly weren't turning out to be what they'd thought we were.

The culmination of the whole escapade was a concert at the Royal Albert Hall, where we played with the band and a complete orchestra behind us. It was loud and over the top, and the strings filled the whole enormous space in a suitably climactic kind of way.

When I was eleven I had appeared in my primary school's production of the musical *Hansel and Gretel*. Since you ask, I played Hansel, never having been a particularly girly girl. Someone provided me with a pair of genuine lederhosen,

which were stiff and scratchy, and the resulting photo of me in
the local Hertfordshire paper is a horrifying kind of paedophile
fantasy. Despite these setbacks, it was my introduction to the
experience of being onstage and, somewhat surprisingly, I
loved it. I clearly remember the moment at the end of the performance when we came to the front of the stage to take a
bow, and the whole hall full of parents whooped and clapped
as hard as they could. I had never experienced that before, and
it was a revelatory moment. I had tears in my eyes, and I
thought, This is a good moment, this should be the end, really,
credits rolling.

That was a bit melodramatic for an eleven-year-old.
Clearly I had watched too many Bette Davis matinees with
my mum on Sunday afternoons, and I had a somewhat cin-
ematic take on moments of emotional impact. But now,
standing onstage at the Albert Hall, singing in front of a full
orchestra and a huge crowd, I was reminded of nothing so
much as that moment on the stage of the school assembly
hall. A slight detachment, looking down on myself inhabit-
ing this particular time and space, but also a complete sense
of engagement. I was in good voice, and felt like I was
singing from somewhere deep inside, and we were making a
big noise for once, which was enveloping the room, and the
crowd seemed spellbound and entirely mine. It felt like an
obvious ending. Cue the swelling orchestra, and ... The End.
Credits.

I went backstage and hugged everyone, gushing about how
it was one of the best nights of my life, then a few minutes later
crept back on to the stage to collect something I'd forgotten.
Already the audience had gone, and the room was empty.
Roadies were dismantling everything, joking and swearing,
and out in the hall bits of litter were being gathered and stuffed
into plastic bags. All the lights were on, and in the flat glare the

room seemed suddenly vast and meaningless. Whatever had happened there a few minutes before was over, the atmosphere evaporated, the space simply dead and neutral, waiting for the next night, the next thing to happen and fill it with some substance. I looked around and wondered, did it mean anything, then, when it was so quickly gone?

I'm getting too used to this way of life
Fame is a baby, she rocks me at night
Far from the cold and the brash city lights
We purchase from sorrow a moment's respite

And each time you smile
I know I would follow you a country mile
For all that I'm chasing is worthless and vile

I was a backwater girl, home most nights
That was before I saw my name in lights
Stardom and squalor were not dreams of mine
But I've seen the Hollywood sign now
And, oh, how it shines

But when you smile
I swear I would follow you a country mile
Please save me before I do things that aren't worth
    my while

'A Country Mile', from
Baby, the Stars Shine Bright, 1986

PART THREE

PART THREE

CONTROL

It's 1987, and I think the wind is beginning to change. Nothing has really gone wrong yet, but there's starting to be a chill in the air, like the first evening at the end of summer when you catch yourself shivering a little and begin to need a cardigan. The days are getting shorter, and the nights are drawing in.

It's 1987. I'm twenty-five years old. Who am I, though? What am I like? I'm a pop singer, in a fairly successful group. We've made three albums, and been in the charts and on the telly. I have gold discs. Am I a pop star? I don't think so; the word 'star' is too big. Madonna is a pop star. Michael Jackson is a pop star. The word 'celebrity' isn't in use, certainly not for people like me. There isn't celebrity news everywhere – no *Heat* magazine, no reality TV with fading stars being taunted for our entertainment.

Basically, I'm a bit famous. I get recognised from time to time, though never enough to be a problem.

I live with Ben, who I've been with since I was nineteen.

We are very domestic. It's fair to say I am not a particularly *young* twenty-five. I am a vegetarian. I don't drive.

My sister has a child now, a little boy called James, and I visit a lot and fall completely in love with him. He is the first baby I've ever known, and I am besotted. I want a baby. But I am a singer in a pop group. We make records and go on tour quite a lot. It's hard to see how that life could incorporate a baby. Ben doesn't want a baby. We get cats instead. It's not a great idea because a) I am allergic to the cats, and b) one of them is mental, and sits on top of the kitchen door waiting for Ben to walk through, then jumps on his head, claws fully extended. We think the cat has issues.

I play tennis quite a lot, with Lindy, though at the end of the year The Go-Betweens will return to Australia, and our friendship will eventually fade away. I read a lot. Rebecca West. E. M. Forster. I think I'm a bit bored.

I've begun to lose touch with the indie scene, the world I came from and which I took so much to heart. I think it's become a dreary and unimaginative wasteland, all shambling, jumble-sale pop, which seems to have descended into a mere parody of the amateurism and naivety of the Marine Girls. I'm twenty-five, and I have lost patience with bands who write songs called 'The Day She Lost Her Pastels Badge'. The Smiths will split up this year, and they leave a hole at the heart of something I once loved, but might not be able to feel the same about again. Perhaps that particular moment has passed. I'm twenty-five now.

I am writing songs, though; lyrics that are more like short stories than pop lyrics. Perhaps they ought to *be* short stories. They don't really have choruses. Maybe I'm just not very good at choruses. Ben is experimenting with synths and keyboards. He buys a drum machine and starts getting into the finer details of how to programme it. I don't know how to operate the drum machine, or how to turn the synths on, and I'm not bothered enough to learn.

There is some disagreement about what our next record should sound like. We keep changing our minds. I still write all my songs on a guitar or at the piano, and so when I play them they sound a bit like my songs have always sounded. But Ben is writing songs with a more modern sound, using his new synths and the drum machine, and I like these too. We veer between these two possible extremes before making a record, *Idlewild*, which incorporates a bit of both. Maybe it's another 'bizarre hybrid'.

When it's finished we go up for a meeting at WEA – the major label who finance Blanco y Negro – to discuss its

marketing strategy, release schedule and musical merits, or lack thereof.

My diary records label boss Rob Dickins's verdict on the album: 'He says it is too miserable, not enough fast songs, too many gloomy lyrics.' (Right, off you go then, Leonard Cohen. That's enough of that, Portishead. Thank you, Mark Eitzel, but will you please stop whining . . .)

We are three albums into our career, and so are in danger of losing the simple power of newness which lets you get away with doing what you want, defying critics and record-company bosses. At WEA, the voices of dissent are getting louder. Rob Dickins had been frustrated by *Eden*, which he had thought would be more like Sade's *Diamond Life* in both sound and sales figures, and now he has lost patience with a band who are clearly not the straightforward pop proposition he had been led to believe they were. Plus, I don't think he likes me. I think he thinks I am a pain. I'm told he is just awkward around women, and that it's not personal. He is one of those men who thinks he's HILARIOUS, and he can say what he likes and no one minds because he's HILARIOUS.

This behaviour makes us feel undermined, and it chisels away at our self-confidence. I arrive at the meeting wearing a hat I've just bought from Kensington Market. He sniggers at me, 'You going to a wedding, Tracey?' Then he tells us everything that's wrong with the record we've just made. Ben and I are floored by the level of disapproval being beamed at us, and are stumped for an answer. After all, what is the right thing to do when confronted with such a bad review from your own record company? Do you go away and start again? Or stick to your artistic guns, hoping that the world at large will feel differently? We leave the meeting, stumble into a bar next door, drink two bottles of wine, cursing and ranting, and stumble home.

And here you come to the heart of the problem. For the next morning, instead of telling WEA to fuck off, we capitulate and write two more up-tempo, 'poppy' songs to try and rectify the situation.

Now, I'm not saying you should never listen to your record company, or that no one ever knows better than the band themselves, but in this instance, IN THIS INSTANCE, that really was not what we should have done. And what's more, it didn't even work. All it did was to further muddy already muddied waters, and left us with a record which we felt we had slightly betrayed before it was even finished.

And the arguments continued. Sensing a chink in our armour, WEA began to push harder. Our choice of single was outvoted. We wanted 'I Always Was Your Girl', but they thought it was 'too sophisticated, too strange'. We let them have their way, and felt that we had surely bent over quite far enough.

No. Not far enough. The song they had chosen to be the single was deemed not *quite* finished. We should 'add an introduction, some backing vocals, a stronger middle eight and an outro'.

Even the album sleeve ended up being a compromise, and the gorgeous, grainy photo of a bridesmaid that I had seen in a gallery exhibiting the work of photographer Richard Haughton was declared too obscure and replaced with a photo, in the same style, of me and Ben.

This is absolutely standard record-company behaviour, and they would argue that it is all necessary and reasonable when you're trying to maximise the commercial potential of bands you've invested in. However, such behaviour also feels like manipulative game-playing when you're on the receiving end, and it takes nerves of steel to withstand it. In calm moods, you argue that you're being amenable and open to compromise.

Other times you curse yourself for being a pushover, and wonder whether along with your copyright you have also signed away your self-respect.

If I had a time machine and could go back in it, to this particular point, where the self-doubt and anxiety was beginning to set in and it felt like the walls were closing around us, I know exactly what I would do. I would invent Twitter.

I firmly believe that Twitter might have been my salvation. For instance, I could have come home from that depressing meeting at the record-company office and tweeted about it and got it off my chest, and you would all have tweeted back at me with supportive comments, witty put-downs and descriptions of similar experiences in your own workplace. We would have bonded over it, and I would have felt less alone and more like there were people out there who understood what I was on about and wanted me to keep going on about it. Just laughing about it would have defused its corrosive potential. Twitter is the arena in which we share all the shit, and laugh it off, and are made stronger. But back then, although I knew there were people out there who liked and bought our records, I couldn't see or hear them; I didn't know exactly what it was they thought or wanted. They were numbers on a spreadsheet, invisible, anonymous. Back in 1987, I couldn't have imagined such a thing as Twitter. These were the days when fan letters were the only means of communication between me and the listener. They were often lovely, and I tried to reply as often as possible, but still, it was not really a dialogue, and certainly there was no way for me to communicate en masse and share stuff with people who bought my records. Instead, Ben and I had to fight these battles alone, not always quite sure which battles were worth fighting.

Idlewild was the record where it all began to get more difficult. WEA wanted a commercial pop record, and we had written something else entirely, a quirky oddity, full of lyrics deliberately written from a very female perspective and avoiding any obvious pop-song subject matter. There are a couple of relationship lyrics (the wilfully anti-romantic 'I Always Was Your Girl' and 'Love Is Here Where I Live'), but there are also songs about growing up in the suburbs ('Oxford Street'), about female friendship ('Blue Moon Rose'), about having babies ('Apron Strings') and about my two-year-old nephew ('These Early Days'). It was all very grown-up, which was both its strength and its weakness. The single, 'These Early Days', had been reworked to within an inch of its life, and yet still proved too awkward for the airwaves. I spent a day optimistically listening to Radio 1, straining to catch a single play, but all I heard every hour, on the hour, was the new Kylie Minogue classic, 'I Should Be So Lucky'. In such a climate, it should have been no shock that we failed to get on the playlist. It seemed, in fact, like a near miracle that we ever got any airplay at all.

Among our fans, though, *Idlewild* has always been a firm favourite, and it was critically well received at the time, getting good reviews in *Q* magazine, *Record Mirror*, the *Guardian* and the *NME*, while the *Independent* commented that 'it is a relief to find anyone in their twenties these days who wants to sound like an adult'. Along with good reviews, it entered the chart at number 13, so despite failing to have anything approaching a hit single, we were by no means 'over'. And yet, and yet. You could feel the atmosphere of *band in decline* that was starting to surround us. You could almost smell it. Our power was waning, and with it our self-confidence.

We became acutely aware of how well our contemporaries were doing, as my diary from February 1988 records: 'Watched Aztec Camera on *Wogan* – Roddy is number 41 this week ... Prefab Sprout went down from 44 to 49 – Morrissey went straight in at number 6.'

We weren't supposed to care about this kind of stuff, and in interviews we would have strenuously denied having any knowledge of anyone else's chart position. But in truth, I think we could probably have placed all our peers and rivals to within a place or two of their current chart status, and given an estimate to the nearest ten thousand of their current album sales.

And if our career was beginning to look a little shaky in the UK, in the rest of Europe it was definitely on the wane and we'd completely failed to live up to the early promise of *Eden* and *Love Not Money*. Commercially we had slipped even further than we'd realised, as we were about to discover when we attempted to tour. Instead of the pop-star tour of the Italian tents we'd done in 1985, this time around we ventured out into Europe as an acoustic duo, being unable to afford to tour with a band. We were booked to play small but bizarre venues, in an attempt to reinvent ourselves as a kind of arty alternative to compensate for the obvious lack of commercial credentials.

So we played a jazz club in Paris, a café in Munich, an arts centre in Bonn (where we were supported by a documentary about Mexico) and a café in the botanical gardens in Hamburg. At an art-gallery gig in Rome, we performed in a tiny but very brightly lit room to an audience of about sixty journalists and TV people, all of them too cool to respond in any way at all. After about forty-five minutes they started wandering into the next room to get more free drinks, and I think for the first time ever we ended up playing to half the number of people who had been there when we began.

The last gig took place, disastrously, in a disco in Stockholm. A disco in Stockholm is not necessarily the ideal venue in which to perform acoustic versions of subtle introspective songs about childhood. It went badly. There was more noise on the dancefloor than coming from us on the stage. Backstage we had a huge row, and glasses were smashed.

In Italy we were particularly traumatised by the sudden disappearance of our former status and all the trappings it had brought. The limos and Hiltons which had previously been booked by the record company were no longer forthcoming, now that we were on a small-scale tour without a hit record. We had never had it explained to us that there was quite such a strong correlation between record sales and record-company expenditure, and we were shocked to discover how far we had slipped in such a short time. Arriving in Rome, there was no car to meet us and the hotel room we found ourselves in was damp and smelly, with a hole in the wall behind the wardrobe. Frustrated and demoralised, Ben kicked out at a metal suitcase. We would spend much of the next forty-eight hours in a rancid Italian health clinic, where eventually Ben had his broken foot strapped up by a chain-smoking 'doctor', while fag ash dropped onto his leg.

It was, to put it in a nutshell, all becoming a bit *Spinal Tap*.

So many things about this life actually turned out to be a bit *Spinal Tap*. It isn't a cartoonish satire at all but in fact the most accurate film ever made about what it's like to be in a band – any kind of band. Being on tour was always a bit *Spinal Tap*. During the UK tour for *Idlewild*, for instance, we drove after a gig from Loughborough to Norwich. As my diary records, we 'all got drunk in the van – I had to stop to pee in a field and fell over and stung my hands really badly on stinging nettles'. A couple of gigs later, we had a day off in the Lake District and drove up into the hills with the band: 'Pearce and Sanger were hilarious, like two lads from the remand home who've never seen the countryside before, running about in leather jackets and trainers, shouting at sheep and smoking in the fresh air.'

And when you're kept up late every night, of necessity, and you're stuck in a Travelodge on the outskirts of a town you wouldn't perhaps choose to spend a night in, let alone on the outskirts of, and you're a bit wound up and want to wind down – what do you do? You drink copious amounts of whatever's going and behave like a bit of an arse.

I always loved this slightly raucous side of being on tour, and the camaraderie of being part of a touring gang. I was quite often the only girl, sometimes spending weeks crossing America on a tour bus watching the boys play with their latest gadgets, or pretend to read a book, or try to make a cup of tea. Everyone in a band had seen the film *Spinal Tap* and recognised themselves in it, and it became like a kind of glue that bonded you with your band members. The characters and one-liners from it became staple parts of every backstage scene or tour-bus conversation. If you started a ballad at a soundcheck, someone would surely comment that it was in 'D minor, the saddest of all keys'. Every town on the US itinerary would be dismissed as being 'not a big college town', and if someone read out a bad gig review you'd all respond in unison: 'That's just nitpicking, isn't it?' We never actually supported a puppet show, but we did go to Belgium to appear on a TV telethon raising money to send doctors to Africa, at which we couldn't help noticing that three people in the front row were asleep.

But what makes the film a work of genius is the fact that it identified the fundamental truth about the whole business of rock 'n' roll, or just showbusiness in general perhaps – which is that beneath the pomposity and delusion and ludicrous self-aggrandisement, it is eventually a levelling experience. Whether you were a successful headline band or the measliest support act, you'd still have to experience many of the same discomforts and indignities. And you'd veer between extreme versions of your apparent status in a way that could be disconcerting, to say the least.

At the conclusion of the *Idlewild* tour we went to Ireland, first playing in Dublin where we were treated like royalty, and were sent champagne and flowers by Bono, who apologised for not being able to make it to the show. We did a cover of 'I Still Haven't Found What I'm Looking For' by way of a thank you.

The next night we were in Belfast, playing a gig at the notorious Europa Hotel, or Fortress Europa as it was nicknamed in those days. The stage had been set up in the carpeted conference room, making it feel less like a gig than a corporate presentation. My diary tells what happened.

A few lads came down to the front of the stage at my side and howled at me unremittingly to 'play fucking "Sean"' [a song from *Love Not Money*, which we didn't intend to perform] and on Ben's side there was a very odd couple baying for autographs. Even while Ben was actually SINGING a song the bloke was standing up, only inches from his face, shouting, 'Ben, Ben, have you got a pen?'

It could all go from the sublime to the ridiculous, you see, in less than twenty-four hours. You couldn't help wondering much of the time if in fact you were as brilliant as some people said you were, or as awful as others thought. After all, it's such a fine line, isn't it, between stupid and clever.

From the top you can see so far into the distance
Look, it's downhill all the way from here
And getting there is quicker, let go and you just slide
Shouldn't take more than a year

I could almost like you
Now it's nearly over
Now you're feeling hopeless
Now you're looking older

I heard what you said and I recognised those feelings
I know how hard it is to watch it go
And all the effort that it took to get here in the first
    place
And all the effort not to let the effort show

I could almost like you
Now it's nearly over
Now you've shown some weakness
Now you're looking over your shoulder

Who's gonna come and find you?
Who's gonna come and find you?

If you can ride the backlash
There's still time for a comeback
You don't have to lie down and die
But Lazarus, he only did it just the one time,
He couldn't face another try

I could almost like you
Now you're falling over
Now you're feeling hopeless
Now you're looking over your shoulder

Who's gonna come and find you?
Who's coming up behind you?

'Downhill Racer', from *Temperamental*, 1999

SUMMER SMASH

Ben got picked up in a taxi from our flat once, a few years ago. He was carrying a guitar case. As they pulled away, the driver slid back the window.

'You in the music business, then?'

Ben nodded, non-committally.

'Yeah, I picked up someone else in the music biz from your block the other day. That skinny bird who sang that Rod Stewart number.'

Ah yes, that Rod Stewart number.

In June 1988 we released a cover version of 'I Don't Want To Talk About It', which had been a hit for Rod Stewart in 1977 and the very record which kept the Sex Pistols' 'God Save The Queen' from the number-one slot in Jubilee week. This should perhaps have given us pause for thought, but to counter its notorious place on the dark side of musical history was the fact that it was a genuinely great song, and had been written by the drug-addled Danny

Whitten of Crazy Horse and so had a kind of pre-punk credibility.

There was also the fact that Rod Stewart had been a heroic figure at home when I was growing up. My brother Keith, ten years older than me, owned those 1970s records he made with The Faces and his early solo albums with grimy-sounding titles like *An Old Raincoat Won't Ever Let You Down*, and *Gasoline Alley*. There was a laddish bravado about Rod in those days, combined with an essentially British rock 'n' roll camp glamour. Keith would go off to watch Arsenal at Highbury with a satin scarf tied round one wrist, possibly wearing something tartan somewhere, along with the red and white, and in my mind Rod seemed to merge with the heroic figure of Arsenal's Charlie George, both of them pure terrace dandies, epitomising the blokey flamboyance of early 1970s fashion. Orthodox opinion has it that by the late 1970s Rod was all over. That the rot set in with *Atlantic Crossing* and it was downhill from there, as the grit got sacrificed in favour of a banal tartiness, all boaters and blondes, streaked hair and silly blazers, LA and champagne. Less football terraces, more *Footballers' Wives*.

I hadn't quite bought into that interpretation of Rod's career, having always liked *Atlantic Crossing*, and in 1977 I still liked the Rod who released 'I Don't Want To Talk About It'. There was a certain degree of family loyalty involved here, a feeling that, for the Thorn household, he was One Of Ours. To me, doing a cover of a Rod Stewart song had connotations way beyond those of simple commercial potential.

So we recorded a faithful and respectful version of the song, acoustic guitar and some strings, vocal up high in the mix – a classic ballad single. On its release, the record leaped out of our hands and on to the Radio 1 playlist as if magnetically attracted. This was something we had never achieved before, the playlist committee usually rejecting our new releases on the grounds of their being too fast, too slow, too obscure or simply too lacking in choruses. Simon Mayo played the single and declared it would be number one ('failure looms ahead, surely' I wrote in my diary), and after a couple of weeks of near-constant airplay, it entered the chart at number 23.

A chart position of number 23 brought us our first ever concrete offer of *Top of the Pops*. This time there was no agonising, no debate – we were on it like a shot. Who remembered any more whether The Clash had ever appeared on the show? Nobody, that's who. We were the last group in the Western world who hadn't been on, and finally it was our turn.

We turned up, and I experienced the exact same disappointment that everyone feels who has ever appeared on *Top of the Pops*. The studio seemed smaller than it looked on the telly, it was poorly lit and entirely lacking in any pop glamour whatsoever. It was like going back to your primary school and realising how small and dowdy it all was, when in your memory it loomed as something huge, influential and vivid. There was no need for a soundcheck as such, there being no actual live element to the performance, so we simply did a couple of camera rehearsals and waited in the dressing room until it was our turn to go on. Then, we were ushered back into the studio, now brightly lit and filled with aimless-looking teenagers. We mimed our song, as everyone did in those days, and wondered whether the kids in the audience were really as bored as they looked – if, in fact, they'd even heard of us – and stood back and watched as they stared with the same dumb blankness at The Communards, Eighth Wonder and Glenn Medeiros, who was, inexplicably, number one.

Following this appearance, the single did what it was supposed to do and climbed seventeen places to number 6. The next week it climbed again, up to number 3. We did *Top of the Pops* again, this time with S-Express and Ziggy Marley, then got the train down to Teignmouth in Devon to film the Saturday morning kids' show *Get Fresh*, where we sang the song again and judged the fancy-dress competition.

The single stayed at number 3 for another week, then slipped to number 8. At one point we sold 45,000 singles in two days, which was more than 'Each And Every One' had sold during its entire release. As the proud new owners of a genuine hit single, we were immediately granted admission to a kind of secret pop-stars' club, being invited to the Prince after-show party at Camden Palace. These were the days when Prince was revered as pop's greatest live performer, and, unable to reign himself in to just one sell-out show a night, he used to do a second, smaller show somewhere else afterwards. We went to the big main event at Wembley, and then on to the second gig in Camden. Boy George was there, dancing to acid

house in a pair of dungarees, and Mica Paris was down at the front of the stage being handed the mic by Prince to sing 'Just My Imagination'. As we left, we were chased along Camden High Street by paparazzi for the first time in our lives.

I'm not going to pretend it wasn't fun. If we had occasional qualms about having had to resort to a cover version in order to infiltrate the charts, these were dispelled by reassurances that we had nonetheless made a good record. I bumped into Alan McGee from Creation on a staircase somewhere, and he stopped me to say he loved it; and *Sounds* made it Single of the Week, describing it as the 'best single since the Patti Smith comeback'. The best part was the moment each Sunday evening when we got the week's chart placing, an hour before it was announced on the radio. I'd immediately ring my family to tell them the news, and there'd be shrieks of delight from the other end of the phone, then all the lines would be blocked for an hour as they called every last relative around the country to spread the news.

But all I will say is that it's a mixed blessing, having a huge hit with a cover version of a well-loved ballad. It takes you places you may not wish to go, and once you've gone there it's quite hard to come back. What I hadn't realised was how quickly the record would be snatched out of our hands and seized upon by an audience who loved it but perhaps hadn't even heard of me before, and what that would feel like. I was happy that it had brought us a bigger audience, but the flipside was that it had brought us a somewhat *different* audience. We had unwittingly steered ourselves perilously close to becoming housewives' favourites.

Sometimes even I couldn't quite see how the record we'd made had led us to such a place – after all, we'd recorded a good version of a cool Crazy Horse song, and yet, through its popularity, it had somehow changed our entire public image and apparent intent. Nick Hornby writes, in *31 Songs*, that after his books became popular, his work 'overnight seemed to go from being fresh and original to clichéd and ubiquitous, without a word of it having changed. And I was shown this horrible reflection of myself and what I did, a funfair hall-of-mirrors reflection, all squidged-up and distorted – me, but not me.'

After 'I Don't Want To Talk About It' was a hit, Ben and I went to a gig at ULU (the University of London Union) one night, to see Galaxie 500. A couple of studenty Beavis and Butthead types recognised us and nudged each other.

'Look, I-don't-wanna-talk-about-it,' chuckled one, and his mate quipped back, 'I-don't-wanna-*hear*-about-it,' and they both snickered, right there in front of us.

Had we suddenly become people who were not supposed to be at a Galaxie 500 gig? Who didn't fit in there any more? Jesus, were we *the enemy* now? This hadn't been the point. How on earth had THIS happened? There were moments when I found myself wondering, 'Was this really what we meant when we said we opposed all rock 'n' roll?'

Come hell or high water
You just do as you please
Waste your time when you oughta
Be charming the birds from the trees
A voice straight from heaven
So you like to believe
And who cares if it's only
Your poor self you deceive

You look in the mirror
And what do you see?
Too much care and scheming
Too little beauty

Come hell or high water
You never will be
A goddess or a genius
A drunkard at twenty-three
And all that you yearn for
Is attention I guess
Come hell or high water
You deserve nothing less

'Come Hell Or High Water', from
Baby, the Stars Shine Bright, 1986

HEY MANHATTAN!

How quickly a pop career goes by. Leaves behind its beginnings and transforms into something you never imagined, never planned for, perhaps never wanted. It was only 1989. Only five years since I'd left Hull University, wrapped in glory, the indie darling. Now the overwhelming feeling I had within the UK music scene – no longer being part of an indie band, not part of the rave culture, nor happily existing at mainstream level, above such concerns – was that of isolation.

It was the Summer of Love. All around me young people were heading out to the countryside to take drugs in fields and dance around in cagoules to loud, repetitive beats.

And what did we do? We headed out to the countryside and . . . bought a little cottage.

Did anyone mention the word retreat?

In a time-wasting fury of DIY mania, we ripped up carpets and threw them from the upstairs windows, stripped off wallpaper and painted bare walls chalky-white, disconnected the cooker and replaced it with an oil-burning stove and water heater that never really worked. I decided to take on the garden as my project and spent whole days, until late into the evening, struggling to clear beds choked with sticky goose grass and stinging nettles. It took me back to my childhood spent playing in the fields around the village, finding dandelion clocks and the papery seed pods of honesty. I knew precisely nothing about gardening, and would rip away at bunches of ground elder till they broke off in my hand, not realising they had an underground root system, which would ensure they came back bigger and stronger by the next morning. Having cleared an area of a few square yards, I filled the space with whatever was in flower down at the garden centre, then left the plants to fend for themselves, till within a few weeks they had wilted, or starved, or been smothered by the weeds which, reinvigorated by my turning of the soil and dispersing of their seeds, had now returned with a vengeance.

After we'd finished with the inside of the cottage, and had removed anything that smacked of suburban modern comforts, we sat down in our newly minimal space and looked out of the window. And got up to rearrange something, and sat back down again. And watched as it got dark at three o'clock in the afternoon.

'Jesus,' I said, 'it's very quiet, isn't it?'

Ben was pacing about a bit.

'What time does the pub open?' we wondered.

This clearly wasn't going to work. It took us about half an hour to discover that we weren't cut out for the country life at all. The silence at night spooked us, and we couldn't sleep without the soothing sound of traffic. When a solitary car would amble down the lane late, and its headlights sweep across our bedroom curtains, I would sit bolt upright in bed, waiting for the smash of the downstairs window as the inevitable axe murderer broke in. It seemed to be dark more or less all day long, and if we arrived for a weekend it would take us most of Saturday and Sunday to get the place warmed up. What had we been thinking? We were townies, through and through; we just hadn't realised it.

Pretty soon we'd sold the cottage and come back to London full time.

But still I couldn't decide what to do next, or how to fill the time while I tried to decide.

I took another very un-rock 'n' roll decision and applied to study for an MA in Modern English Literature at Birkbeck College. I went up for an interview, at which they eyed me suspiciously.

'So, you say you're in a pop group?' A little glance off to the side, a suppressed smirk.

'Ye-e-es, that's right. But it doesn't take up all my time, and this is a part-time course . . . '

'And do you . . . go off on . . . tours?' Barely keeping a straight face now.

'Well, yes, but I can read on the bus.'

By October 1988, I was spending Monday evenings in tutorial sessions, talking about Yeats and Pound, Leavis and Empson, Foucault and feminism.

None of these projects or diversions solved the problem, though, or answered the basic question that was nagging away at us both – how we should make another record. And there was no doubt that we would make another one. The dilemma was fundamentally a musical one, and could only be answered in those terms. We'd lost our place within the UK music scene, partly because it had moved away from what felt instinctive to us, but also because we'd drifted into making careless mistakes. And now we felt rejected, misunderstood and blameless, and extremely sorry for ourselves. And so, like many before us, feeling scorned in Britain we went to America to feel forgiven.

It was different there. As an English band you always felt glamorous anyway. It was only a slight extension of the way in which all English people are made to feel – smart and sophisticated.

When we toured there, I always felt I was regarded as cooler, cleverer, classier than I was at home. And in the late 1980s we were still seen as being part of a pop avant-garde, experimenting with and updating classic elements from jazz and soul and stripped-down songwriting. Having not had any hits in the US also meant that we were not at all mainstream. Given that we now felt we were widely perceived in the UK as being a bit naff, this was enormously appealing.

We decided it was time to return a phone call that had first come in a few years ago. Soul/jazz producer Tommy LiPuma, who had worked with a catalogue of greats from Horace Silver and Miles Davis through to Randy Newman and George Benson, and who had recently contributed production to Aztec Camera's *Love* album, had said long ago that he had an interest in producing us. At the time it hadn't seemed the right thing to do, but now we took a leap of faith, contacted him and asked him if he wanted to hear some demos.

Tommy, who came from the old school in the strictest sense, said that he wasn't interested in hearing demos, he just wanted us to come out to New York and play him the songs we had. We obediently got on a plane and went to meet him at his Upper East Side apartment, which oozed Manhattan class, with fine art on the walls and a huge wine fridge in the kitchen. From there, we all went to a downtown studio, where he led us into a small recording room containing just a piano and a mic.

'OK,' he said, 'just play me what you got!'

Fuck, this was just like the Brill Building come to life! We were Leiber and Stoller! We were Gerry Goffin and Carole King!

We spent the whole day round the piano, hammering out every song we'd written in the last year, till I had no voice left and no idea whether I was any good or not.

'That's terrific,' said Tommy. 'Now we just pick the ten best and get started.'

So it was as simple as that? Apparently so.

This was a whole new approach for us, a kind of Tin Pan Alley tradition of record-making. We were the 'talent', in the sense that we wrote the songs and sang them, but beyond that we were not expected to come up with much else in the way of making the record. It was decided that we would record in LA, using classic studios like Sunset Sound and Ocean Way. The song arrangements were written for us by Larry Williams and Jerry Hey (both of whom had been instrumental in creating those Quincy Jones–Michael Jackson records), the band

was put together for us and consisted of Omar Hakim on drums, John Patitucci on bass and Larry Williams on keyboards, with Ben playing guitar and piano. We simply gave ourselves up to the experience, happy to have been relieved of some of the burden of decision-making.

As for these musicians we were working with in America, they knew little of our background, or the esoteric British scene we'd emerged from, and why on earth should they? They could not have begun to comprehend how convoluted our ideas were about this record we were making, or about records in general. Though fairly diluted by this point, I still carried around a certain amount of attitude that was basically grounded in a punk sensibility. When Larry Williams, for instance, found out that we had recorded at Abbey Road, he was immediately impressed because it fitted us into a Great Tradition of record-making.

'Oh wow, guys,' he'd say, 'Abbey Road. The home of the Beatles!'

'God, I HATE the Beatles,' I replied.

There was a stunned silence.

'You ha-a-ate the *Beatles* ...?' he faltered. Clearly this wasn't a stance he had ever encountered before, whereas I had grown up around people who thought there was no greater fun to be had than dissing the Rolling Stones, or saying Bob Marley was crap. A certain iconoclasm was in the very air I breathed back home, but here it seemed it just didn't translate.

If we'd thought that we might be about to recreate some classic 1970s grooves, though, we soon found that we were sorely mistaken. These guys were all fully locked into the rhythm and production ideas of mid-1980s US jazz–soul fusion, and thought the 1970s were old hat, while many of the current innovations seemed to them to be a mere flash in the pan. A bit too trashy, too 'pop' even, to appear on a serious record. Hip hop and house beats were for kiddies, while they were going to show us how to make a record for grown-ups.

Starting work on a track in the studio one day, Ben tentatively suggested that he'd always heard it with a kind of swung beat, which he thought would sound great played in real time by a real drummer. They burst out laughing, and began to play the rhythm he'd suggested.

'Shit, man, that's a boogaloo!' they chuckled.

'People gonna say, "That's hysterical! You got Omar Hakim playing a boogaloo!"'

Whatever a boogaloo was, clearly it wasn't cool.

Another time, they started up a cabaret-style version of a current popular beat. Again, they obviously thought it was pathetic.

'New Jack Swing?' they declared. 'Noo Jack Shit!'

And we were on their turf, after all. We had come here specifically to buy some of what they were selling. There didn't seem to be much point in flying all the way out to LA and then demanding we make the same record we could have made back home. So for once, we kept our mouths shut and let ourselves sink into what was actually an extraordinarily easy and enjoyable experience.

We were innocents abroad, in many ways. We decided it would make sense if we stayed at the same hotel as Tommy LiPuma, so we checked into the Four Seasons Beverly Hills and stayed there, in a luxurious corner room with a wraparound balcony and a view, for eight weeks. Being in a hotel meant that we had to send our clothes off to the hotel laundry service, and at the end of the first week I asked to see a running total of the bill, just to keep a check on things. The laundry bill alone was equivalent to the entire recording budget of my earliest records.

For the next eight weeks there were dinners every night in

fancy restaurants. Anyone who happened to be in the studio was invited along. Tommy would order the wine and we would all drink it. We learned about Californian chardonnays and Caesar salads and grilled swordfish, when these things were unheard of in England. Ben hired a car and drove us through Laurel Canyon every day to the recording studio, and at night would drive it back to be valet-parked at the hotel. On a weekend off we drove up to the San Ysidro Ranch in Santa Barbara, where Laurence Olivier and Vivien Leigh had got married, and stayed in a bougainvillea-draped cabin with a wood fire burning. Another weekend, we flew out to the Grand Canyon and stayed in a hotel right by the rim, over-whelmed by the vastness of the landscape outside. I took photos of the view and of cactus flowers that looked like birth-day candles on a cake, and in the clear desert air the damp and chill of England seemed a long way away.

In LA, in the hotel pool in my bikini, I was Joni Mitchell in the photo on the back cover of *The Hissing of Summer Lawns*. The hotel smelled of lilies, and every time we wanted to leave we called down to reception for the car to be brought to the door. It was impossible not to be seduced by the California sun and the luxury lifestyle.

Back in the studio, it seemed Tommy only had to pick up the phone and any musician we wanted would come along to contribute. We needed a sax solo on one song and I said, 'We sort of need someone who plays like Stan Getz.'

'Stan, it's Tommy here,' he said into the phone. 'Listen, I got a song I want you to hear . . . '

And I was very much 'just the singer'. I played not a single note on a guitar or piano, and so long hours were spent sitting in the control room while the tracks were recorded. Then, when the record was being mixed, I realised that I couldn't, as I would do in London, pop home for a few hours and come back to hear more finished results. I've never been able to sit in the room while a bass-drum sound is laboured over for six hours, and have always thought that I could offer more by returning with fresh ears and being the one to say, 'But the vocal's too quiet!' or, 'What have you done to the piano? It sounds like a hurdy-gurdy.' Here, in LA, I had to retire to the lounge while Ben sat in on a lot of the mixing. I learned to play *Super Mario Bros.*, and in the evenings Joe Sample would tap on the door and come and sit with me, having had a row at home.

But the whole project was expensive, and who on earth did we think was paying for all this? I certainly never gave the matter any serious consideration. I knew enough to realise that ultimately we ourselves paid the full costs of any recording budget. But I hadn't stopped to think that being away from home meant that all these extra expenses – every hotel room, every breakfast, every car-parking bill, every bottle of wine – became part of the recording budget. When we got back home, we had two things under our arm: a fully realised, immaculately performed and produced modern American soul–pop record, and an enormous bill, which we were going to have to sell a lot of records to pay off.

I know you'd rather talk instead
About the things inside your head
But everything, everything that I overheard
Tells me you just don't have the words

'Cause you never learned to speak the language of life
And here you are a grown man
Who can't talk to his wife
And the children you don't understand

You think you've come on pretty far
Still got the job, the house and the car
But there's one thing, one thing that you never get
A grip on life's sweet alphabet

'Cause you never learned to speak the language of life
And here you are a grown man
Who can't talk to his wife
And when things get out of hand
And the kids you don't understand
Love is a foreign land
Over words you have no command

It's not that you don't care
Admit it, baby, and you're halfway there
'Cause you know, you know that you feel much more
Than you ever have the words for

'Cause you never learned to speak the language of life
And here you are a grown man
Who can't talk to his wife
And the children you just don't understand

'The Language Of Life', from
The Language of Life, 1990

I'M SO BORED WITH THE USA

Coming back to England, I knew we wouldn't be in for an easy ride. We could see ourselves to be part of a pattern that included groups like Scritti Politti, Prefab Sprout and Aztec Camera – contemporaries of ours who'd all started out making somewhat ramshackle records at an independent level, but had then gone on to make the leap into glossily produced pop music. But would anyone else see it like that? Or would they just hear an overproduced AOR album, a sell-out of all our supposed realist values?

The answer to that question was a bit of both.

To British ears, *The Language of Life* sounded like a very slick piece of work indeed, but those who liked it homed in on the strength of the songs contained somewhere within all that sumptuous production. *Q* magazine gave it four stars, declaring that 'there's not a duff song on the album'. *Smash Hits* liked it too, awarding it nine out of ten, 'full of brilliant songs'.

Andrew Collins came to interview us for the *NME*, and he too focused on the fact that the best aspects of the album were our songs, and more specifically the caustic lyrics to a couple of them. He made his point quite forcefully by contrasting the lyrics of my song 'Me And Bobby D' with a cover we'd done of Womack and Womack's 'Take Me'. 'Lyrically speaking,' he wrote, 'the former is complex, original, inspired and provocative. The latter is shite.'

We were lucky to get off as lightly as this with the *NME*, to be fair. By now the acid-house revolution, and the Madchester scene it had given rise to, was no marginalised alternative fad, but dominated both the rock press and the charts. Andrew Collins had turned up for that *NME* interview wearing baggy dungarees and a smiley badge, and I remember thinking, 'Bloody hell, the game's up if this is how they dress at the *NME* now.' In the UK we were more out of step with the prevailing musical mood of the times than perhaps at any other point in our career, and what this meant was that the record was doomed to be disliked by anyone under the age of about thirty.

In the US the scene was different, and *The Language of Life* was seen as being a hip English update of a tradition that stretched from jazz through funk and disco and into the highly polished soul records of the 1980s made by Luther Vandross or Anita Baker, or produced by Jam and Lewis. The single 'Driving' was highly regarded among many in the US dance scene.

Feeling cold-shouldered by the British press and public, we turned gratefully to an audience in America that seemed to be welcoming us with open arms. Up until now we'd largely been played on 'college radio' in the US, and as such were part of the alternative scene, which afforded such respect to British bands of varying styles. American radio has always been a bizarrely Balkanised world, with a set of categories and definitions that are incomprehensible to outsiders, and it was simply taken as read that you had to inhabit one or other of the various ghettos on offer in order to get any airplay at all.

'Pop radio', which to us in the UK really meant *all* radio, meant something very specific indeed in the US (HITS!) and was entirely out of our reach. And by the beginning of the 1990s the world of college radio, which had formerly been our home, was now the domain of the new grunge movement, which sounded suspiciously like heavy metal and was exclusively American. British alterna-pop suddenly sounded fey and over-conceptualised to American ears – the very qualities they'd always liked in it before – and was suddenly not so welcome. In among all this we found ourselves being offered a new radio home, within a new format called New Adult Contemporary, or NAC, which would turn out to be a very scary place indeed.

Some of the stations had previously been what was described as 'Quiet Storm', playing slow, subtle soul records. Others had been part of the 'New Age' format. Now they were rebranding themselves as a genre that was supposed to attract a stylish, high-end type of consumer, offering soothing sounds for stressed-out professionals, playing what Ben describes as 'an ambient jazz lite soup of Michael Franks, Earl Klugh, Kenny G, Donald Fagen and Enya'. 'Driving' duly became a massive airplay hit on the NAC radio format, while also sneaking onto a few Urban stations, like New York's WBLS. At the beginning of a promotional tour in the US, we'd been encouraged by our management to attend a music-biz convention at which the future of NAC radio was being discussed. Someone made a short speech about how the format needed to be rebranded. 'What we need,' he said, 'is an injection of hip new talent like ... like ... ' and he cast his eyes around the room before alighting on us sitting sheepishly at the back. '*Like Everything But The Girl!*' An entire roomful of smilingly sincere bearded men stood up and applauded us, and by the following Monday morning 'Driving' was smeared thickly over the whole of NAC radio like jam on toast.

No, no, wait – this wasn't what I meant either. I wasn't like Enya, for God's sake! Couldn't people tell the difference? Didn't they know there was more to records than just what they sounded like? There was what they MEANT. And we meant something different from Enya. Or at least, we meant to.

You could begin to get a bit impatient with us at this point, I think. Christ, I feel impatient with myself just thinking about it. There's an element of randomness, chasing one idea after another with diminishing commitment and no real goal in sight. If the goal was just commercial success, then we had certainly found some ways in which to achieve it. But, crucially, they weren't the right ways. The swanky LA lifestyle was all well and good, but the trouble was, nothing seemed to *connect*. The success we'd managed to come by in the last couple of years had been seemingly at our own expense, in that it left us feeling impoverished.

Was I just unnaturally, indefensibly picky about it all? Along with the Smiths, we'd been tagged as 'miserabilists' by the UK press back in the mid-1980s. Could that be true, after all? Was I just a misery who couldn't enjoy even the good bits when they were thrown at me? Was it all there on a plate, and I was just too damn fussy to get stuck in and enjoy it? Was I my own worst enemy – or the only one who could possibly save the situation?

Me and Bobby D don't get along that easily
You told the world, 'Be free, love life'
Tell me, is it true you beat your wife?
You see, me and Bobby D don't get along that easily
You told the world, 'Skip rules, have fun'
Knocked her from here to kingdom come
How many girls have you had today?
And how many bottles have you downed today?
And while you're on the skids, who's minding the
    kids?

Go to sleep, Bobby D, here's a kiss,
Don't worry your pretty head about this

Me and Saint Jack K never had too much to say
It's easy driving with your feet
With some good ol' girl in the passenger seat
Watching the road all day
'Oh honey, what funny things you do say'
But while you're out of your head
Who's making the bed?

Go to sleep, Bobby D, here's a kiss
Don't worry your pretty head about this
Go to sleep, Saint Jack K
Don't worry your tiny head today

Me and old Bobby D don't get along that famously
A saviour and a seer? Maybe
But he never meant that much to me
Sure, I'd love a wild life
But every wild man needs a mother or wife
The seven seas you roam
And who's waiting at home?

'Me And Bobby D', from *The Language of Life*, 1990

EXPRESS YOURSELF

When Lady Gaga performed on *The X Factor* in 2009 wearing a tight, reflective leather cat costume and dancing inside a giant ten-foot bathtub, she was briefly interviewed afterwards and asked what advice she had for the contestants. 'Be yourself,' she answered, without a moment's hesitation or a flicker of irony.

Being yourself, and being able to reveal your real, authentic self to an audience, have become glib mantras of the modern pop industry, most often heard in those very circumstances where artifice and concealment seem most in evidence. And yet, there remains something true and elusive in those two words, and it was the very thing I struggled with most throughout many years of being a performer. Not at the moment of songwriting; not at the moment of singing in the studio, where I was always happy and comfortable; but at the point of performance – whether that was in a TV studio, or on a film set making a video, or onstage in front of an audience.

I wrestled constantly with the problem of how to be myself, and whether or not that self would be good enough; whether it could ever compete in a world of bigger and brasher selves. Since the days of singing from inside the wardrobe I had never learned to enjoy being looked at. Being listened to was OK, but the public gaze, so empowering and enriching to the natural extrovert, to me was kryptonite.

When we were touring in 1990, after *The Language of Life* album came out, I began to go into a complete decline about it all. We were playing at large, seated venues – Nottingham Royal Concert Hall, Edinburgh Playhouse, Manchester Apollo – culminating in three nights at the Royal Albert Hall, but the tour was plagued by sound problems. The audience who had come to these gigs wanted the live show to sound EXACTLY like the CD, and were disappointed. There were shouts of 'Turn the drums down!' and, more often, 'Turn the vocal up!' One night, at Preston Guild Hall, the sound was so bad that people asked for their money back at the end of the night, prompting us to postpone a few gigs and start again with a new sound engineer.

All this was simply rocket fuel for the self-doubt and neurosis which were taking me over. I'd never been able to hear myself onstage at the best of times, and now the swaggering drums and lush keyboard arrangements on many of the songs were completely drowning me out. The sound engineer out front had my vocal cranked up to eleven, but it would help him enormously if I could only sing louder. I couldn't, though, not for any sustained period of time, and so the upshot was that I felt inadequate onstage.

I'd suffered from stage fright since those days of throwing up at the Moonlight Club with the Marine Girls in 1981, but the doubts about my vocal abilities had become almost paralysing.

This level of self-criticism had begun, really, during the making of *The Language of Life*, where the recording sessions threw me into the company of musicians with whom I felt I simply couldn't compete, and compared to the other singers they'd all worked with – Michael Jackson! Chaka Khan! Anita Baker! – I thought my inadequacies must be glaringly obvious. The punky spirit I might embody in conversation went out of the window when I was put in front of a microphone, and now all I could hear were my limitations. A vocal range which barely spanned a hand's width on the piano seemed laughably meagre, and while I'd defended Morrissey in the past for those three notes his career depended on, I was beginning to forget all that and was turning into my own worst critic.

Up onstage in front of an audience is a place where neurosis meets narcissism, and these two competing forces were fighting a constant battle inside my head every night.

'Look, they love me, I'm fabulous and I have a gorgeous voice . . . '

'Oh, shut up, they're bored, and you're out of tune.'

'But that girl down there, she's crying, my singing is so moving.'

'Yeah, but you're tired, aren't you? Your voice is going to go in a minute . . . '

I couldn't shut those inner critics up any more. When we got to the US to tour, we had Kirk Whalum on saxophone, and in the middle of the songs he would step forward to play searingly raw, deep soul solos, tearing the place up and, in many US cities, bringing the crowd to their feet. Then I'd take the mic for the next verse with a sinking feeling of 'How do I follow that?'

Along with the vocal anxiety, I'd also lost confidence in what I looked like and what I meant. There seemed to be a dearth of female role models with whom I identified. The late

1970s indie scene I'd sprung from had been full of women who were great examples of how you could be a) quirky-looking, and b) an unconventional performer and yet still get on and form a band. Among my heroines had been Siouxsie Sioux, Pauline Murray, Poly Styrene, The Slits, The Raincoats, Lesley Woods and Alison Statton. Women like Patti Smith and Chrissie Hynde were a godsend to someone like me, who was a natural tomboy in appearance, and at the moment when I was trying to forge a self-image they seemed to beam the empowering message that you didn't need to be 'pretty' or take your kit off in order to get attention.

But the 1980s had become a very much more conservative decade. The female icon you were supposed to revere above all others was, of course, Madonna, and no one could have seemed more alien to me. A shiny, brash, Teflon-coated embodiment of AMBITION, she was absolutely a version of feminism but not the one I felt I'd signed up for, and the pouting and flirting of songs and more particularly videos like 'Material Girl' and 'Like A Virgin' left me cold. Manipulating men, using your feminine wiles 'to your own advantage', above all exploiting a simplified version of your own sexuality was suddenly the name of the game again.

But I didn't want to be a cartoon woman. I didn't want to be an Iron Lady, or a Sex Kitten, or a Diva, or the Madwoman in the Attic. If I'd been nineteen at this moment, I think I would have been full of a defiant self-confidence that would have fired me up to resist this rebranding of female performers. But I was at a low ebb as it was, and so it all conspired to make me feel out of step with the times, still banging the same drum and ranting on like an old harpy.

Self-doubt is common among performers, I suppose, and can be a positive spur, pushing you to do better, to want more; the antidote to complacency. But it becomes crippling when it veers off into paranoia, and by 1990 I was rapidly turning into someone who shouldn't have been anywhere near a stage. It was the place where I was perhaps *least* myself, where I could not be 'the real me' at all. During this last year, as a kind of diversion from the semi-detached feelings I was beginning to have about the music business, I'd been a part-time student at Birkbeck University. By the end of the US tour I was ever so slightly on the verge of a nervous breakdown, so when we got home I switched off the whole internal drama about being a pop star and got on with writing my thesis on Samuel Beckett's Trilogy. From the outside, it may have looked as though I regarded myself as being too good for this silly pop world. In truth, I felt I was probably nowhere near good enough. And that was crushing.

Frances, keep your mouth shut dear
We don't want the neighbours round
With their ugly little schemes
They make the pretty world go round
And there's a place in it for every one of us
I'll keep the home fires burning
Only don't make a fuss

And if you're not impressed
With the wares life has to show
You can take them or leave them
They choose their own fate who say no
There's some ugly little dreams
For pretty girls to buy
It's enough to make you mad
But it's safer just to break down and cry

It's a battlefield, Frances
You fight or concede
Victory to the enemy
Who call your strength insanity
What chance for such girls?
How can we compete
In a world that likes its women
Stupid and sweet

I bet you rue the day
The angels gave you your share
Of bright cornflower-blue eyes
And golden hair

There's a lot of ugly little dreams
For pretty girls to buy
It's enough to make you mad
But it's safer just to break down and cry

'Ugly Little Dreams', from
Love Not Money, 1985

There are a more night night dreams she...
For those who sleep to her who...
....
But how much is to see down on her...

Ngũgĩ ... , from
... November 1935

THIS IS A LOW

'Don't confront me with my failures /
I had not forgotten them ...'

I imagine all artists can look back at their work and admit that there are low points. It doesn't take an enormous amount of soul-searching to own up to the simple fact that some records are better than others. Often this signals the beginning of an inevitable decline, which is really the normal trajectory of a pop career. Pop careers, after all, are normally fairly short-lived affairs. There's some good stuff at the beginning, maybe a period of commercial success, then some not-so-good stuff, then really bad, then it fades into silence.

Because I had a long career by pop standards, I think the shape of my graph is different. And now, in 1990, I was right at the bottom of that big dip in the middle, which perhaps started sometime around *Idlewild* in 1987 and which I would not fully climb out of until 1994. I'm not really talking about commercial success here, either – after all, *The Language of Life* sold over half a million copies – I'm talking about the records I made, and even more about the pleasure I got from making them. Something was missing, and it was this: it was the feeling that I was expressing what I intended to express, and that I had an audience with whom I was in sync, who understood me, got from me what they wanted and what I wanted to give. It was the feeling of belonging.

I hadn't belonged anywhere for a few years now. Ben and I just existed inside our own little bubble. I wasn't part of any scene, and for quite a while hadn't even tried to be. As a band, we probably meant more in the US now than we did in the UK, and that was strange, not having a comfortable foothold in the country I lived in. Having to go abroad to feel loved made home feel unwelcoming and alien. Like a lot of groups, we were Big In Japan, and would play much bigger venues there than we could in England. Strange, sedate early-evening gigs, where we'd perform on freezing-cold air-conditioned stages to neatly groomed young professionals who adored us but had no apparent means of showing it. Their responses were confined to a code of behaviour which seemed designed to quash any outpouring of spontaneity or joy. So at the end of each song they would clap hard and rhythmically, but in unison, which made it sound insincere and forced. The applause would stop as abruptly as it started, leaving long silences between one song and the next. Where an audience's response should be like a gust that buoys you up and sustains you through the performance, these audiences seemed, however unintentionally, to drain the very lifeblood out of the evening. The gigs would be cold, stillborn affairs, where nothing went wrong, but nothing of any value happened, or seemed as if it could happen.

But I was caught now, in the machinery of a career in motion. There was more to it than just the two of us, making up our own rules as we went along. There was a manager, with a manager's office, and musicians to pay, and a record contract to fulfil, and expectations to meet, and so I simply moved forward with the impetus that all this had created. Where once I had written songs and recorded them because I *had* to, and couldn't get them recorded fast enough to keep up with myself and everything I wanted to do, now I was in danger of making records simply because I *had* to; it was what I did, it was the day job. And in this kind of fatalistic mood, in early 1991 we started recording the next album, *Worldwide*, working again with Jerry Boys at Livingston Studios where we'd recorded *Idlewild*. It came out in September of that year and was our sixth album, and in many ways it was absolutely invisible. I imagined there were lots of bad reviews lurking somewhere, but when I went to dig out the press for that period I could find none. There were simply hardly any reviews of it anywhere at all; it was just ignored. And the truth is, it really *isn't* a dreadful record, just a not-good-enough record.

I didn't completely believe in it even at the time, and I'd spent weeks in the studio making the thing. We were by now so out of step with any UK audience that we didn't even tour with the album. It wasn't successful enough for us to play the concert halls, and our ageing audience seemed unlikely to be prepared to come and stand up at small clubs or university gigs drinking warm beer and sticking to the greasy carpet. We were trapped in a complete limbo.

Despite all this creative paralysis, I don't think I was actually personally unhappy at this point. I'd finished the MA at Birkbeck University, and was considering carrying straight on with a PhD. I had some discussions with my tutor there, and began to make some provisional notes with the idea that I might write a thesis on Anthony Powell's *A Dance to the Music of Time*. Life was becoming perhaps more domesticated than ever: Ben and I moved into a new house in London, for the first time a house with a garden, and I set about learning how to grow things properly, instead of just attacking the outside space with all the skill and discernment of an out-of-control combine harvester, which had been my approach up to now. Of course, this domesticity was part of the problem – a life apparently free of conflict, while enjoyable to live, provided little in the way of raw material to inspire the kind of lyrics I was best at writing. Contentment replaced urgency like a warm blanket which I tucked around myself, comforting, snug, but deceptively stifling. If I complained of anything, it was of boredom. Too much of the time I was bored, possibly because I was being boring.

But how little I knew. How ironic it is to complain about such contentment, given what was about to come. It was the calm before the storm, and we were of course entirely ignorant of how abruptly this calm was about to end. Aside from the musical impasse, there was another problem we were trying to ignore – the fact that Ben was feeling increasingly unwell. He was suffering from asthma, which seemed to be getting worse, and between January and May 1992 I can count around twenty doctor's appointments in the diary. We were trying to soldier on, imagining that somehow we would manage to sort out both Ben's poor health and the health of our musical career. We agreed to fly out to Portugal in July to support Elton John and then we planned to go to America to play as an acoustic duo, promoting an album of covers and acoustic tracks which was being released. Instead, during June, Ben's health took a turn for the worse, and by the end of the month he was in hospital and all the touring was cancelled.

We were at the lowest point of our entire career, the point at which it may have looked as if it was all over. We'd had a reasonable run at it, all told. The band had lasted eight years and made six albums. The last one had been a bit rubbish, and we were running out of steam.

Luckily, Ben decided to contract a life-threatening illness, and in doing so, saved us.

What is it that I think I need?
Is there love in me that wants to be freed?
Or is it selfishness and ego
We carry with us everywhere that we go?

And this feeling that life's incomplete
Do you feel that too?
Do you want what I want?

And if I should start to cry
And I can't begin to tell you why
And I stumble when I begin
It's 'cause I don't understand anything

And people say that we're so close
How can there be something that I don't know
Oh, but even though I share your bed
Baby, I don't get inside your head

And this feeling of some mystery
Do you feel that too?
Do you know what I mean?

And if I should start to cry
And I can't begin to tell you why
And I stumble when I begin
It's 'cause I don't understand anything

'I Don't Understand Anything',
from *Amplified Heart*, 1994

PART FOUR

PART FOUR

HOSPITAL

On a morning in June 1992, Ben went off for another doctor's appointment to try and get to the bottom of the mysterious symptoms that had been plaguing him for months.

He'd been suffering from asthma. But asthma that got worse and worse, and was untouched by the strongest asthma drugs available. Endless visits to the GP, and then to specialists, seemed to offer nothing in the way of a concrete diagnosis.

Then the strange and sudden hot flushes began. And when they were accompanied by equally strange and sudden excruciating pains, a doctor finally took some notice and suggested that a visit to a cardiac specialist might be a good idea.

After Ben had been gone about an hour, he phoned me from the clinic where he had just had an ECG. 'They think I might be having a heart attack,' he said calmly. 'D'you think you could come over?'

I tried not to overreact, but my own heart was suddenly hammering inside my chest. All the anxiety I'd been suppressing for months was unleashed in a single moment.

'Don't move,' I said, 'just stay where you are and I'll be right there.' I thought that if he stayed still he'd be safer, that any movement might be hazardous. He'd sounded relaxed, though, so maybe it wasn't really as serious as it seemed. I jumped in a taxi and crawled through London traffic to the clinic, only to find that the doctors had become concerned about him in the meantime and, not wishing to have him drop dead in the corridor, had packed him off in an ambulance to Westminster Hospital.

I hailed another taxi, restrained myself from yelling, 'Follow that ambulance!' and raced after him.

Arriving at Westminster Hospital, I asked at reception for the Coronary Care Unit. It was upstairs, left out of the lift, down a long corridor, through some swing doors, right into the next corridor ...

I couldn't find it. The hospital seemed huge, and if you looked closely at the gloomy corners and curtain-less windows, slightly decrepit. Everyone else there knew where they were going. Or they were patients in wheelchairs who had nowhere to go, and just seemed to be killing time in doorways, like extras waiting to be called into action.

Then round another corner and through some more doors, and there he was, sitting on a bed, with his chest shaved and nurses sticking heart-monitor patches to him. Suddenly it all seemed very real, and at once entirely unreal, like being in an episode of *ER* and not being able to get out.

Over the next ten days Ben experienced a lurching descent into what was an obviously serious, though as yet undiagnosed illness. It wasn't a heart attack, or apparently a heart condition of any kind. Nor was it an acute gall-bladder infection. It wasn't AIDS, or a rare and strange parasitic infection. He got gradually sicker, then suddenly much, much sicker, and meanwhile every invasive test, all involving needles, pain and fear, came back with inconclusive but alarming results, all pointing at some kind of unidentifiable multi-system disorder. Doctors scratched their heads and said they were baffled, which is really the very definition of what you don't want doctors ever to be.

Surgeons arrived – the mechanics of the medical profession – and called time on all this namby-pamby tests business, declaring that it was time to operate. 'Open this man up,' they said, 'and let's see what's going wrong.' And so one morning Ben was wheeled off to the operating theatre for exploratory surgery. Unable to sit by his empty bed waiting, I took myself for a walk, pounding mindlessly along beside the river, crossing and recrossing the Thames at every bridge, looking at my watch every thirty seconds. Finally I deemed it long enough since I'd left and returned to his room, where I found two nurses matter-of-factly stripping his bed and sweeping the personal items from his bedside table into a plastic bag.

One of them turned and caught sight of my stricken face. 'No, no!' she cried. 'It's not what you think. He's been taken into intensive care. Sit down, I'll get the doctor.'

So not actually dead then, but in intensive care. That was nearly as bad. The doctor arrived and gave me a synopsis of what had happened. They'd found a lot of internal damage to Ben's intestines, caused by a rare inflammatory condition, and he would require a lot of further surgery and medication if he was to recover.

On telly, people always ask the bluntest questions. They say, 'How long have I got, doc?' or, 'You can tell me straight, doctor, is he going to die?' I couldn't bring myself to be that direct, so I asked, 'Could this kill him?'

That sounded suitably hypothetical. After all, almost anything *could* kill you.

'Well,' the doctor replied, 'yes, it *could*, but,' more brightly now, 'we're here to make damn sure it doesn't!'

Later, I sat with the surgeon who had operated and tried to ask again, brutally this time.

'Is he going to die tonight?' I was crying as I said this, which can't have made it easy for him. With the benefit of hindsight, I know now that he thought this was a distinct possibility, if not a probability, but all he said to me after a pause and a deep breath was, 'He's a very, very sick man.' From a surgeon, I think that comes as close as you'll ever get to an admission that things are bad.

Later that night I blagged some Temazepam from one of the nurses, went off to the relatives' room and fell fast asleep. Another nurse came in and shook me awake very early the next morning. Again I felt sure Ben was dead, but she was just asking if I wanted a cup of tea.

It would be a long time before I could get over that state of appalled expectation, and break the habit of holding myself braced for bad news at any minute. In the end, it simply became too exhausting to sustain that level of anxiety. It faded, or hardened, or settled somewhere inside me, and I got used to living with the possibility of disaster without being overwhelmed by it. As Ben lay unconscious in intensive care, I sat beside his bed, doing jigsaw puzzles and reading P. G. Wodehouse novels, gratefully losing myself for hours in the comforting world of stories where the worst disaster that could befall a young chap was the unexpected arrival for lunch of a fearsome aunt. I'd burst out laughing at inappropriate moments, then look up guiltily to see if anyone had noticed.

In the evenings I'd sit and talk to whichever nurse was on duty. Often it was Martha. She'd hand me cups of tea, and hold my hand for a bit if I was crying. And patiently listen while, for the first time ever, I talked to a virtual stranger about Ben and me, and what we had together, and everything it meant.

*

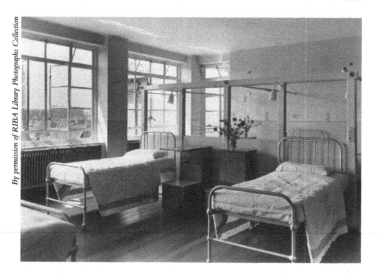

By permission of RIBA Library Photographs Collection

When Ben wrote *Patient*, his book telling the story of his ill-ness, a few people commented to me that one of the reasons it was so moving was that it was a great love story, as much as it was a story about an illness. And it was a story that hadn't ever been told before because we'd always found it impossible to talk in public about our relationship, or to describe to jour-nalists what it was like living and working together for all those years.

We often used to say in interviews that to us it just seemed normal because it was all we'd known, and that was true. Though, of course, there was nothing very ordinary about our relationship. We'd met aged nineteen and started living together, and formed a band together, and so had spent an awful lot of our time together ever since. An *awful* lot of our time – more than is normal. And so people wondered. Did we hate each other, really? Was it all a front? Or were we, actually, just a bit weird? There were no stormy bust-ups in the press,

or tempestuous public rows, so people often assumed our relationship was a bit too good to be true. But in reality, we'd had
as many ups and downs as any other couple.

There was a trip to Japan in the late 1980s when we were
sleeping in separate hotel rooms, not getting on well at all. In
the hotel's bland conference room, we sat next to each other
all day giving interviews to earnest, smiling Japanese women
dressed like newsreaders. We put on a united front and acted
normal, but upstairs we were tense and bickering. In the
middle of one night there was an earthquake. Waking up in a
gently swaying hotel, at first I wondered where Ben was. Then
I remembered, and thought, 'Oh, great. After all these years
we're going to perish fifty yards away from each other in a
Japanese hotel.' I went out and groped my way along the corridor to Ben's room. The experience had, quite literally,
shaken us up a bit, and we had a word with ourselves.

Often in interviews we would be asked: 'What's the secret of
your success as a couple?' and it would be impossible to answer.
Sometimes we'd make a joke: 'Well, I'm extremely vain and
shallow,' one of us would say. 'And I'm exactly the same!' the
other would finish. Or we'd give some long-winded, serious
reply till the interviewer's eyes glazed over. We were wary of
being slushy, or sleazy, or just plain boring. The ever-present
danger was that we'd give Too Much Information, and that
however much people might imagine they wanted detail, it
would actually prove to be a bit creepy and intrusive.

Recently, though, I was asked by a magazine to fill in a
questionnaire about my favourite films, and while I was rack-
ing my brains for an answer I remembered an anecdote that
says something about the two of us.

On one of our first dates, back in 1981, we went to the
cinema, but when we got there we couldn't agree on what to
see. So Ben went into Screen One to see the gothic

Deliverance-style horror flick *Southern Comfort*, while I went into Screen Two to see the girly option, *Tess of the d'Urbervilles*. We met up outside afterwards, and had our date. My point being that perhaps the only secret of success in any relationship is to agree to differ.

Accept that you are not the same.

Grasshopper.

And we were different, in so many ways. One Sunday afternoon recently, Ben dug out the box of his old family photos. There were his parents through the 1960s and 1970s, all boho jazz glamour. His dad in sharp, tailored suits, always with a little ciggie. And his mum, who is half Romany Gypsy, doing the full 1970s exotic actress look, channelling Liz Taylor, who she in fact interviewed many times while doing celeb journalism for *She* and *Cosmo*. Headscarves and hoop earrings. Tanned after only two days on holiday. Bottles of wine on the Formica tables. Showbiz pals – Trevor Howard, Billie Whitelaw, Brian Rix. Everything about his family seemed to be verging on the extreme, a bit larger than life. There was an uncle who'd committed suicide. Half-brothers and a sister who were triplets. Strange Gypsy ancestors called things like Woodlock and Ezekiel.

Compared to the box of my family's pics, the contrast could not be more striking.

My parents look cool too in their 1960s clobber – shades, narrow trousers, neat hair. But there's a basic and insurmountable culture gap, a yawning gulf between the grooviness of Ben's snaps and the small-town conformity of mine. Kaftans in Tangier versus windcheaters in North Wales.

By the time I met Ben's parents in the early 1980s, a little of the glamour had worn off. A few too many gins before dinner made evenings unpredictable and stormy. Ben's dad enjoyed confrontation, and one of his opening gambits to me,

aged only nineteen and used to grown-ups who were con-
ventionally polite and inhibited, was to fix me with a steely if
inebriated stare and demand: 'So, Tracey, how long have you
been a socialist?'

My parents, on the other hand, couldn't quite cope with
Ben's forthright stance in the company of adults. Still adher-
ing to old-fashioned rules of decorum, they expected him to
sleep in the spare room when he first came to visit. Finding
him in my bedroom, my mum wasn't impressed, and spoke
to him in a tone he wasn't used to. He responded by writing
a letter, which arrived a few days later. 'If you think I intend
to use your house as a knocking-shop', it began, before continuing in the same spirited manner. My parents had the good
grace to be amused, but really he was a little too much for
them. It would be a year or more before they met again, and
allowances had to be made on both sides before the permafrost
thawed.

After a few years together, we probably became more alike,
and found we'd developed that communication shorthand that
couples share. We could make decisions in the studio or
onstage with just a nod and a wink. Message understood.

The weird hours and crazed obsessiveness of making records
were also things we shared, so there was no partner back home
demanding attention or questioning the need to be in the
studio ALL night. On tour, we would watch other band members fall into a slump of loneliness, missing partners back
home, feeling torn between the freedom that travelling offers
and the duty not to enjoy it too much – a constant battle
between solitude and guilt. They'd go back to hotel rooms
alone and we wouldn't have to, and that was cool.

We were lucky, too, in being a showbiz celebrity couple
before there was really a celebrity culture. Or perhaps we were
only ever a minor celebrity couple. We once glanced over the

desk to check our reservation at a restaurant, only to see the words 'semi-VIP' next to our names.

Nowadays, pop music inhabits the tabloids on a daily basis, and entire magazines devote their energies to snatching pictures of you with sick down your front. That didn't happen in our day. There was barely even any paparazzi. We kept our heads down as much as possible, and stayed under the radar most of the time.

To journalists who liked us we were 'the Damon and Justine of their day'. Or Sonny and Cher.

For those who didn't, we were smug marrieds; the Richard and Judy of pop.

Much of the time interviewers were too nice to ask really probing questions, and the music press would falter at any hint of intrusiveness, lest they be seen to be gossipy and trivial. In the 1980s the *NME* was a deadly serious publication, with the sales figures to prove it.

An early Paolo Hewitt article was one of the exceptions. He came along to interview us in 1984 with the intention of trying to find out what we were like as people, and get a sense of our relationship. We completely stonewalled him and were humourless and earnest. The article makes me cringe now. He was trying fairly harmlessly to get us to admit we fancied each other, but we were too wrapped up in our right-on sexual politics to talk about such a thing, so he came to the conclusion that we were more friends than lovers.

Nothing could have been further from the truth. Like any self-respecting new couple, we had spent the entire previous year in bed, but it didn't seem cool to tell that directly to the *NME*. We gave off the opposite impression – of being coy and sexless, and having a slightly suspect brother–sister type relationship, like the White Stripes.

We'd never succeeded in conveying to the media any sense

of what we were really like. It was both a strength and a weakness to have been so elusive. It meant that we'd avoided the pitfalls that await those who try to live their lives in public. But it also meant that our story seemed to be lacking in the drama and passion that would have entertained the public and probably made us more popular. The glamorous version would have been more Burton and Taylor, the archetypal couple held up to represent true love; an enviable larger-than-life style of romance. Not only had we never divorced, we'd never even got round to marrying each other. Nor had we got round to having babies. And now, as Ben lay at death's door, it seemed as though we might have left it too late to do any of those things. I felt a nagging sense that we had wasted time, and that I'd missed countless opportunities to shout from the rooftops about how much I bloody loved him, as if it was somehow crucial that the world know that.

Ben spent nearly two weeks in intensive care, some of that time kept artificially unconscious so that his body could rest between further bouts of surgery. He'd finally been diagnosed with Churg–Strauss syndrome, an auto-immune disease which had caused vascular inflammation. Much of his small intestine had been irreparably damaged, and had to be removed bit by bit, in a series of operations. During the first couple of days, when he was fighting peritonitis, there was a distinct possibility that he could take a sudden turn for the worse at any moment. The doctors told me that if this happened, and the infection suddenly swamped his system, he would die very quickly. I sat and numbly watched the glowing LED readouts of his temperature and heart rate, knowing that an increase in either could spell disaster. Little bleeps and alarms would suddenly go off and I'd jump out of my skin, until a nurse would come by and flick at a drip line with her fingernail. The alarm would reset itself, and a kind of sickly calm would settle over the room again.

After the extreme danger of the first few days, Ben's condition stabilised and, though it would still be weeks before he came home, with many relapses and recoveries in between – surgery on a huge abdominal abscess, then a bout of septicaemia that nearly killed him – life began to settle into a kind of routine. I spent the first week or so sleeping in the relatives' room, but then went back home and spent part of each day travelling backwards and forwards between Hampstead and Westminster. I did nothing else at all but get up, dress, travel to the hospital, sit by Ben's bed all day, go back home, eat a takeaway and go to bed. Whole days would pass when I'd barely speak to anyone, and I would forget to eat, till by the end I had lost nearly as much weight as Ben, and the two of us looked like a poster campaign warning young people to Just Say No.

If you lose your faith, babe
You can have mine
If you're lost I'm right behind
'Cause we walk the same line

Now I don't have to tell you
How slow the night can go
I know you've watched for the light
And I bet you could tell me
How slowly four follows three
And you're most forlorn just before dawn

So if you lose your faith, babe
You can have mine
If you're lost I'm right behind
'Cause we walk the same line
When it's dark, baby
There's a light I'll shine
If you're lost I'm right behind
'Cause we walk the same line

And I don't need reminding
How loud the phone can ring
When you're waiting for news
And that big old moon
Lights every corner of the room
Your back aches from lying
And your head aches from crying

So if you lose your faith, babe
You can have mine
If you're lost I'm right behind
'Cause we walk the same line
When it's dark, baby
There's a light I'll shine
If you're lost I'm right behind
'Cause we walk the same line

And if these troubles
Should vanish like rain at midday
Well, I've no doubt there'll be more
And we can't run and we can't cheat
'Cause, baby, when we meet what we're afraid of
We find out what we're made of

'We Walk The Same Line',
from *Amplified Heart*, 1994

STILL ILL

Ben wrote in his book about the glamour of being an extremely ill patient, and the same holds true to a certain extent for the partner by the bed. Films and TV shows like *ER* abound with images of the suffering husband or wife sitting beside the wired-up patient in intensive care. There is a clearly defined role to be played, and it brings with it the consolations of sympathy and attention. I felt quite important while Ben was in hospital. For a start, I was needed – anyone who has been in hospital for any length of time will recognise the fact that with a regular and assertive 'visitor' beside you, you're much more likely to get a fresh pillow, a drink of water or a wheelchair to get you to the loo, than if you're on your own trying to get the attention of a harassed nurse. In hospital, I was also the one the doctors talked to, the recipient of all the difficult news and appalling information. Often this was because Ben was unconscious, or drugged, or just too ill to take anything in, and so I was the one in a fit state to receive the latest update.

But that important supporting role changes outside the walls of the hospital. There are no saintly images to sustain us once we get home; there is no glamour attached to the grinding boredom of recovery. In many ways, living with a depressed and traumatised convalescent is a far more difficult and lonely experience.

In the immediate aftermath of his illness, after he had come out of hospital, Ben retreated into himself, often not speaking for hours, and when we did speak it was to replay the events of the previous months, over and over again, clutching at meaning, gruesomely fascinated by the extremity of what had happened. I had kept a diary much of the time, just to get it straight in my own mind, and I suppose in an attempt to impose some kind of order on events that had spiralled so far out of control. I would fill him in on all that had happened while he was in surgery, or sedated, and tell him the things the doctors had said to me, and what they'd thought his chances were. He both did and didn't want to know everything, and was drawn towards every detail only to find that it then added another layer of horror. For a long time he seemed distant and strange to all our friends. Some thought he had maybe changed for the better, and for a while we mistook that detachment for a new calmness and acceptance of life.

Zen Ben, we called him, as he seemed to have lost some of the furious drive and competitiveness which had always spurred him on. But we were wrong: those aspects of his character hadn't gone away, they were just suppressed by other concerns, and the reason he seemed not to connect with things or people was that for a while he cared about nothing except the narrative replaying inside his own head. He was self-centred to a degree that I suspect is common in anyone recovering from a trauma. Flashbacks: the word is in common parlance now, but I don't suppose many of us understand what the word really entails, and how debilitating it is not to be able to switch off images inside your head that you'd rather forget.

After a while I welcomed the re-emergence of his old, sometimes slightly manic self-motivation; that fighting spirit was, after all, what had kept him going in hospital – and now had him roaring up the M1 in a new sports car when he could barely walk, and would in a little while have him going back on tour despite brief hospitalising relapses.

'I'm gonna be the sickest patient ever and make the biggest recovery' seemed to be his motivating philosophy, and it was amazing to witness, if a little hard to share.

'You haven't changed at all,' I'd say. 'You were mad before, and you still are. Aren't you supposed to have discovered some inner peace?'

He'd laugh, somewhat ruefully, and shake his head, and go back to wondering about himself.

Ben had been in hospital for nine weeks over the summer of 1992, finally coming home over the August bank holiday weekend. In October he had a relapse and was back in for a few nights, then again in November. These relapses were terrifying in themselves. Sudden agony; ambulances called. Was this going to be the pattern for ever?

I wondered if we were going to have to resign ourselves to a semi-invalid lifestyle, never venturing too far from home, certainly never too far from medical help. Ben's diet was incredibly compromised, and so it was easier for him to eat in our own kitchen than anywhere else. Life shrank a bit, became confined to quarters. I became protective of him, ever anxious, a little fretful. It was like a foretaste of old age.

Yet below the surface, something was stirring. Physically we were weakened, had been dealt a near-knockout blow. But at the same time, a kind of mental steeliness had developed in both of us. When we talked about music again, I was aware of a new kind of determination creeping into the conversation. The change wasn't immediate by any means, but if Ben's near-death experience had taught us anything, it was perhaps the somewhat obvious lesson of not wasting time and energy doing things we didn't want to do, or didn't believe in. We had spent the last few years chasing something intangible – a level of success, perhaps, that was forever out of reach? An idea of ourselves that had formed in someone else's imagination, not our own?

And we had lost the ability to make our own decisions and stick to them. Instead, we had begun to believe more in other people's versions of what we were and what we should be doing. None of this had made us happy, nor had it led us to produce good records. If Ben's survival, and being given a second chance at life, meant anything at all, then surely we should wipe the slate clean of all that rubbish and try to settle for ourselves what it was that we wanted.

For now, though, we had to wait until Ben's gradual physical recovery could catch up with our sense of being on the brink of something new. At this stage, the idea of recording a whole new album seemed laughably implausible with the state we, and our career, were in, so instead we compiled a *Best Of* collection, in order to regroup and buy ourselves some time. One small step at a time, we thought. Songwriting was proving difficult, so we recorded a cover of 'The Only Living Boy In New York', and the one song we had managed to write since Ben had come home, 'I Didn't Know I Was Looking For Love' (which would end up being a big hit for Karen Ramirez in 1998). Adding these two songs to the compilation meant that at least we had a record under our belts again, and could dip a toe back into the waters of being an actual functioning group who did things like touring and making videos.

The making of videos wasn't something I usually looked forward to. It had, in fact, become an absolute millstone round my neck, and we'd made a fair number of shockers since The Incident With The Well And The Bell. It had been a long time since I'd had the confidence to insist to our record company that I knew better than they did, but that was all about to change.

Having fallen in love with the early films of indie New York film-maker Hal Hartley, who had dance routines set to Sonic Youth tracks in his coolly funny, literate movies, we decided he'd be great to work with, and so Ben faxed him and asked if he'd be interested in making a video for 'The Only Living Boy In New York'. He got straight back in touch expressing his enthusiasm, but with two caveats attached that were never going to endear him to the record company:

1 He had never made a pop video before, nor had he ever wanted to;
2 He could not in all conscience film a lip-synched vocal performance, so there would be no shots of us singing in the video.

I thought that was all fine. WEA blew their stack, but for once we brazened it out. Summoning up all our courage, and trying to dispel all our fears about travelling, we flew to New York, reasoning that if Ben were to fall ill he would at least be within reach of top-notch hospitals. With a cast of actors dressed as 'poet–thug' characters, we filmed a kind of hammed-up, choreographed performance of the song without ever opening our mouths. It was the first video we'd made and liked since about 1985.

Later that year, we would do a gig at the Everyman Cinema in Hampstead, where we screened Hal's film *Simple Men* then performed an acoustic set, with the video Hal had made for us on a permanent loop in the bar. The money raised we donated to the cinema, and they bought a new screen with it. Afterwards, whenever we went to the cinema, I would look up at the screen like it was one of those benches on Hampstead Heath that commemorate someone who used to sit there. 'There should be a plaque under the screen,' I said to Ben. '"In memory of Ben and Tracey, who liked to look at this view".'

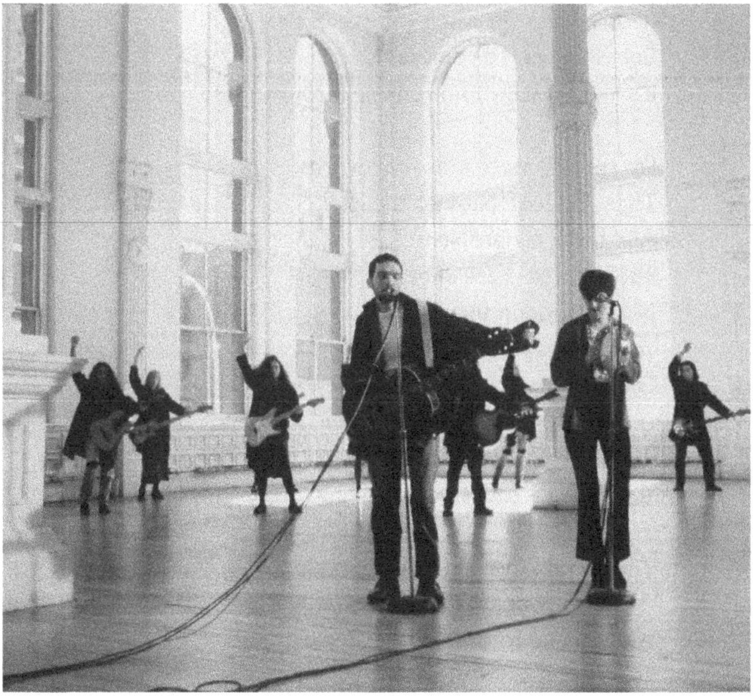

Don't say one thing one day
Then something else the next day
I'm trying to keep up with you
It's hard enough when you speak clearly
But when you're confused
It's like a goods train running through these rooms

I'm reading more into your words
Than you have put into them
And that's my problem
But you tied these knots
Now you undo them
You undo them
Oh, and think before you speak my darling

'Cause with your troubled mind
You're like a goods train running through my life

We all walk through this world alone
We keep ourselves untouched, unknown
You look up to the sky above you
Read this there – I love you
You know I love you love you love you love you

But with your troubled mind
You're like a goods train running through my life

And when you're down
You bring me down too
And, babe, that's something
I would not do
I know it's hard, yeah I know it's hard
And, baby, that's something I don't disregard

But with your troubled mind
You're like a goods train running through my life

'Troubled Mind', from *Amplified Heart*, 1994

BETTER THINGS

It's the summer of 1993, and Ben and I are sitting in the homely, country kitchen of Dave Pegg, bass player with the legendary Fairport Convention. We've come out to Oxfordshire on the introduction of our live sound engineer, Rob Braviner, who has worked with Fairport for years, and the idea is that we are going to rehearse a couple of songs and then appear with them at their annual Cropredy Festival, which is really more of a kind of souped-up village fete than an actual proper rock festival.

The band all seem to live in the same small village. It's like folk music's *Stella Street*. So we find ourselves sitting in Dave Pegg's kitchen, with pints of beer in front of us, and I can't help noticing that in the corner of the room is the computer from which Dave seems single-handedly to run their career – booking gigs, organising their festival, selling their merchandise. The whole shebang is run from home, like a little cottage industry, completely independent of any interference from record companies or the obvious trappings of the music business. Do they even *have* a record company? I don't think so, and there is no visible manager, either. Yet they still connect with a huge and devoted audience, and seem, after all these years, genuinely to be doing it for the love of it. I follow them into the barn next door, and rehearse for a bit, reverentially trying to fill Sandy Denny's shoes on the standard end-of-set 'Who Knows Where The Time Goes'. Then we stop, and go and drink Guinness in the pub down the road.

This, I realised, was how you could carry on making music without constant compromise and meddling. Fairport Convention were not of my punky generation: they were dyed-in-the-wool, ale-drinking, jumper-wearing old folkies, but they were as DIY and indie as anyone I'd ever met. It was inspiring. It was all starting to come back to me now, like I'd been asleep for a long while and had woken up, struggling to remember who and where I was.

And so, while some people will claim that Massive Attack saved my life, and others might say that it was Todd Terry, I also want to let it be stated for the record that Fairport Convention played their part, too, and were instrumental in bringing about a huge change in our attitude which in no small part contributed to everything that happened next.

The juxtaposition of events is lovely, though; you couldn't make it up. One day I am onstage in a country field in front of a crowd of bearded, real-ale folkies, euphorically singing a Sandy Denny anthem as the late afternoon sun dips behind the trees and hedgerows. And then, almost the next day, or so it seems, there is a phone call from Massive Attack asking me to collaborate and sing on their second album. To say this comes as a surprise would be putting it mildly, but it transpires that there is some method in their madness, and they are looking to make a sideways move from what Geoff Travis describes as the 'Motown reggae' of their first album. They are, in fact, in

the process of inventing trip hop, and reaching out to a 'rock' audience as a way out of the Brit soul-group ghetto, which had consigned so many before them to one-hit-wonder status. All this will only become clear long afterwards. Another message comes through to me saying that they are big fans of my *A Distant Shore* album, so I say OK, why not send me a tape of some stuff?

A cassette duly arrives as Ben and I are leaving the house one day, and I pick it up off the mat and take it with me. In the car I stick it on, still expecting something frantic and grandiose, along the lines of 'Unfinished Sympathy'. Instead, the first track slowly begins.

And it goes BOOF CLACK diddle-iddle-ick ... (pause) BOOF CLACK diddle-iddle-ick ... (pause), at the approximate pace of a snail. A stoned snail at that. It carries on like this for six or seven minutes, then stops. I look at Ben. I've just had my first introduction to trip hop, and the track I've heard is

'Protection', though without any title, or vocal melody, or lyrics, or indeed any indication as to where those things might go. There is no real beginning, middle or end. I'm not sure whether I have ever heard a piece of music this slow and empty before, and when the next one starts in just the same mood, I realise that a whole new thing is happening here.

I carry the tape around with me for a while. At first I can't get anywhere with it. Then it starts to seep into my brain, insidiously digging in under my skin until I know it so well it feels like a part of me.

A few days later, I put on the Massive tape again, get out some paper and a pencil and almost in one go write the entire song, 'Protection'. It starts off with the story of a girl some friends had told me a few nights before, then moves on to deal with my protective feelings towards Ben since his illness. Within about ten minutes I've written the whole thing, and will never change a word. When I send the tape back with the vocals, it's exactly what they wanted, and I'm summoned.

Encountering Massive Attack is both a hilarious and a daunting experience. They exude all the confidence and insularity of a true gang, speaking in an apparently private code much of the time. Despite possessing bona fide gang-style nicknames, they choose to ignore these and all address each other as 'Jack'.

It's all quick-fire repartee and banter. Lots of in-jokes and piss-takes, private remarks and snide one-liners. By the time of this second album, the original members of the old Bristol Wild Bunch sound system who had mutated into the Massive Attack of the *Blue Lines* record have been whittled down to just three: Daddy G, Mushroom and 3D, plus producer and original Wild Buncher Nellee Hooper. But as an outsider, what are you supposed to call them? Do I call 3D by his real name, Robert, or do I call him 3D, or Jack? And is Daddy G to be called Grant, or Dad, or what? In the end I take my lead from other outsiders, and end up calling them D, G and Mush. It all seems to go down OK. I kind of wish I had a nickname, too.

Journalists meeting Massive Attack at this time experience the same slight disorientation as I do. Simon Reynolds writes about his encounter in *Melody Maker*.

> Interviewing Massive Attack is a bit like being a supply teacher drafted in to supervise an unruly class. Mushroom is the superficially docile but slyly subversive pupil ... Daddy G is the intransigent type at the back of the class ... And 3D? Well, he's the closest to teacher's pet, good-naturedly attempting to answer questions. All this is accentuated when Mushroom actually asks for permission to go to the toilet!

Nellee and 3D seem to be the driving forces behind the recording process; Nellee, a somewhat raddled pixie-like creature, exudes an atmosphere of imminent debauchery, as though he can't wait to conclude this recording session and get back to the real business of ... well, God knows what. 3D appears to be the most serious about it all, and is the aesthetic brain of the band, producing all the artwork and seemingly trying to steer the creative ship. He's earnest and committed, but changes his mind a lot; it's a bit like working with Paul Weller. Daddy G is the calming, fatherly figure in the background, saying little whenever I'm around, but clearly an important and steadying presence.

Mushroom, on the other hand, is a complete enigma. I get the feeling he's suspicious of me, perhaps unsure about why I'm here. Was he party, I wonder, to the choice of me as singer on this track? I later find out that 'Protection' is one of his tracks, so it's perhaps not surprising that he feels possessive of it, and I'm not altogether sure he's bought into this concept of genre-bending juxtapositions. Would he prefer Mary J. Blige? He seems to be under the impression that I am Mary Hopkin, and have lived in an isolated croft in the Orkneys knitting my own muesli for the last ten years. I try to make conversation with him at one point by asking if he likes the new Craig Mack record, and he squints at me even more suspiciously, as if I'm deliberately trying to confuse and upset him.

Musically, they seem to be pulling in different directions, but for the time being this is creating a dynamic tension that is productive at least as often as it is destructive. Crudely speaking, Daddy G brings the reggae input, Mushroom the hip hop and 3D seems to want to be The Clash. The disagreements are spectacular – and I only witness a fraction of them – and ultimately the centre will not hold, but for this brief period it just about works. The tension between them all is personal as well as musical, and again seems to stem from the kind of playground relationships they are locked into. Laura Lee Davies interviews them for *Time Out* and experiences a typical scenario:

> In the middle of Naples airport, Mushroom and 3D ... are squabbling. The cause of their disagreement is a glossy football magazine Dee has just bought ... Mushroom tells me that Dee wants him to fold it very carefully and bend it the other way every ten minutes so that it won't crease.

Can these guys really be the saviours of modern dance music? Maybe so. Out of all this childlike behaviour comes the album *Protection*, which will change everything for a lot of people, myself included.

This girl I know needs some shelter
But she don't believe anyone can help her
She's doing so much harm, doing so much damage
But you don't want to get involved, you tell her she
    can manage
Now you can't change the way she feels
But you could put your arms around her
I know you want to live yourself
But could you forgive yourself
If you left her just the way you found her?

I'll stand in front of you, and take the force of the blow
Protection

You're a boy and I'm a girl, but you know you can lean
    on me
And I don't have no fear, I'll take on any man here
Who says that's not the way it should be

And I'll stand in front of you, and take the force of the
    blow
Protection

She's a girl and you're a boy
But sometimes you look so small, you look so small
You got a baby of your own
But when your baby's grown
She'll be the one to catch you when you fall

And stand in front of you, and take the force of the
     blow
Protection
You're a boy and I'm a girl
You're a boy and I'm a girl

Sometimes you look so small, you need some shelter
You're just running round and round, helter skelter
And I leaned on you for years, now you can lean on me
That's more than love, that's the way it should be
Now I can't change the way you feel
But I can put my arms around you
That's just part of the deal, that's the way I feel
I'll put my arms around you

And stand in front of you, and take the force of the
     blow
Protection
You're a girl and I'm a boy
You're a girl and I'm a boy

'Protection', from *Protection*, 1994

ON THE ROAD AGAIN

Some writers carry a notebook with them at all times; you never know when you might need to jot down a sudden idea, a great line that comes to you. Waking in the night with the best ever album title in your head, which has just come to you in a dream, you need to have that notebook right there, on the bedside table, to capture it before it's lost. Some songwriters try to enforce a kind of work ethic that has them sitting down at the piano every morning, without fail, facing the silence and the blank page, trying to get something down, get some work done every day, in order to keep the creative juices flowing. Or to prove that it really is a full-time, demanding job, requiring hours at the coalface like any other, and not just the occasional besotted moment of inspiration where a song alights on you as if from above, no effort required. I always mean to do all these things, but never quite succeed. I can't seem to control or coerce this writing business – the ideas either come or they don't – and there are long periods of silence when, far from lyrics welling up in my brain and demanding an outlet, simply nothing comes at all. My head, as I've said to Ben on occasion, is just 'empty, like a sieve'.

During the years when I 'retired' from music, between 2001 and 2006, I wrote not a word. They were the baby years, and I was happy and content, absorbed beyond reason in the minutiae of every single day. But there was simply nothing interesting to say about that time, and I didn't have the energy to think about anything else. Writing vanished from my life. I honestly thought I might never write anything again, but then, strangely, the germination of this book set about reminding me who I used to be and where I'd come from, and why I'd spent all those years writing and recording songs. It triggered in me the desire not to let that person disappear for ever, and so I shelved the book without finishing it and returned to songwriting instead. But still, even now, the writing ebbs and flows; a song might appear almost without warning, the silence descends again, and nothing I do can force anything into life.

In 1994, though, I was in full flow and so was Ben. Having finally unlocked the pent-up emotions of the last year, we had each written a flood of songs, which came in a rush like tears held back after a sudden shock. They were raw lyrics, uncensored outpourings from the insides of both our confused heads. With an urgency that came from their needing to be written, they sounded less detached and mature than anything we had written for a long time. Like in the old days, we were making a record again because we NEEDED to.

As well as the inspiration provided by the seismic events of the previous couple of years, we were musically inspired by the collaborations with both Fairport and Massive, and so settled on the concept of creating a kind of modern–retro hybrid. A combination of acoustic, woody instruments, with lots of crunchy-sounding analogue samples. The resulting album,

Amplified Heart, was our seventh, and we recorded some of it at Livingston Studios, with Jerry Boys engineering, and a band consisting of Dave Mattacks from Fairport Convention on drums and the legendary Danny Thompson on double bass. An arrangement was written for us by Harry Robinson, who had written the strings for Nick Drake's 'River Man'. At the same time, we were also recording tracks with John Coxon, who at the time was famous for having produced Betty Boo, but who would go on to form drum-and-bass duo Spring Heel Jack. Once again, there are elements of the 'bizarre hybrid' in this approach, same as there ever was.

With John we recorded the songs 'Get Me' and 'Troubled Mind', both songs stripped to their acoustic bones, under-pinned by stuttering, scratchy drum samples. And we had an idea for another song, too, which we'd been playing at home over a loop of the rhythm track from Raze's 'Break 4 Love'. We hadn't got a whole song yet, just a few lyrics that I had found scrawled in a notebook at home. 'I step off the train / I'm walking down your street again . . . ' It needed some kind of lyrical conclusion, a hook to hang the whole thing on. When that came later, it formed a simple chorus – 'And I miss you / Like the deserts miss the rain' – and the song took its place on the album.

In August 1994, after *Amplified Heart* had been released and we'd done some touring, 'Missing' was finally released as a single. Progressive house duo Chris & James did a mix for the UK clubs, and a more alternative version was provided by our Blanco y Negro label-mates Ultramarine.

The Chris & James mix got a respectable amount of play in UK clubs, but the single stalled at number 69 in the charts. I'd long since stopped thinking of ourselves as a hit-single group, and though it had worried me for a while, I was now far less concerned. Hell, I had my own plans now; I felt like we'd seized back the means of production. We booked a tour, of clubs not concert halls, playing as a revved-up acoustic duo, deliberately visiting every tiny dive you could think of. The Moles club, Bath, Liverpool's Lomax, King Tut's in Glasgow. Looking at these tour dates, you could have been forgiven for thinking, 'Poor old EBTG, what a comedown, eh? Albert Hall a few years back, now it's the Old Trout in Windsor ...' I didn't see it like that at all – I was having a whale of a time, feeling nineteen again, eyeball to eyeball with a wide-awake, enthused crowd, steaming in front of me in some sweaty dive. Fired up and running on adrenalin, I had a crusading zeal to seize back my career, and it felt like I'd rediscovered the rawness of what I'd always done. Both newly skinny and crop-haired, we'd returned to our roots.

This is from an article I wrote at the time:

Halfway through our current tour of small clubs, we've finished our set at Manchester University's Hop & Grape and are about to leave the stage. From the front row, a fan extends his hand and I cheerfully reach down to shake it. He grips hard and doesn't let go; instead, he pulls me down towards him. This is not a handshake, I realise, but a confrontation. Looking at him closely now I can see that he sports a kind of ageing-Ted-meets-Morrissey look of quiff, sideburns and denim, and that he is perilously drunk. 'I've driven all the way from High Wycombe,' he hisses, managing to make this sound at once like an act of devotion and also a kind of vague threat. 'And I want you to play "I Don't Want To Talk About It".' I'm trying to free my hand and smile, and Ben is trying to leave the stage, and the audience is stamping and cheering. 'Thanks,' I mutter at him, 'yeah, yeah, sure, OK.' He lets me go. We weren't intending to play it, but now I feel somehow obliged, even intimidated.

We come back on and do our usual first encore of Robert Forster's 'Rock 'n' Roll Friend', and then I whisper to Ben that we should play 'I Don't Want To Talk About It'. He's surprised, but begins the song. As we start singing, I remember how much I love it and I'm almost grateful to the guy for asking for it, and I look down to the front row, hoping to be rewarded by his gratitude, and of course, he's gone . . .

Our next gig is at the Lomax, a new club in Liverpool. We arrive early in the afternoon for a soundcheck, and lying on the stage is a set list left behind by some previous band. Their song titles include 'Suck Me Dry' and 'Bend Over Bitch'. This is hilarious, in a daunting kind of way – what kind of psychotic crowd do you get in here on a Saturday night?

In the end, of course, what we get is an EBTG crowd, good-humoured and attentive, and it's a great gig. There are two bars at the club, one up on the balcony and one downstairs, so inevitably there's a constant low murmur and some background noise of glasses shattering, but not enough to bother us onstage. Some of our fans, though, can be fiercely protective of us, and when we come back for our encore we are just about to start the song when someone yells, 'Shut the fuck up while they're playing.' The crowd falls silent, half laughs and looks at us for our response. Ben creeps towards his microphone. 'Sorry,' he whispers, 'we'll be as quiet as we can.'

This DIY cottage-industry approach extended into our next tour of the US as well. Instead of trying to tour with a hired band and fill concert halls, we set off again as an acoustic duo, to play in small clubs using in-house sound systems, travelling much of the time in a self-drive van, just me and Ben, our sound engineer/tour manager and one roadie. No PA or equipment; a few guitars and suitcases in the back. It wasn't a glamorous way to tour, but it kind of suited the zealously combative mood I was in. The gigs themselves were fairly extreme, too, partly due to the proximity of the audience in such small venues, who were sometimes casual observers and sometimes scarily manic fans.

In one town, the posters put up around town called us the 'legendary British duo', presumably in an attempt to whip up some ticket sales. It felt like quite a lot to live up to, but for some of our US fans, who'd seen a lot less of us over the years than their counterparts in the UK, we did genuinely seem to have a status that went way beyond what we were used to.

When we played at the Magic Bag in Detroit, an old 1920s converted cinema with posters of Miles Davis and Kurt Cobain in the dressing room, the show had apparently sold out in a few hours on the day the tickets were announced. When we went onstage the audience were beside themselves, and the air of devotion in the room was palpable. One man in the front row gasped audibly at every introduction. Another guy, who looked like Allen Ginsberg, nodded sagely to himself at what he considered to be good chord changes. Couples linked arms on the ballads. A girl mouthed every lyric. Another fan leaped to his feet and punched the air when we began 'Driving'. Their combined focus was at once disarming and uplifting in its concentrated intensity.

Afterwards a crowd built up outside, and people were shouting in the side alley. Someone banged on the door to the fire exit. I was too tired to stay and talk to fans this time, so we got a taxi to pull up right outside the back door and bundled in and raced off with people hammering on the roof. Unbelievably, two cars managed to follow us back to our hotel, which was half an hour away via freeways and multiple junctions. On the

everything but the girl

saturday sept 17 with guests

the starfish room

tickets at ticketmaster and track records or call 280-4444

doors 8:30pm • show 10pm

Z95³

perryscope '94

forecourt outside the hotel, they pulled up behind us. A guy with every record we have ever released under his arm jumped out of the still-moving car and approached us. For a moment I was quite scared.

'Hey, Ben. Hey, Tracey. Will you sign a few things? Oh, Christ, I can't believe this is happening. Pinch me, someone. Lord, will you pinch me.'

'It's OK. Take it easy.'

'You should know for every sleeve you sign, I will have a frame made and hang it in my shrine.'

'Your what?'

'Shrine. To Everything But The Girl. It is just beautiful. Are you going into the hotel now? I saw you in 1990. Some people tonight have waited ten years. Are you? Upstairs? To your room? Oh, Christ, I can't believe this is happening.'

It was all a very intense experience. We were like a band at the beginning of their existence in terms of the scale of the work we were doing, and yet behind us was the accumulated baggage, good and bad, of a long and convoluted career. Where that baggage used to weigh me down, it now seemed something I was strong enough to carry, and none of the mistakes of the past could touch me any more. At the end of the tour we treated ourselves to a first-class flight home from Tom Bradley International Terminal at LAX. It was my birthday, and somehow Ben's mother had managed to hack into the British Airways computer system and a birthday greeting came up on the screen when we collected our boarding passes. The cabin crew presented me with a cake and a congratulatory bottle of Krug.

When that summer sun comes down
When the season comes around
There will be no end in sight
We will be besieged by light

When we shake off winter's chain
We will see the point again
Right now we are just keeping afloat
But soon we'll be swimming
Soon we'll be swimming

It's all over so let's go on
There's nothing left so let's go on
We can't keep on, so let's keep on
There is no reason so let's make our own
Let's make our own

When the hurricane dies down
And everything lies on the ground
There will be no end in sight
We will be besieged by light

It's all over, let's carry on
It's all over, let's carry on
Right now we are just keeping afloat
But soon we'll be swimming, swimming
Soon we'll be swimming

'Swimming', from *Love and Its Opposite*, 2010

YES SIR, I CAN BOOGIE

Once upon a time, and quite out of the blue, when I was least expecting it, I had a huge worldwide hit single. And I'm going to tell you how it happened because it is a strange story, with unlikely twists and turns, and it says something yet again about how peculiar and unpredictable and *uncontrollable* a career in the music business can be.

The story begins in late 1993, with the recording of the album *Amplified Heart*. The song 'Missing' was released as a single from the album and, like most of our singles, failed to be a hit. The remixes we'd had done had got a certain amount of club play, but nothing to set the world alight. For the US, though, Johnny D at Atlantic Records wanted to get a new mix done, one that could move an American dance-floor. He approached Todd Terry, legendary house DJ and remixer, who came up with a version of the track that changed almost nothing from the original except the rhythm track. Todd himself says of the mix: 'I didn't have to do a lot. They use a lot of melody flavour with the vocals, which makes my job much easier. They did the production; I just made it dance.'

It was added to the US release of the single, along with all the other mixes, and again, nothing much seemed to happen and we carried on with our new plan of working like maniacs in the sure and certain knowledge that something brilliant would ultimately come of it.

Perhaps to test this new self-confidence of ours, WEA, the company who had bankrolled Blanco y Negro all these years and had been the major label behind everything we did, decided to drop us. Having heard *Amplified Heart*, and then the tracks I'd done with Massive Attack, and the remixes of 'Missing', they decided in their wisdom that our career was over, and – not entirely against our will, it must be said – let us go, just at the moment when our self-belief and drive was probably at its highest point ever.

As Oscar Wilde might have said, you'd have to have a heart of stone not to laugh.

At the beginning of 1995, I found myself in New York doing promotion with Massive Attack. There were some interviews, a live radio session – well, I was live. The boys sat in the control room bickering, and watched me sing over the backing track – and an album release party. It was a glamorous little trip, New York was snowy and we stayed in the Philippe Starck redesigned Royalton Hotel, where my minimalist room made me feel lonely and rudderless, and inspired me to write the song 'Single'. At the release party we were feted and fussed over, and I had the slightly strange experience of feeling like a 'new' singer with a 'new' band.

But Massive Attack still didn't know what to make of me, or what on earth I stood for.

One day we were all in a taxi, heading off to a photo shoot, when Daddy G leaned over and said, 'Trace, I was out last night and I heard a remix of one of your songs by Todd Terry. Did you know he'd done that?' He looked a bit concerned.

'Well, yeah,' I replied, and then explained that, contrary to their unwavering impression of me, I had heard of the notion of remixes, was not opposed to them and yes, had willingly agreed to the Todd Terry remix of 'Missing'. And liked it.

They were surprised, but nodded politely.

'Well, it sounded good,' said G. 'You know, bit of a dance-floor hit.'

In April, Ben and I decided to up sticks and go and spend some time in New York ourselves. We rented a huge but completely knackered loft apartment down in Tribeca. It had a standard NY heavy steel door, with bondage-style locks and bolts studding it from top to bottom. Inside was one huge dusty space, bereft of furniture, a slightly grimy kitchen at one end and then off that, one small, windowless bedroom. We started working on some new songs, believing that the last album had run its course now, and set about recording new demos, gathering ideas for the next record – moving on again.

And it was while we were in this flat in New York in 1995 that we began to get the first intimations of something happening with our old single 'Missing'. The same single that I thought was long dead and buried, months having passed since it was remixed and sent out to clubs and radio stations. Unprompted by any record-company promo machines or advertising, DJs around the world had started playing the Todd Terry mix and it was going down a storm. It had apparently become some kind of hit in Italy, but I couldn't quite get the full details. An airplay hit, or just in the clubs, or what? I made a few phone calls, but no one was sure.

Then I opened up *Billboard* magazine one day, and there it

was in the US club charts, largely on the basis of the massive amounts of play it was receiving in Miami. Ben called up Atlantic Records – still our label in the States – to see if they knew what was going on, but our main contact there at the time was someone who had little connection with the dance department, so he was somewhat dismissive of the frivolity of a Miami dance hit, and the idea of it having any serious significance was pooh-poohed.

We couldn't ring up WEA in the UK to see what they knew because they'd just dropped us. We no longer had a record deal, so how could we possibly be having a hit?

Gradually the full picture emerged. Though some people at Atlantic seemed unaware of its bubbling-under status in the US, Johnny D in the dance department knew every DJ who was playing it, and how often, and probably deserves more credit than anyone else around us for spotting the potential of this record early, and refusing to give up on it long after it might have seemed reasonable to admit defeat. He made us realise that the song really was taking off in a big way, and wasn't just a weekend sensation but was on its way to establishing itself as a true anthem.

Back in the UK, our ex-record company began to sit up and take notice. We were now officially an unsigned band outside the US, but WEA still had the rights to the track, and, never ones to look a gift horse in the mouth, the label who had so recently dropped us decided to set about rereleasing it throughout Europe. By June it was number one in Italy, and remained so for weeks. Other European countries followed suit. In October 1995 it was rereleased in the UK by WEA, who presumably at this point were feeling a bit sick. They owned the song but they no longer owned us, and we were looking dangerously like being on the verge of a late comeback.

You probably don't need me to tell you that 'Missing' was a hit – though it was a hit of spectacular proportions. Eleven weeks in the Top Ten in the UK. Number one in Italy, Germany and across Europe. And then in the US it began to pick up radio airplay across the board, spreading like a virus throughout the whole of America, gradually emerging as a fully-fledged pop hit. By November it was number 23 in the US pop charts, then it crawled upwards – 14, then 12, up to 10. Then another leap up to 4, then 3, then up to 2. Could we really do it? Have a number-one single in the US?

No, we couldn't. It stopped at number 2, only making it to number one on the airplay charts.

But it had broken more or less every rule of pop marketing and strategy, and proved that even the modern, ultra-controlled music business was still subject to the subtle and unpredictable

whims of public taste. By the end of its extraordinary second life, 'Missing' had sold around three million copies.

With the benefit of hindsight, the track looks and sounds like a predestined hit, something that was always meant to be, but it's salutary to remember that it didn't strike everyone that way on first hearing. I think it's interesting, too, that it took an American remixer to find in 'Missing' the elements that crystallised into its success, where British remixers had wrestled with its 'songiness'. In the US, where rave culture had nothing like the same impact as it did in the UK, a whole generation of DJs had a lot of love and respect for our single 'Driving' and *The Language of Life* album, and to them 'Missing' seemed like a natural development of what we'd already been doing rather than a complete volte-face.

In retrospect, its mega-success conferred upon it near-mythical status, and inspired my favourite ever piece of EBTG hyperbole in a review by James Hunter in *Village Voice*, which I quote for you here in full:

> Fifty or sixty weeks ago, EBTG released 'Missing', a track from *Amplified Heart*, as a single. Todd Terry masterminded a charging remix. Miami radio started playing the shit out of it. Across the country, slowly but surely, the track continued to build. And for the past few weeks, the single's been at or near the top of the American charts.
>
> It's not a good thing. It's a great thing.
>
> Originally, 'Missing' was rage rearranged as calm, rain reimagined as sand ... A woman takes a train to her ex-lover's house. He's gone – 'disappeared somewhere', she fears, 'like outer space'. As Thorn's voice remains moored and intact, full of her radical midrange rationality, she wonders, 'Could you be dead?' What Terry put back into the song was the

founding panic, the hell of abused sleep and liquor cabinets that put the woman on the train in the first place. He gave the part to a kind of loud post-disco tech shuffle, an ongoing beat of changing volume that sounded like a new character called Trouble who shows up at the ends of the verses, just before the 'And I miss you' choruses, kicking over seats, cursing at the conductor ... The Remix EP proves that behind tonal modesty can lay stuff so devastating that it could level the forces of distorted guitars.

I wish I'd said that.

I step off the train
I'm walking down your street again
And past your door
But you don't live there any more
It's years since you've been there
Now you've disappeared somewhere
Like outer space
You've found some better place

And I miss you
Like the deserts miss the rain

Could you be dead?
You always were two steps ahead
Of everyone
We'd walk behind while you would run
I look up at your house
And I can almost hear you shout
Down to me
Where I always used to be

And I miss you
Like the deserts miss the rain

Back on the train
I ask why did I come again
Can I confess
I've been hanging round your old address
And the years have proved
To offer nothing since you moved
You're long gone
But I can't move on

And I miss you
Like the deserts miss the rain

'Missing', from *Amplified Heart*, 1994

FROM THE RIDICULOUS …

Of course, 'Missing' being such a success means that everything will be different, and I will be treated with a level
of respect bordering on reverence. I will no longer be expected
to perform at humiliating and ridiculous promotional events;
instead, I will take part in occasions which are worthy of me
and which showcase my talents in an appropriate manner.

With all this in mind, in the summer of 1995 we go to Italy
to appear at one of their regular TV pop extravaganzas –
'Festivalbar'. These are uniquely Italian phenomena, song con-
tests at which pop groups from all over Europe who have
current Italian hits are gathered together to mime them in
front of a huge, screaming teenage audience. It's like a pop festival, but drained of any performance, substance or meaning.
I've appeared at several of these over the years – San Remo and
Saint-Vincent, for example – with fellow guests ranging from
Mandy Smith and Simply Red to Patsy Kensit and Kim Wilde,
via Bros and Nick Kamen. Often I have shared dinner tables
and backstage areas with these acts, who have usually been

charming company. For me, it has sometimes been a dispiriting experience, consisting of being half recognised while
performing a song that isn't quite a hit. Now, though, I have
a single, 'Missing', which has been number one in Italy for
weeks, and is being referred to as '*il disco per l'anno*'. Surely
things will have changed, and this year the festival will prove
to be some kind of reward for all the years of indignity? Surely
I'll discover what it's like to be a real pop star?

In fact – and it's possible to find this vaguely reassuring – it's
all much the same as it ever was. The location this time is the
curious medieval hill town of Marostica, where the stage for
the whole show has been set up in the chequerboard central
square, beneath the ramparts and in the shadow of the
portcullis. Our dressing room is hung with pikes and staffs and
shields, with a chunky oak table for make-up. After hanging
around for a while, we go down to the stage to rehearse, enter-
ing from beneath a neon-lit arch, which makes the stage
resemble Bournemouth pier. I am miming, of course, and Ben
has a Korg keyboard to 'play', despite it having no mains cable
attached, while I have a Fender Telecaster with no guitar lead.
The camera rehearsal is always the most undermining moment
of the day, when self-doubt can overwhelm all sense of your
own value or purpose or desire to live, and today, pretending
to sing and play the guitar while a fag-smoking stage manager
stares blankly at me, is no different.

Also on the show with me is the current Italian pop star,
Irene Grandi, who is performing her hit, the improbably titled
'Bum Bum'. She makes a much better show than I do of actually enjoying herself, and wanting to be in this environment,
cavorting happily round the stage in a suitably skimpy outfit.
In the break between rehearsal and performance we go to a
pizzeria for dinner, and finally some hint of my current fame
in Italy reveals itself. I am gradually recognised by the waiters,

then 'Missing' comes on the radio to confirm their suspicions, and soon the whole place has degenerated into an orgy of gawping, autograph-collecting and Polaroid-taking. Some can think of no response other than to point at the radio and back at me, while I smile and nod and feel stupid.

Later, after a torrential thunderstorm almost causes the whole event to be cancelled, momentarily raising the awful possibility that we might have to return tomorrow to repeat the whole day, we finally get to go on and perform the song. And yes, there is a sense that the crowd do genuinely know and love this song, but still I feel I am curiously peripheral to their experience of it. Their excitement is about the record, not about us – which is as it should be, really – and proves that, in the most basic and obvious way, we haven't changed at all. Our huge images are projected onto an enormous screen, and the lights bounce and reflect off the illuminated pink castle, while Ben pretends to play and I pretend to sing.

On the way home Ben comments that, although it's called a festival, it feels less like appearing at Glastonbury and more like being on *Jeux Sans Frontières*.

...TO THE SUBLIME

It's June 1995, and I'm about to experience my first ever Glastonbury. I have never been to the festival, and as a band we have never performed there. In fact, since that disastrous late-1970s visit to Knebworth, I don't think I've been to a festival at all. For my generation they have held none of the allure they do now, in my mind being for ever associated with hippies, boring old farts, long hair, mud, prog rock and guitar solos – everything I hated and was bent on destroying. I've always thought gigs should be things that happened at night, after dark, in cities, preferably in front of a crowd of no more than a few hundred. And that bands should be viewed, ideally, one at a time, close up, with a drink in your hand and someone else's cigarette smoke in your face. But here I am, it's the mid-1990s and festivals have had their comeback and are now a fixture on the live circuit, deemed suitable even for a band such as ourselves. Or Massive Attack, who I am also booked to be appearing with, on the Friday night, in the dance tent. Ben and I arrive at the site in the middle of Friday afternoon.

In the backstage area I meet up with 3D, Mushroom and G and the rest of the Massive crew, and we sit around drinking beer in the afternoon sunshine. It feels to me nothing like being at a gig at all; there's a sort of holiday, campsite atmosphere which I simply can't associate with the idea of bands and performance. As the light fades, we all make our way to the dance tent and the band begin their set. The tent is huge and packed with bodies – a thousand people? two thousand? – and is midsummer-steamy, like being in the garden as a child and sweating it out in the confines of a small cave instead of enjoying the fresh air. The air is hot and thick with the smell of cut grass and damp canvas.

The pattern of Massive Attack's gigs is that various singers come on at points throughout the set to perform their songs. Horace Andy is there, and Deborah, who sings the Shara Nelson hits, and then halfway through I come on to sing 'Protection'. As I walk onstage I realise that the volume in this space is ear-splitting, and the sound seems to swirl aimlessly around inside the tent, coming and going in waves, gathering momentum like a whirlpool. I open my mouth to sing the first note of 'Protection' and the vocal level in my monitors has simply vanished, or been swallowed up in the volume both on and off the stage. There is simply nothing there – I am singing as if special earplugs have been designed to filter out the sound of my voice. Being an experienced veteran, I do what you must never do in these circumstances and fly into a complete panic, shooting desperate glances at the monitor man to the side of the stage. He is aware of the problem, and shoots desperate glances back at me while he tries to fix it, managing to blow me backwards with a howl of feedback from the monitor in front of me. It soon becomes clear that there is nothing much he can do, and I am left with no audible vocal to work with onstage. All I can hear is the sound bouncing back at me from the walls of the tent, with a two-second delay, and so I simply carry on, hoping and praying that I am not too far out of time or out of tune. As the song finishes I take my bow, leave the stage and burst into frustrated tears.

Luckily, we are due to return tomorrow to perform as Everything But The Girl, so there may still be time to redeem things. We are booked to play an acoustic set on the main stage at midday, and so, having spent the night at a hotel in Bristol, we return and are shown to our 'dressing room', a kind of workman's hut standing on wooden duckboards. Inside is a table spread with Ben's standard post-operative food supply – a roast chicken, some white bread, a bit of salad and a bottle of brandy. I am wearing a long, sleeveless thin cotton dress and turquoise Mary Jane shoes. But it has turned out to be a cold morning, and I am underdressed. My confidence has been shaken by last night's events, and I need to warm up. Thankfully I have recently discovered that brandy is a miracle cure for the stage fright I've always suffered from. At first, just a medicinal nip before going on worked wonders. Then that wore off a bit, so now a little more is needed. It is only eleven in the morning, and I haven't eaten yet, but I slug back a couple of large brandies anyway, and hey presto! I feel much warmer and braver.

At that moment, Jeff Buckley appears unexpectedly in our cabin.

In New York in April 1995, we had done an acoustic gig at a little club/café in the East Village called Sin-é, for the sole reason that Jeff Buckley had, in 1993, released his first EP of live recordings made there. After it was released, and following tip-offs from Geoff Travis, we went to see Jeff play live in London, and at first I had mixed feelings of awe and impatience. He was so good, but he could be *so* self-involved onstage it was almost impenetrable, and the self-love was off-putting. Then he'd open his mouth to sing, and you were lost. I think he took his shirt off at this gig, too, and that may have played a part in the rapture. In 1994, his first album *Grace* was released, and confirmed everything.

Out in New York I wanted to play where he had played, and so we booked a gig at Sin-é, which really was just a café where they pushed the tables back and you set up in a corner of the room. We lugged our own gear down there, turning up with a couple of guitars and a tiny amp, and set up and played to a packed and amazed room, with the pavement outside crowded with those who couldn't get in, noses pressed against the windows, watching from the street.

Our friend Valerie had a small hairdressing salon in the East Village, and Ben wandered down there one day to get a haircut. By magical coincidence Jeff Buckley, who was also friends with Valerie, was in there at the same time getting a trim. Valerie introduced them to each other and they started chatting, and soon discovered that we were all booked to play at that year's Glastonbury. Jeff suggested we team up and do a song together. Sounds like a great idea, said Ben, and thought no more about it. When he came home and told me about the encounter, I made a mental note to accompany him to his hair appointments in future.

And now, without warning or preamble, at eleven o'clock in the morning here is Jeff Buckley standing in front of me in my workman's hut of a dressing room, and he has come to remind me that we have agreed to do a song together. We are due onstage in about half an hour.

'Bloody hell, isn't it a bit late now?' I ask. He doesn't think so. With a kind of gauche enthusiasm that makes him seem like a spectacularly gorgeous younger brother, he produces a guitar and begins to throw ideas at us. We swap titles of songs we might all know, and uncover a shared love of The Smiths. At random, we settle on 'I Know It's Over' from *The Queen is Dead* album, with its awful, prophetic lyric: 'Oh, Mother, I can feel the soil falling over my head ... '

We run through it a couple of times in the dressing room, trying to work out who should sing which bits and when. It sounds OK, but then I am, frankly, a bit pissed.

Suddenly it's time to go onstage, so out we go, in broad if somewhat cloudy daylight, in front of the just-waking-up Glasto crowd. It is one of those chilly summer days, a stiff breeze blowing the grey clouds about. Set lists are flapping at your feet. You're wishing you had a fleece on. By late afternoon, when Polly Harvey appears in her pink catsuit, it will be a fine day, but for now we have to contend with the gloom. I do my best to connect with the audience, who are several miles away from the stage, but it does feel as if it is falling a bit flat. Then, like the magical moment when Paul Weller joined us all those years ago at the ICA, Jeff Buckley, this year's heart-throb hero, comes onstage and the mood lifts. Never one to shy away from a song's potential for emotion, if not downright melodrama, Jeff attacks the vocal as though his life depends on it. Together, the two of us howl our way through The Smiths number – 'It's so easy to laugh / It's so easy to hate / It takes guts to be gentle and kind' – crashing into each other's ad-libs, wandering in and out of tune and hilariously stepping on each other's toes. At the end, the audience look more startled than anything, but it has at least woken them up. A great, if chaotic moment, entirely true to the spirit of Glastonbury.

Later that afternoon, Jeff is onstage with his own band, and we are watching from the wings. At the end of one song he looks over to us, catches Ben's eye and starts beckoning him onstage with furious jerks of his head. It's the scene at the end of *Spinal Tap* when the band reunite onstage! Ben picks up a guitar, gamely ambles on and plugs in.

'OK,' yells Jeff, 'we're gonna do "Kick Out The Jams". One–two–three–FAWH!'

Now, Ben may well be the only guitarist in rock music who had never heard MC5's punk anthem, let alone played it. Still, he's nothing if not a quick learner, and after about eight bars he has sussed it and is off and running. Jeff's set is one of those being filmed for TV broadcast that day, and watching at home, one of our friends sits bolt upright to get a closer look at the *Zelig*-like moment unfolding on screen in front of her. Is that Ben there, on the telly, onstage at Glastonbury, standing behind Jeff Buckley, playing an MC5 song? Before she can get a clear view, the camera swings back to Jeff, and by the next song Ben is gone.

HERE'S WHERE THE STORY ENDS

'**M**issing' had been a huge hit. My career was saved . . . hooray!

From here on it should be easy, no?

Well, no, of course you have realised by now that it doesn't work like that, and that the moments of success, when you glide along with swanlike grace, conceal the same frantic amount of paddling going on beneath the surface as ever before.

I'd had a hit single before, remember – admittedly, not on this scale – and it had led me nowhere. By now I was old enough and wise enough to know that one hit did not last for ever, and you were only ever as interesting as your *next* record, not your last one. This time, though, that very fact seemed less like a daunting recipe for disaster and more like a challenge, which I at least had a chance of rising to. We were still racing along with that second wind in our sails, full of purpose and direction, an entirely different band from the one we'd been a few years earlier. People said that at this point we 'reinvented ourselves', and that the reason for the sudden about-turn in our fortunes was that we completely and utterly changed in a way that could not have been foreseen. But that sounds so calculated and opportunist, it just doesn't ring true. And even the word 'reinvention' had become a trite cliché, often seeming to refer to nothing much more profound than the notion that Madonna changed her hair colour every time she had a new record out. Did that really constitute reinventing yourself?

It wasn't so much that we turned from an acoustic band into an electronic one, as that we turned from a band with no confidence back into a band who believed in themselves. And while it's true that we changed, what also happened – and this is the most overlooked factor in the story – was that the world changed, again, and like the magical lands at the top of the Faraway Tree, the music scene swung around and landed back at our feet.

By the mid-1990s grunge had finally died, and dance music had experienced something of a post-rave comedown. 'Missing's success came about in part because it brought a moment of melancholy and heartbreak back to the dancefloor, a combination many people had always loved but perhaps forgotten. With artists like Massive Attack and Tricky, Portishead and Björk came an evolution in expectations of electronic music with beats. It could be melodic and heartfelt, as well as experimental. Slow and moody. Atmospheric. All the things I'd always been good at.

The press were also beginning to employ new terms like 'sleazy listening' and 'loungecore', which sounded a whole lot more hip and, well, hardcore than easy-listening background music. Music that might formerly have been defined sneeringly as 'dinner-party music' was suddenly being redefined as 'chill-out'. All these changes meant that suddenly, me doing what came naturally was regarded in a very different light.

*

In 1995, just before 'Missing' really took off, we had left New York and come back to London, lured by Ben's growing sense that the drum-and-bass scene was the most exciting thing he'd heard in years. As soon as we got back, Ben started going to the club Speed, which LTJ Bukem had started in 1994 at the Mars Bar. He was totally enthused by what he was hearing, and one night he persuaded me to come along too. I was apprehensive at first – Will we fit in? Will we get pointed at? – but at this moment, just before the huge success of 'Missing', we were still quite anonymous and so were able to get back to being participants in a music scene, part of the crowd, rather than famous representatives of something else entirely. We queued up at Speed and weren't really spotted. In fact, if I got recognised at all at this point, it was for being the singer with Massive Attack. I was surrounded by a new generation who only knew me for the good stuff I'd done recently. There was no history or baggage weighing me down. It was fabulous – a completely clean slate.

We got into the club early and sat drinking beer, and got up to dance while Doc Scott was DJing. It was mostly blokes, I noticed, but the atmosphere wasn't laddish, more muso. Everyone was pretty dressed down: jeans, hoodies, cool trainers. On the dancefloor there were a few high-speed breakdance experts, but most of the rest of us were doing a kind of half-time skinhead skank. It was a bit like being at a postmodern Specials gig. It wasn't a rock gig, and it wasn't a rave – it felt like something new again. Strange and yet familiar, it felt *possible*.

Ben in particular was completely inspired by what he was hearing because alongside the beats, in the acres of empty space, he could hear room for a big fat vocal like mine. At home, in the basement studio of our house, he began working on new tracks, almost writing in reverse, creating the mood first and writing the song later. The guiding ethos was 'electronica with songs' – and although today that sounds like a fairly common-place idea, in 1996 it was less so. John Coxon, who produced some of the *Amplified Heart* album, including the original ver-sion of 'Missing', had by now formed drum-and-bass duo Spring Heel Jack with Ashley Wales (who, in another extraor-dinary example of the wheel coming full circle, had played in a band called Crazy About Love with the teenage Ben). They sent us a piece of music they had created and Ben wrote a song over the top of it, in much the same way that I collaborated with Massive Attack. The track was 'Walking Wounded', and would be the follow-up single to the smash hit 'Missing'.

One thing this approach did mean, however, was that I really was not involved at all in the creation of the music. For a technophobe like me, there was no appeal in trying to get to grips with sequencing and programming, the creation of music in an electronic context. I loved the results, but had to take a complete back seat when it came to the making of this sound. The fact that I didn't entirely mind says something about where I was at this point. We were in the middle of a career high point, and though I was excited about it all, I was begin-ning to feel a bit less involved, less entirely engaged, than I had for a while. We'd talked on and off over the years about the possibility of having children, but various things had kept deferring the decision. At the end of the 1980s we toyed with the idea, but decided to carry on touring instead. 'Apron Strings' was written when the first stirrings of maternal feel-ing were aroused by my sister having babies. I had wondered what it would be like, what kind of mother I'd be, but the wonderings were vague, a bit idealised. Motherhood was a theoretical concept to me; children I had almost no experience of. Then Ben's illness intervened, and after his recovery it was more the salvaging of our career that energised us than the idea of slowing down and starting a family.

But it began to nag away at me, a little barely acknowledged gap at the centre of everything. I hinted obliquely at it on *Amplified Heart* – 'What is it that I think I need / Is there love in me that wants to be freed?' – but shied away from addressing it too directly.

Now, in 1995, I was beginning to wonder whether the repeated deferrals might just go on for ever, and whether we might agree in theory to the idea of having a family but simply never postpone our career for long enough to actually get round to it. This was starting to worry me, and I was feeling that in the end it might have to be a unilateral decision, that I might have to put my foot down at some point and say, 'Enough!'

All of this was preoccupying me. And the record we were making was ultimately more Ben's baby than my own, however much I loved it.

Still, despite my distraction, I had to admit this next step in our musical career was exciting. There were no certainties involved in any of it, no sense of treading familiar ground; rather, a strong feeling of heading out into uncharted waters. Just before *Walking Wounded* came out, I remember thinking that it could go either way. We might triumph, or we might fall flat on our faces. We worried that we would annoy some of the drum-and-bass underground by making a pop version of a sound that was still so new, but in the end even that never really happened. When the single 'Walking Wounded' was released, *Mixmag Update* acknowledged that 'this record's very existence is going to upset some people', but they took an early and decisive stand by making it Single of the Week.

On its release in April 1996, the single entered the charts at number 6, our highest ever chart entry. No doubt this was partly off the back of 'Missing', but even so, it's a long time since any band could take for granted the fact of one hit single leading to another. The follow-up single, 'Wrong', went in at number 8, and the album itself charted at number 4.

To our relief, most of the media greeted the whole project with amazed delight, and we were suddenly press darlings in a way we hadn't been since the early 1980s. Every magazine wanted to talk to us again, from *Time Out* and the broadsheet papers through to *Q* and *Spin*. We were interviewed by *The Face*, *i-D* magazine, *Dazed & Confused*, *Jockey Slut* ... The kind of magazines who would have killed themselves laughing if you'd suggested an EBTG feature a few years earlier.

Six years before, we had released an album, *Worldwide*, which had been non-reviewed, considered worthy of no one's attention, about which there was simply nothing to say. Some artists might have resented the fact that the very same magazines who had ignored me back then were courting me, hanging on my every word. But I don't think I've ever had much of a sense of entitlement about any of it. And I've always been able to see, perhaps a little too clearly for my own good, that there was no point at all in defending records that just weren't quite good enough. We'd once written a letter to *Q* magazine denouncing a *Best of Everything But The Girl* record that had been put together without our involvement, because it consisted of material that just wasn't our best. *Q* thought this was hilarious, that a band would actually write in to the letters page to slag off their own record. Now, we felt no bitterness at all; it seemed entirely logical to us that the press liked us better because we had made a better record.

The reviews were resoundingly good, and at the end of the year we featured in most of the Best of Year round-ups in the press. We were played on the radio, appeared on all the TV music shows from *Top of the Pops* to *Later . . . with Jools Holland*, and life in general became more pop-starry. Having watched them at home on TV for years, we started getting invited to awards ceremonies. In February 1995 we'd been to the Brits with Massive Attack, when 'Protection' was up for a couple of awards, and though it was the height of the Britpop Oasis vs Blur battle, I felt that ours was the table to be on, with Massive and Tricky and Björk. The rock kids seemed to be trapped in a dreary rehash of the past, still repetitively harking back to the yawn-inducing 1960s, while we were with a group of people who were looking forwards, and I felt proud to be part of it. By 1996, 'Missing' was up for Best Single at the Brits, and later in the year Ben would be nominated for Best Producer at the Q awards, and we attended as nominees in our own right.

I'd been to events like this a few times down the years – the infamous Brit Awards presented by Sam Fox and Mick Fleetwood, for instance, where I embarrassed myself by mistaking one of the penguin-suited heads of our record company for a waiter and ordering a glass of wine from him – and they were always strange affairs. Though there's been an attempt in recent years to Hollywoodise the presentation of the Brits, turning them into a pale approximation of the Oscars, it doesn't really work. It somehow goes against the grain of British sensibility, especially the music-biz sensibility, to be so slick and stage-managed. I've been to the MTV Awards in New York, and the event runs like clockwork: you are terrorised into being in your seat on time and at all times throughout the show, and it is boring in the extreme. The Brits, on the other hand, can be guaranteed to produce some moment of loutishness, unpredictable bad taste, drunken rebellion or sheer amateurism. Every year the event moves a little closer to blandness and becomes less likely to throw up moments of absurdity like the Jarvis Cocker incident or the brilliant sight of Björk and Polly Harvey performing 'I Can't Get No Satisfaction'. But those aspects are only the public face of the whole show anyway. When you're actually present, the most bizarrely memorable moments are usually the unpredictable encounters with other pop stars.

One night, at just such a ceremony, I had a long and heart-felt chat, before either of us had kids, with Liam Gallagher about his deep and unsuspected yearning to be a father. It was all he wanted to talk about, and while onlookers may have thought he was slagging off Damon Albarn or offering me a line of coke, he was actually saying to me, 'I'm desperate to have kids. Desperate.' In fact, I think he may even have said, 'I'm mad for it.'

Sometimes these meetings could be joyous, and leave you with an anecdote you couldn't wait to share. Like when Thom Yorke came and told me that back in 1985 he'd been thrown out of an EBTG gig for DANCING. Other occasions were shudder-inducing catastrophes. Like the time I found myself sitting next to Lenny Kravitz. I was wearing a dress covered in little sequins, and at this point Lenny still had those long dread-locks. He was joking with the person next to him, swinging his head flamboyantly as he laughed, and – you can see what's coming next, can't you? – he threw his head round towards me, and his dreadlocks got stuck to the front of my glittery dress. He was caught fast, with his head slightly bowed before me, more or less in my lap. Picture the two of us, embarrassed beyond words, fumbling and fiddling to get his hair free. We coughed politely, turned aside and never spoke of it again.

But I should stress again: this really isn't the pattern of most pop careers. Some fourteen years after our first release together, 1996 was our biggest year ever both critically and commercially.

It reminded me of a conversation producer Robin Millar had told me he'd had many years before with Seymour Stein from Sire Records.

'I don't know when it's gonna be,' Robin had told Seymour,

'it could be their second album, or it could be their seventh or eighth album – but one day, Everything But The Girl are gonna make a really successful record.'

Seymour's response was a clear indication of the way the music business was going at the beginning of the 1980s. 'I haven't got time to wait for eight albums,' he declared. 'Gimme success now! Gimme Madonna!'

Robin had been uncannily prescient. *Walking Wounded*, which went on to sell 1.2 million copies, was our eighth album.

My greatest stroke of fortune was to be given success when I was old enough to enjoy it and not take it for granted, or fritter it away, or be contemptuous or arrogant or supercilious about it. And I was lucky to have achieved my greatest success with a record I was proud of, and finally to reach a place where I felt understood and liked for who I really was. All the doubts that had set in from around the time of *The Language of Life* – were we just the kind of people who couldn't enjoy success, perhaps couldn't enjoy *life*? – were answered now. It turned out it was possible after all, and I saw it, and it was good.

At the same time, being that much older prevented me from being dazzled, and I knew only too well that there were limits to the fulfilment that success and acclaim could bring. It was great; it was certainly better than *not* having success and acclaim. But it wasn't everything.

We'd been working pretty much solidly for the last three years, recording, touring, promoting. If it hadn't been for our resurrection I don't imagine we would have carried on at such a furious rate. After all, without the new motivation and direction, we would have been in danger of turning into our own tribute band, hauling ourselves round the country year after year to play songs we'd written back in the days when we were young and inspired. That would never have appealed to me, any more than taking part in those gruesome revival tours appeals to me now. But becoming unexpectedly cool again was a blast, I have to admit. In terms of my public persona I felt reinvigorated, young again. I'd stayed skinny – had in fact got skinnier, thanks to Ben's illness and the resulting trauma – so I could get away with wearing the same kinds of clothes. Many of our fans were younger than us, which kept us on our toes and energised us.

But still, dragging ourselves out of the deep dark hole we'd fallen into had been time-consuming and exhausting, and though I felt rejuvenated, I wasn't actually getting any younger. I was thirty-five years old, and though I'm loath to reduce myself to a magazine cliché, my biological clock was ticking as loudly as Liam Gallagher's. My friend Lindy Morrison, some years older than me, had reached a point in 1990 when, as she says, 'I was desperate to have a baby. I had it tattooed on my forehead, DESPERATE TO HAVE A BABY!'

By 1997 I was in exactly the same state, and I think it was only because I was working in an almost exclusively male world that those I was surrounded by didn't notice or couldn't read those words that were printed on my own forehead. What looked like the opening move in a whole new career actually felt to me like the endgame.

March 1997, and I'm in a hotel room in Perth. I've just been told by Ben that we've been offered the support slot on the upcoming U2 stadium tour of America. U2 at this point are going through a period of dancefloor-inspired reinvention themselves, so I can see why they've made the connection, but it is nonetheless a jarring juxtaposition in many ways. While U2 might be the most open-minded of musical magpies, I'm not sure that the whole of their US audience is ready to embrace UK drum and bass, or tolerate the kind of small-scale, deliberately minimalist non-performance I would most likely offer. The thought of stepping onstage in a 60,000-seater stadium somewhere in the Midwest in front of an impatient rock audience and attempting to sing 'Missing' at them, fills me with a kind of stomach-churning horror.

And yet ... Everyone else around us is beside themselves with excitement at the prospect. This is the kind of opportunity people pay for, and we have just been handed it on a plate. If you were being properly ambitious and careerist, you would regard it as the perfect stepping-stone leading to bigger and better things, opening doors, propelling you one rung higher up the ladder. I have never been totally immune to this way of thinking, nor have I ever been fully able to believe in it. I've got into the habit these days of always seeing the pitfalls along with the potential. This time, though, I think Ben really is going to leave the decision up to me. I think he knows that I'm the one with the strongest feelings about what has to happen next.

I look around the room, at the view, the grand piano, every-thing.

I'm really glad the phone call came in – it'll be a good story to tell everyone later, something to show off about. But here's what I say.

'Actually, babe, d'you know what? I think I want to stop now.'

Apron strings hanging empty
Crazy things my body tells me
I want someone to tie to my
Apron strings

Apron strings waiting for you
Pretty things that I could call you
I want someone to tie to my
Lonely apron strings

Your baby looks just like you when you were young
And he looks at me with eyes that shine
And I wish that he were mine
Then I go home to my

Apron strings, cold and lonely
For time brings thoughts that only
Will be quiet when someone clings to my
Apron strings

And I'll be perfect in my own way
When you cry I will be there
I'll sing to you and comb your hair
And all your troubles I will share

For apron strings can be used for
Other things than what they're meant for
And you'd be happy wrapped in my
Apron strings
You'd be happy wrapped in my
Apron strings

'Apron Strings', from *Idlewild*, 1988

PART FIVE

PART FIVE

IT'S ALL OVER, LET'S CARRY ON

January 1998. Less than a year later.

I'm lying on a table in the operating theatre, about to give birth to twins by Caesarean section. I've had an epidural, which has taken hold down one side of my body better than the other. This will prove to be less than ideal towards the second half of the procedure, when I'm being stitched up again. There will be tears, both of joy at the arrival of these, our first children, and also of pain. It will be the most memorable day of my life so far, and one I would happily revisit at a moment's notice.

But the one thing – THE ONE THING – that is marring this otherwise perfect moment, and setting up a memory that will linger and compete with all the profound and meaningful memories, is the fact that in the heat of the moment I have forgotten to bring a CD with me to the hospital. Forgotten to bring any music of any kind. And then, also in the heat of the moment, I have agreed that the nurse can choose a CD to put on. And she has selected some kind of compilation, possibly entitled *One Hundred Songs You Most Love to Hate*, so that as my first child enters the world – and bear in mind that I am someone to whom music has always been of some importance – the song that is playing is 'Where Do You Go To My Lovely?' by Peter Sarstedt.

I'd always sworn that I would be a non-neurotic, very laid-back mother. My babies would sleep in a drawer! I wouldn't obsessively sterilise everything! They'd eat whatever we ate! And I would get on with my life, exactly the same, just with a baby strapped to my back. I planned to be a kind of cool, semi-detached parent, and Ben and I would go back on tour with a couple of rugrats crawling round the tour bus, raising free-range children who would just uncomplainingly fit in with our way of life.

But now I had two actual, real babies to care for. Two small, premature babies. They'd been born six weeks early, and after the Caesarean were immediately whisked away in wheeled incubators to the neonatal intensive care unit. When I next saw them, they were both hooked up to monitors, being fed by tubes up their noses, their tiny arms bound with splints to hold drips in place. Here I was, once again, sitting beside a bed – or in this case, two incubators – in an intensive care unit. Back to the crazed fixation on pulsing lights and sudden bleeps of alarms, back to scanning doctors' faces for a hint of untold bad news amid the positivity, back to washing my hands with super-strong detergent a hundred times a day till they were raw and cracked.

I felt responsible for these little people to a degree I simply hadn't anticipated, and the idea of handing them over to nannies while I got on with my career was all of a sudden unthinkable. The experience of Ben's illness a few years earlier had stripped off an outer layer when it came to my feelings about those I loved, and there was a fierceness there now, a kind of fighting spirit that seemed to believe that if anyone I cared for was in danger or in need, I had to be there, absolutely full time, and no one else would do.

Even once they were out of hospital, that state of mind didn't switch itself off, and I found I was turning into the kind of domesticated, child-centred, stay-at-home mother I'd never had any time for. I didn't really know what to make of myself; all I knew was that wild horses wouldn't drag me out of the house. Meanwhile Ben, devoted dad though he was, had not had the same kind of epiphany and did not believe that having children spelled the end of everything else. Not wishing, or perhaps not daring, to intrude upon my slightly nutty one-track-mindedness, he quietly busied himself for a while with other projects, focusing on the DJing that had become a passion and starting up a club night, Lazy Dog, which would end up running for five years. Also reluctant to let the momentum we had built up over the last couple of records just dribble away to nothing, he set about beginning our next album, not really knowing for sure whether I would be participating at all. Downstairs in the little makeshift basement studio in our house, he got on with writing and creating music and lyrics.

At the same time, I was totally and utterly wrapped up in the world of babies, happy as a clam, content to slob around the house all day in baggy track pants, wander up to the shops with a pram and then settle down in front of afternoon telly while I fed them both. After some pushing from Ben, I somehow produced a few lyrics, though because motherhood had made me so happy I found I had absolutely nothing to say about it, so I just ignored the whole subject. Ben, interestingly, wrote a set of lyrics which were mostly about going out. In the evenings, after the twins had fallen asleep in their cots, I would drag myself downstairs, set up the little winking baby monitor

in the corner of the room and record the vocals, having to stop in time for the last feed of the night at around eleven. I loved all the music Ben was creating, but I just wasn't in the right state of mind to contribute much of any value, and in a sense, I ended up being guest vocalist on someone else's album.

The problems really started when the record was finished, and I found I had no appetite at all to jump back into the gruelling schedules of promotion and touring. I conceded that I would do some interviews at the record-company offices, but I would give them only a short period of time each day, so that I wouldn't be away from the kids for too long. The timings in my diary are very specific, and say things like: 'Interviews at Virgin, 2–4 p.m.', or 'Photos for US, 12–4 p.m.'. In August, Ben went to New York for five days without me to cover all the US promotion. In between times, he was spending hours on the phone to journalists in every corner of the world, doing phone interviews for every music paper that now wanted to talk to us, just when I'd decided I no longer wanted to talk to them. I was feeling guilty, and committed to a project that really my heart wasn't in, but I couldn't pull out and leave Ben in the lurch, so I tried, half-heartedly, to carry on. It wasn't my finest moment. There was an element of prevarication and cowardice involved, and when I should have been saying, 'I don't want to do this any more,' in fact, I ummed and ahh-ed and pretended it would all be fine. I was desperate for someone else to tell me I could stop, that it was OK not to want this, when in reality only I could make that decision.

Instead, I said nothing, and with the girls aged eighteen months, we set off on a UK tour, taking them with us. It was a complicated set-up, as any tour where the band are a couple with twin toddlers is going to be. It wasn't just that it was exhausting; all tours are exhausting, that's half the fun. But the family element removed some of the frisson of being on the road, which at best enables you to live out an almost comically alternative lifestyle. This was the least rock 'n' roll tour of all time. We took a nanny along with us to help, but if I was awake and visible, the girls wanted me. During the day we'd take them out to a nearby park in whatever town we were in, then try to make the journey to the next town coincide with their afternoon nap so that they'd sleep in the tour bus. Then go to the soundcheck, where they'd run around and shout into microphones from the stage, being made a fuss of by all the crew, and eat their tea in the backstage dressing room. Back to the hotel, where I'd help give them a bath and get them set-tled in bed. At that point I'd have to try and turn myself into someone else. Someone less like a mum with sick down her T-shirt and more like a pop star. I'd put my make-up on and get into a change of clothes, race back to the venue and do the gig. Back to the hotel, hoping not to be woken in the night, and up toddler-early in the morning to start all over again.

No, it wasn't just the exhaustion. It was more the split-personality thing of having to be two different people at different times of the day. 'Mummy' in daylight hours, except when I was also called upon to do my job of soundchecking for the night's gig. Then, later that night, when the audience had arrived and the lights were down, I'd go onstage and have to become someone else, a character I'd never been that com-fortable with anyway – a singing show-off – only now I felt even more of a phoney and a fraud than ever before. It was all my onstage nightmares rolled into one.

At the end of the UK tour I agreed to do one show in New York and, not wanting to make the girls travel all that way, but also not wanting to be away from them for any length of time, I flew out on Concorde on the day of the gig and flew back home, on Concorde, the next day. It wasn't really being on tour, and it wasn't really being at home with the kids. The record company were moaning that I wasn't promoting the record, and the kids moaned if I went out the front door. This couldn't go on. The budget wouldn't stand it, for one thing. Back in that Perth hotel room I'd said I wanted to stop, and then I had wobbled and thought maybe it would be possible to do both – to have kids and carry on doing music, recording and travelling round the world. I suppose it is technically possible – other people manage it, after all – but it didn't seem to work for me. I was doing neither thing very well, and I was miserable.

We tried to come up with a compromise: play festivals instead of touring. That way we could reach a large audience in a short space of time, reducing the travelling and the time away from home. So we played at the Roskilde Festival in Denmark, and then the Montreux Jazz Festival, taking the girls with us and staying in a beautiful hotel overlooking the lake. That little trip was actually quite enjoyable. It was only spoiled by the fact that I began to feel sick the morning after the gig. On the way home, at the airport, I felt worse – sick and faint. It passed as the day wore on, but the next morning I woke up and felt sick again. Eight months later, our son Blake was born, and that gig at Montreux in July 2000 became the last gig I did.

The dog days of summer
Heat haze and bad temper
And whole days of shouting
'Would you listen to me!'

See, I'm the one in charge now
What happened to me?
I turned into someone's mother

Really someone should give me a uniform
Or someone should show me where is the door
Or someone should come around and explain
How it is that love forgets to speak its name

And then you turn on the news
And it's somebody else's news
And it's always such bad news
And I'm no good with sad news any more
Gets me running upstairs
To count heads in tangled beds

And someone tears up that uniform
And somewhere gently closes a door
And I'm right here once more
Crying, confessing and counting my blessings

Don't let go
'Cause we'll never know
And even when the sky is clear
And the moon looks really close
Well, it's nowhere near

'Nowhere Near', from *Out of the Woods*, 2007

THE SOUND OF SILENCE

It's December 2004; four years since that last gig. I haven't performed at all in that time. Or recorded, or written a song, or sung. I'm beginning to wonder myself why exactly this is.

After all, it's what everyone asks me nowadays, and I'm not sure what the true answer is.

'What are you doing at the moment?' they say. 'Haven't heard anything of you for a while.'

'I've had three kids,' is my standard answer.

Sometimes it's met with immediate and clear understanding. A kind of, 'How wonderful, but yes, of course you can't combine that with a pop career!'

Sometimes there's just a sense of amazed bewilderment.

Tonight I'm at an EMI party, where the question seems to hang in the very air around me.

I'm back in the kind of setting I spent years in. A smoky, noisy party, surrounded by record-company execs and other recording artists. Free drinks. Supermodel-style waitresses slinking through with trays of designer nibbles: satay and sushi.

Wraps and dips. There's bound to be a vodka luge somewhere, I just haven't seen it yet.

I'm introduced to Moby, who grumbles about the cigarette smoke and is very charming in a nervous, nerdy way, claiming to be a long-time fan since the Marine Girls days, and to have seen an early solo gig by Ben. He disarms me by declaring that I should record an album of old jazz standards – the last thing I want to do. He defends this by saying that he loves melancholic ballads best of all, and I reply, yes, but there are always new ones to be written. Hah! As if I've been writing any.

I spot Neil Tennant across the room and want to say hello to him. We've met before, and I think of him as some sort of kindred spirit. Same generation and motivation. The Pet Shop Boys could probably tempt me back, I think. I'd like to follow in Dusty's shoes. I sidle up next to him, and he's also charming. But, like Moby, he immediately asks what I am doing these days 'with my lovely voice'. 'Shouting at the kids,' I answer. It's meant to be wryly funny, but comes out sounding like Waynetta Slob. He looks dismayed.

I tell him I've had the idea to try and write a book telling the whole story. He reminds me of his review of 'Night And Day' for *Smash Hits*, which I have recently unearthed in my trawl through the cuttings collection. 'It wasn't even in the pile for review,' he says. 'I dug it out specially.'

While we're chatting, a flash goes off as someone takes our picture – I turn to see that it's Erlend Øye from Kings of Convenience, who comes to say hello and kiss my hand devotedly. He has recently found a vinyl copy of *A Distant Shore* and has been listening to it. He too wants to convey to me the significance of things I've done. Reminders of my past are everywhere this evening. Everyone here seems to have a clear sense that I should still be singing, and cannot quite understand why I'm not. Momentarily, while I'm actually in their company, I start to feel the same. Something stirs.

But by the time I'm in the taxi going home, I've already forgotten. I don't seem to feel any need. I think I'm just fine as I am. I'm happy. Content. In these driven times of binge-working, I'm left feeling inadequate.

So yes, four years without singing a note. Sometimes when people asked me about it I said, only semi-joking, that I had completely retired. I would then rationalise that statement by arguing that in a long career – seventeen years – I had achieved everything I wanted to achieve; there was nothing left for me to prove, and I was happy now to leave it all behind. I had three small children, and they were as time-consuming and fulfilling as I could wish anything to be. And it certainly wasn't the case that I was at home with the kids because I had to be. Ben was there, helping through it all, and the truth is that we could have afforded an army of nannies. I could have been back on tour, or out every night, whatever I wanted. But it seemed that what I wanted was to go to Gymboree and sing 'The Wheels On The Bus', and then come home and have some lunch, watching *Little Bill* on the telly.

I have a couple of friends who had kids and felt this way too. Took their maternity leave, then never went back. Equally, I have friends who were crawling up the walls by week twelve, and skipped back to work with barely a backward glance the day the nanny arrived. And, of course, yet other friends who had no choice in the matter. They had to go back to work, and did the juggling that most women do. The last thing I have ever wanted to be is a poster girl for the stay-at-home mum brigade, many of whom scare me beyond belief with their non-stop breastfeeding and organic cupcakes. No, I didn't feel that I was representing anybody: I just wanted to hang out with my kids, I was temporarily bored with being in a pop group, and I had the luxury of being able to make that choice.

Once I had disengaged from the music business, I began to relish living a more completely anonymous life. The kids weren't used to me working, or familiar with my identity as a pop star, and so they would be completely baffled on those occasions when someone would come up and ask for an autograph. They would look bewildered and ask, 'What are you writing on that bit of paper, Mummy? But why, WHY does that lady want your name written down?' Like all mums, I sang to my kids at home, so they knew what my voice sounded like, and once when I walked into a branch of Gap, pushing Blake in a pushchair, 'Missing' was playing loudly. He twisted round to look at me, little finger pointing upwards towards the source of the music. 'Mummy!' he exclaimed in a tone of pure amazement. 'You are singing in the shop.' When he started at school, he came home one day and said to me, 'Mum, did you used to be famous?'

'Um, sort of, a bit,' I replied.

'It's just my teacher says she's got all your records.'

The kids found it slightly confusing and strange, but above all, just not that interesting. It wasn't who I was to them. 'Tracey Thorn' was someone they didn't know, who seemed to belong to strangers. Meanwhile, I was Mum.

I turned forty, and realised the life I was living now felt more grown-up than any life I'd led before, and I began to look down on the world of pop music with a kind of disdain born of my newly acquired maternal wisdom. Being at home all day with the kids, I felt more in control than I had for years. I wore what I wanted, ate what I wanted, made no effort at all beyond what was strictly necessary and got on with looking after myself and the kids. Like a proper adult. And far from finding it a more boring, constrained or lonely existence, I was able to make a lot of friends. For the first time in my adult life, I was living in a mostly female world. For years I had inhabited the almost exclusively male domain of the music business. It had been hard to make women friends when there just weren't that many women around. Now I had a whole new female gang, and I was defiantly enjoying it.

I wasn't always sure whether these other mums knew 'who I was', or what my job had been before. Often it wasn't discussed at all, and so I assumed my anonymity was complete. But it was sometimes a bit like living in disguise, wondering whether at any moment my cover would be blown. I remember when the kids were very small standing outside school, Blake in a pram, waiting for the girls to come out. I was with a group of mums, talking about teachers and playdates and school dinners, when suddenly a huge, gleaming Range Rover with black-tinted windows slowed as it neared us and then pulled over to the side of the road. The window whirred down and a voice called out, 'Tracey! Tracey! Hi, how are you?' In unison, all heads turned towards the car and the familiar face that leaned out, the stubble and sunglasses confirming the almost unbelievable fact that, yes, it was George Michael.

Sometimes it reminded me of those days up in Hull, where I was a sort of part-time pop star and, in true English fashion, everyone was too polite to mention it.

But all this time I was playing house, Ben had carried on a kind of parallel life, establishing himself as a DJ and remixer, then as a club owner and finally, and perhaps most importantly, starting his own dance label, Buzzin' Fly, and its subsidiary alt-rock imprint, Strange Feeling. In 1998, very soon after the girls were born, he'd set up the club night Lazy Dog at the Notting Hill Arts Club, and he DJed there on alternate Sundays right through until 2003. After that he went into partnership with a couple of friends as club owners, and they first opened up the tiny basement club Cherry Jam, also in Notting Hill, then moved onwards and upwards by buying the old Subterania space and reopening it as Neighbourhood. It felt quite glamorous, having a partner who was a DJ and club owner; a little bit underworld. We went down to Neighbourhood early one evening, before it was properly open, and one of the bouncers was standing outside. 'Evening, boss,' he greeted Ben as we went by.

I liked the contrast. Up until now we'd worked together, done the same job, lived in each other's pockets. But now Ben had a separate life from me, and I was grateful for the glimpses of the outside world that he brought into my little domestic set-up. None of the other mums I knew had a kitchen cluttered with twelve-inch vinyl that had just come in the post and needed listening to urgently before Saturday. None of my kids' friends had to ask their dad to turn the bloody music down because they were trying to do their homework. And none of them had to creep round the house till lunchtime some mornings because Dad was asleep upstairs, having DJed till 5 a.m.

And while many of my friends had understandably reached the stage in life where their interest in music was waning and their ability to 'keep up' had hit a brick wall, and the latest new genre left them feeling defeated and old, I was still in the curious position of being incredibly well informed about the current state of music, despite apparently paying no attention to it whatsoever. I didn't go out very regularly, but when I did I went clubbing, at whatever club Ben was DJing at, with a small group of like-minded friends. I remember dancing round my handbag at the early days of Lazy Dog, before I even had a mobile phone, with an old-fashioned pager clipped to my belt in case the babysitter needed to reach me. I'd go to Neighbourhood on big nights like my birthday and New

lazy dog

DEEP HOUSE MUSIC FORTNIGHTLY SUNDAYS NOTTING HILL ARTS CLUB
21 NOTTING HILL GATE LONDON W11 020 7460 4459
4PM - 11PM £5 DONATION (FREE BEFORE 6PM)
DJS BEN WATT AND JAY HANNAN
APR 2 16 30   MAY 14 28   JUNE 11 25

WWW.LAZYDOGCLUB.COM

Year's Eve, and it was still close enough to the heady days of 'Missing' that when I took to the dancefloor I would be treated like a local superstar, being semi-mobbed and often dancing euphorically with complete strangers.

Eventually, in 2004, Ben even persuaded me to come and DJ a couple of times at Cherry Jam, saying casually to me at dinner one night: 'Come down and play your old Delta 5 records.' We put on a night, calling it A Different Kitchen, and I DJed alongside Ben, playing a mixture of stuff from the Buzzcocks and The Specials, through Eighth Wonder, Cameo and Freeez, to Fonda Rae, Shannon and Evelyn 'Champagne' King.

Because he worked from home so much of the time, Ben was there to share much of the childcare stuff. From the outside, it might have looked as though I had given up my career to take sole charge of the kids while he carried on regardless. But he was there pretty much all day, every day, and as hands-on as you could wish any dad to be. Bizarrely, there were old and loyal 'fans' who decided to get upset on my behalf, and posted vitriolic messages on the EBTG website message board haranguing Ben for keeping me at home chained to the kitchen sink while he gallivanted round the world living the life of a superstar DJ. He was blamed for the demise of EBTG, when in truth he had always been keener on our trying to carry on, even with the kids. I had taken the unilateral decision to 'retire' and he had to make the best of it, carving out for himself a new job and a new creative life, and he did so without ever questioning my choice to be at home most of the time.

Boy, I think you've come home
Open up the door and step inside
So many people who feel the way you do
Whose sweetest dreams have always been denied
Lock the past into a box and throw away the key
And leave behind those days of endless night
Everyone is waiting
Everyone is here
Step out of the woods into the light
Everybody loves you here
Everybody loves you here

Boy, you've been on the wrong road
Wearing someone else's shoes
Who told you you were not what you were meant to
    be?
And got you paying someone else's dues?
This is the place for you, just look around this room
Is anybody here made out of stone?
Down among the heretics, the losers and the saints
You are here amongst your own
You've come home
You've come home

Look at this hole inside your heart
No one can ever fill
It's like the Grand Canyon
Look at this gap that's opened up
Between you and the world
It's like the Grand Canyon
Look at this hole inside your heart
It's like the Grand Canyon
The Grand Canyon
Everybody loves you here
You've come home

'Grand Canyon', from *Out of the Woods*, 2007

BACK FOR GOOD

People kept asking me to sing, and instead ... I wrote a *book*?

It sounds like the wrong answer to the question, but in fact it was just more of a roundabout way of getting to the answer.

'Why don't you sing any more?' people said, and I realised that I wasn't sure, but that maybe one of the reasons was because it had always been a strange thing for me to be doing anyway – a job I wasn't really cut out for. I'd never quite fitted in; none of it had ever quite added up. It had been a career that often fell down into the gaps, and didn't connect with the official version of pop's history during the period when I was part of it. So I thought I'd set about exploring it and see whether, if I could begin to explain it to myself, it would then be explicable to others.

And the process turned into an act of remembering.

The more I trawled through my past, reading my old diaries and listening to the records, the more I began to remember what it had all been about and what it had felt like, and why I'd done it in the first place.

People asked, 'Do you *miss* singing, now that you don't do it any more?' I'd laugh and answer, in complete honesty, 'No, not at all.'

Until suddenly, one day, I really really did. I missed it badly, and couldn't imagine why I had stopped.

So when, at more or less that precise moment, I was sent yet another request to sing a vocal over a dance track, I was primed to give a different answer to the usual blanket 'No, thanks'.

These kinds of requests came in all the time. I would be sent a backing track, which was usually a generic, house-music-by-numbers kind of affair dispatched in the opportunistic hope that having me sing on top of it would transform absolutely any old piece of crap into the next 'Missing' and bingo, another massive hit.

This time it was different. The track that Ali and Basti Schwarz, aka Tiefschwarz, sent me was a dark, moody piece of electro-house that inspired me to write the first song I had come up with in five years. Ben recorded the vocal for me in our studio at home.

It felt good. It felt totally familiar, easy. I liked the paraphernalia of it all, the putting on and adjusting of the headphones, setting up the vocal level, adjusting the reverb. I thought, 'I know how to do this,' and it was like rediscovering a craft that had lain dormant for too long, like remembering that you know how to wire a plug or fix an engine. And the realisation of how much I had missed it was like a physical pang.

The song, 'Damage', came out in June 2006, and doing this one small project flicked a switch inside my head back to On. I came up with the brilliant plan that I would make a solo record.

Ben was far too busy with his other projects for us to make an Everything But The Girl record, but more than that, it was time for a bit of self-assertion again. This was all about me emerging from a period when I had submerged myself in favour of others – the kids – and so there was a strong element involved of having something to prove. I wanted to make a statement, that I was still that girl who'd gone and bought an electric guitar aged sixteen and formed bands. Having grandly stated that I was going to do it by myself now, I had to work out how on earth to put that into practice.

Technology had never been my strong point, so despite having a fully functioning recording studio in our house, where Ben had done many remixes and I'd recorded the Tiefschwarz vocal, I decided I would go nowhere near it as I couldn't even turn the lights on without asking for help. Instead, I bought myself a little four-track Tascam cassette recorder, no more advanced than the one I'd used a hundred years before to record the first Marine Girls songs, with a manual only four pages long that even I could understand. I set it up in the front room with the piano and my desk, and decided that this would serve as my demo studio. Then I went onto eBay and bought a harmonium and an omnichord, and with the door shut I began, very quietly, to write some songs, and record primitive demos of myself playing and singing them, with only room for the barest of overdubs and with maximum tape hiss included.

The record I ended up making, *Out of the Woods*, was more of a pop record than those beginnings would ever have led you to imagine. I realised pretty quickly that I didn't actually want to remake *A Distant Shore*, so I got some electronic producers on board to help out: Tom Gandey, Alex Santos, Charles Webster and Martin Wheeler. Ben also said the name Ewan Pearson to me, and when I checked out his website I found him referencing both Dusty Springfield and Rufus Wainwright. 'Sounds like a kindred spirit,' I thought, and indeed he was, his contributions proving invaluable to the continuity of the whole project.

A lot of the work was done at one remove, with tracks and ideas being sent via email, worked on and then sent back. That allowed me to go on feeling independent, and not have the sense that anyone else was possibly stamping themselves on the record too much. Despite all the outside input, I still felt it was a solo record, and very much my concept of what I'd wanted to do. A little bit acoustic, a little bit electronica and ten new sets of lyrics from me – more than I'd written in a very long time.

In the middle of 2006, with the record half finished, I went to have a meeting with Virgin (still my record company, despite the years of silence) to tell them what I was doing. Tony Wadsworth, the label boss, sat and listened patiently while I told him that I was making a solo album, but didn't want to tour, or appear in videos, or do much in the way of promotion. He'd had the same conversation with Kate Bush when her album *Aerial* had come out the year before, so he must have wondered why on earth all his female artists were suddenly becoming hermits, but to his credit he agreed that I could do what I wanted and they'd put the record out on those terms.

By December, *Out of the Woods* was finished and ready for release, and I was halfway back to the old life, filming a video for the first single 'It's All True', doing an interview with Sheryl Garratt for a cover feature for the *Telegraph* magazine and a photo shoot with fashion photographer Valerie Phillips. I did press interviews at the super-glamorous, hi-tech EMI offices in west London, where I spent the day in a glass-walled corner room while journalists from various international locations were ushered in and out every half-hour in order to quiz

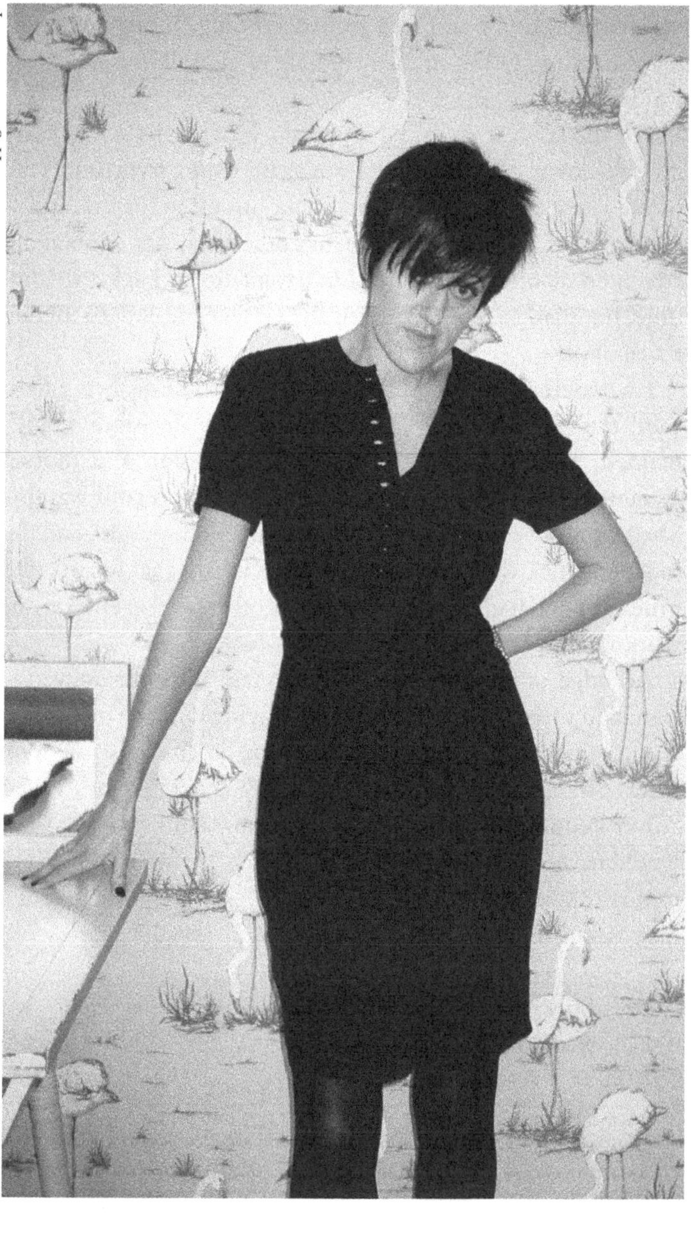

me about a) my long break from recording, b) my return to recording and c) the strange absence of Ben. 'He is Missing!' I quipped.

For the last few years, I'd spent much of the time in a fairly dressed-down state, and here I was again with a stylist and a rail of the latest clothes, having my make-up done for me. It was like a mums' spa-weekend dream come true; not a job at all. I realised at once that I wouldn't want to go back to it full time, but that, to dip into, it was the perfect antidote to midlife melancholy.

I wondered if it would feel strange not to be working with Ben, but in fact it was liberating to make decisions single-handed, rather than as the result of discussion and mutual agreement. I had played him nothing until the record was finished so as not to be overly influenced by his responses, and the independence we had from each other meant that for the first time ever we had things to tell each other at the end of our working day. It was a novelty.

An edge of competitiveness even crept into our conversation, and often it was as if we were playing a new game called Competitive Airplay. Ben's first release on his new alt-rock label, Strange Feeling, was a track by the Figurines called 'Silver Ponds' and as our promotional campaigns coincided, we would have conversations at dinner which were very polite and mutually supportive but with a subtle – and hilarious – edge only detectable to each other.

Ben: So we got three plays on Steve Lamacq this week.
Me: Wow, that's fantastic.
(Pause)
Me: My video is going down very well at MTV.
Ben: Great news!
(Pause)

Ben: So, did I tell you? The band are doing a session for Xfm.

Me: Fantastic!

(Pause)

Me: Dixon is really playing the Martin Buttrich remix of 'It's All True', apparently!

Ben: That's excellent.

Out of the Woods was well received by the press; many of the reviews seemed to refer to me as cruelly underrated, a kind of buried treasure of British pop. I thought that was sweet of them, though if I was a buried treasure I possibly had only myself to blame, as I had rarely courted publicity or chased fame, and for the last five years I had quite successfully buried myself.

And after all this time, many of them were still flattering in the extreme about my singing:

'Tracey Thorn could sing the speaking clock and it'd send tingles down my spine'
'Thorn's distinctively sultry alto voice'
'One of the unique British voices, up there with Dusty'
'Thorn's voice is still uniquely, deliciously forlorn'
'Tracey's voice – for ever one of British pop's better instruments'

It's what Ben calls 'The Voice of Thorn'.

Only he and I are allowed to make the kind of jokes we make about my voice. Only he knows how totally self-deprecating I can be, how mixed my feelings. It is a voice which inspires reverence in certain listeners, and yet about which I have so many reservations. I still really think of myself as 'someone who sings' rather than 'a Singer', and have a very clear-sighted awareness of my limitations. I know what I *can't* sing, as well as what I can. To be mentioned in the same breath as Dusty makes me swell with pride and pleasure, but only momentarily. I'm not Dusty, and I never will be. The End.

And the voice sometimes feels separate from me, something over which I have no real control, and for which I can take no real credit. A glimpse, perhaps, of how it must feel to be truly beautiful and be gazed at and revered for your beauty, a quality you were simply granted by some gracious fairy godmother, for which you have not worked or strived and which you did not create.

But I'm not an idiot. I also know that to have 'a sound', a distinctive sound, which is yours, not borrowed and not easily copied, is the most fundamental building block of any life in music. And so above all I am grateful to be able to open my mouth and make a noise which is my own. There are many singers who are 'better' than me, but they are not always unique. And uniqueness is all in this game.

Above all else, it has been the thing that has allowed me to survive this long, and to find myself here, in 2007, aged forty-five, on what was effectively my *thirteenth* album release, invited to appear alongside a group of female singers mostly twenty years younger than me to film a short Channel 4 ad.

February 2007

It's nine in the morning, and I'm being driven through the gates of Pinewood Studios. The driver points out to me a kind of huge aircraft hangar over to our right. 'That's the James Bond stage,' he says. We drive past workshops and storage areas. It's like a small town in here. There's one signposted Shed 7 – is that where the band got their name from?

I'm here to do a filmed ident for Channel 4. Idents are those little clips that get shown in between programmes after the ads, so that just as you're settling down to watch *Ugly Betty* you get a thirty-second clip of someone or other off the telly or the radio doing nothing much. It gives you a chance to find the remote so that you can turn the volume down, or race to the kitchen for a biscuit.

Anyway, the theme of this one is – guess what – 'Female Singers', and I'm here to be filmed both on my own and then in a group setting, with Corinne Bailey Rae, Mutya, Lady Sovereign, Natasha Bedingfield and Sophie Ellis-Bextor. I told Ewan Pearson the line-up last week and he kindly said, 'Well, you are the coolest by a mile.' 'Ewan,' I said, 'I am the OLDEST by a mile.' I am flattered to be asked, actually, but I must admit that I do feel a bit generationally discombobulated.

I film my solo bit first, and it's very straightforward. I sit in a nice 1960s-looking armchair and stick a cassette into an 1980s-looking boombox. 'It's All True' blasts out into the studio, the camera pans round me and then whooshes up to the ceiling, revealing a giant neon figure four. Done and dusted in fifteen minutes.

The group scene takes a little longer. For a start, that's six women who have to be ready at the same time, happy with their hair and make-up. Eventually we all arrive on set, and there's a bit of skirting round each other. Corinne and I have the same shoes on, so to break the ice I go over and say hello and point at our shoes. It could be a ghastly moment but she's very sweet, even offers to change, but the director tells us that our feet will not be visible, so we have in fact both lost the chance to show off the best pair of Christian Louboutin patent wedges you will ever see.

We're all wearing different styles of headphones, the idea being that each of us is listening to our own track. The director says, 'As we film you, you will hear your own track in your headphones and we want you to move along with the song a little.'

I gently explain to him that the wires to our headphones have been neatly clipped off by the assistant director, who was worried they were getting in the way, so that unless they are somehow able to beam the tracks into our ears, we will be hearing only silence. He is taken aback by this technical information, goes off to have a huddle, comes back and says, 'Well, we will just have to pretend.'

It turns out, of course, that all the others are basically very nice. Mutya is a little guarded, Natasha the most primped and backcombed. Lady Sovereign is the one I warm to. She is probably the youngest of all of us, and is clearly feeling a little out of place, but even in her discomfort she's sharp and funny. We're all in frocks and heels, she's in streetwear, ponytail scraped tightly to one side. She's twitching and fidgeting, worried she looks no good, uncertain as to what this kind of thing means, how it will make her appear. The camera pans round from behind her, catching her in close-up from the side.

'Don't film me from the side, man,' she complains. 'I look like a fucking peanut. This side of my head, man, it looks BALD.'

'No, no,' says the director, 'you look nice.'

'NICE?' she wails. 'Jesus, I feel like fucking Gollum.'

My heart goes out to her in her self-consciousness and self-doubt and inability to go with the flow, her determination to let everyone know that she is more than this. I remember feeling like that; trying to act tough, coming over as edgy and angry because you're trying to deal with the anxiety about what it all means, whether you're going to be understood or misunderstood. The constant alertness, and the attention, trying to dodge the pitfalls.

I'm not so much like that any more, I realise. I'm easier in my own skin. Finally. But, for so many years, I WAS like that. I identify with her completely, and at the same time, I feel like her mum. And I quite like the feeling.

Just this once
Let me tell you you're the sweetest thing
The love in every song I sing
The music in my ears and everything
Happiness writes white
Maybe that isn't true tonight
And things you know you might forget
And other things I haven't told you yet

Close your eyes
Count to ten
Turn around
Back again
Hit the floor
Then once more
I'm still here
And it's all true

We don't need any kind of big parade
Just this once a little serenade
To celebrate this love we've made
We don't need, don't need a big fanfare
This is just my heart laid bare
For anyone who might care

Go away
Round the world
Talk to all kinds of girls
But it's me you won't find
And you're mine

Close your eyes
Count to ten
Turn around
Back again
Hit the floor
Then once more
I'm still here

And it's all true
And it's all true
Tell me do you feel it too?

'It's All True', from *Out of the Woods*, 2007

POSTSCRIPT

You may wonder why this book ends where it does, six years ago in a TV studio with Lady Sovereign. I'd started writing it in 2005, when I genuinely believed that I had retired for good from making music. And the very act of writing it triggered in me the desire to return to music. So when I recorded *Out of the Woods*, I put away the pages I had written and forgot all about them, deciding that, after all, I'd rather make records again than write books. I went on and recorded another solo album, *Love and Its Opposite*. I wrote a gardening column. I frittered away whole evenings on Twitter. Time ticked by.

Then, in 2011, as we packed up in preparation for a house move, I found a box file with MY BOOK scribbled on the outside. I opened it up and had a look and couldn't believe how much I'd written. I'd put hours and hours of effort into it, and then just shoved it away out of sight. Suddenly that seemed a waste, and as I reread the pages, it seemed to me that it was a good story and deserved to be told.

But still, the point where it ended seemed like a good place to end. The story had a trajectory: the early upward curve, the terrible crash in the middle, the unexpected resurrection, the inevitable retirement, and the final return. To bring it up to date would spoil that.

And so, the book ends in 2007, and because of the gap between the starting and the finishing, there are some moments in the telling when timings shift about a bit; the age I say I am 'now' isn't always consistent. I've let the inconsistencies stand. You're a grown-up, I know you won't mind.

ACKNOWLEDGEMENTS

I want to thank a few people who agreed to talk to me while I was writing this book: Mike Alway, Geoff Travis, Ade Clarke, Richard Norris, Jane Fox, Alice Fox, Gina Hartman, Dave Haslam, Huw Davies. They all appear in this story and helped jog my memory about things that happened hundreds of years ago.

I also want to thank Kirsty McLachlan, my agent, for her invaluable contributions and suggestions. And for being the first person to read the book.

Thanks to Rowan Cope, my editor, and the rest of the team at Virago for welcoming me with such open arms.

And finally, biggest thanks of all to Ben, for being there during most of it, and for letting me tell a story that is half his as though it were all mine.

SONG CREDITS

'Getting Away From It All':
Written by Tracey Thorn. Copyright ©. Used by the author's permission.

'Marine Girls', 'Honey', 'On My Mind', 'Flying Over Russia', 'Plain Sailing', 'Small Town Girl', 'The Spice Of Life', 'Mine', 'Ugly Little Dreams':
Written by Tracey Thorn. Copyright ©. Licence issued courtesy of Complete Music Ltd / Universal Music Publishing Limited.

'Each And Every One', 'This Love (Not For Sale)', 'Trouble And Strife', 'Apron Strings':
Written by Tracey Thorn and Ben Watt. Copyright ©. Licence issued courtesy of Complete Music Ltd / Universal Music Publishing Limited.

'A Country Mile', 'Oxford Street', 'I Don't Understand Anything', 'We Walk The Same Line', 'Hands Up To The

PUBLISHER'S NOTE